British Nuclear Mobilisation Since 1945

This book explores aspects of the social and cultural history of nuclear Britain in the Cold War era (1945–1991) and contributes to a more multivalent exploration of the consequences of nuclear choices which are too often left unacknowledged by historians of post-war Britain.

In the years after 1945, the British government mobilised money, scientific knowledge, people and military–industrial capacity to create both an independent nuclear deterrent and the generation of electricity through nuclear reactors. This expensive and vast 'technopolitical' project, mostly top-secret and run by small sub-committees within government, was central to broader Cold War strategy and policy. Recent attempts to map the resulting social and cultural history of these military–industrial policy decisions suggest that nuclear mobilisation had far-reaching consequences for British life.

The chapters in this book were originally published as a special issue of *Contemporary British History*.

Jonathan Hogg is Senior Lecturer in Twentieth Century History at the University of Liverpool, UK. He is the author of *British Nuclear Culture: Official and Unofficial Narratives in the Long 20th Century* (Bloomsbury, 2016), and editor of the e-textbook *Using Primary Sources* (Liverpool University Press, 2017).

Kate Brown is Professor of Science, Technology and Society at Massachusetts Institute of Technology, Cambridge, USA. Her numerous books include *Plutopia: Nuclear Families, Atomic Cities and the Great Soviet and American Plutonium Disasters* (Oxford, 2013), *Dispatches from Dystopia: Histories of Places Not Yet Forgotten* (University of Chicago Press, 2015), and most recently *Manual for Survival: A Chernobyl Guide to the Future* (Allen Lane, 2019).

British Nuclear Mobilisation Since 1945

Social and Cultural Histories

Edited by
Jonathan Hogg and Kate Brown

LONDON AND NEW YORK

First published 2021
by Routledge
2 Park Square, Milton Park, Abingdon, Oxon, OX14 4RN

and by Routledge
605 Third Avenue, New York, NY 10158

Routledge is an imprint of the Taylor & Francis Group, an informa business

© 2021 Taylor & Francis

All rights reserved. No part of this book may be reprinted or reproduced or utilised in any form or by any electronic, mechanical, or other means, now known or hereafter invented, including photocopying and recording, or in any information storage or retrieval system, without permission in writing from the publishers.

Trademark notice: Product or corporate names may be trademarks or registered trademarks, and are used only for identification and explanation without intent to infringe.

British Library Cataloguing-in-Publication Data
A catalogue record for this book is available from the British Library

ISBN13: 978-0-367-74311-6 (hbk)
ISBN13: 978-0-367-74315-4 (pbk)
ISBN13: 978-1-003-15709-0 (ebk)

Typeset in Myriad Pro
by codeMantra

Publisher's Note
The publisher accepts responsibility for any inconsistencies that may have arisen during the conversion of this book from journal articles to book chapters, namely the inclusion of journal terminology.

Disclaimer
Every effort has been made to contact copyright holders for their permission to reprint material in this book. The publishers would be grateful to hear from any copyright holder who is not here acknowledged and will undertake to rectify any errors or omissions in future editions of this book.

Contents

Citation Information	vi
Notes on Contributors	viii
Introduction: social and cultural histories of British nuclear mobilisation since 1945 *Jonathan Hogg and Kate Brown*	1
1 Weaponising peace: the Greater London Council, cultural policy and 'GLC peace year 1983' *Hazel A. Atashroo*	10
2 '… what in the hell's this?' Rehearsing nuclear war in Britain's Civil Defence Corps *Jessica Douthwaite*	27
3 Mass observing the atom bomb: the emotional politics of August 1945 *Claire Langhamer*	48
4 Resist and survive: Welsh protests and the British nuclear state in the 1980s *Christophe Laucht and Martin Johnes*	66
5 'Nuclear prospects': the siting and construction of Sizewell A power station 1957–1966 *Christine Wall*	86
6 Britain, West Africa and 'The new nuclear imperialism': decolonisation and development during French tests *Christopher Robert Hill*	114
Index	131

Citation Information

The chapters in this book were originally published in *Contemporary British History*, volume 33, issue 2 (June 2019). When citing this material, please use the original page numbering for each article, as follows:

Introduction
Introduction: social and cultural histories of British nuclear mobilisation since 1945
Jonathan Hogg and Kate Brown
Contemporary British History, volume 33, issue 2 (June 2019) pp. 161–169

Chapter 1
Weaponising peace: the Greater London Council, cultural policy, and 'GLC Peace Year 1983'
Hazel A. Atashroo
Contemporary British History, volume 33, issue 2 (June 2019) pp. 170–186

Chapter 2
'…what in the hell's this?' Rehearsing nuclear war in Britain's Civil Defence Corps
Jessica Douthwaite
Contemporary British History, volume 33, issue 2 (June 2019) pp. 187–207

Chapter 3
Mass observing the atom bomb: the emotional politics of August 1945
Claire Langhamer
Contemporary British History, volume 33, issue 2 (June 2019) pp. 208–225

Chapter 4
Resist and survive: Welsh protests and the British nuclear state in the 1980s
Christophe Laucht and Martin Johnes
Contemporary British History, volume 33, issue 2 (June 2019) pp. 226–245

Chapter 5
'Nuclear Prospects': the siting and construction of Sizewell A power station 1957-1966.
Christine Wall
Contemporary British History, volume 33, issue 2 (June 2019) pp. 246–273

Chapter 6
Britain, West Africa and 'The new nuclear imperialism': decolonisation and development during French tests
Christopher Robert Hill
Contemporary British History, volume 33, issue 2 (June 2019) pp. 274–289

For any permission-related enquiries please visit:
http://www.tandfonline.com/page/help/permissions

Contributors

Hazel A. Atashroo completed a PhD at the University of Southampton, UK.

Kate Brown is Professor of Science, Technology and Society at Massachusetts Institute of Technology, Cambridge MA, USA.

Jessica Douthwaite completed a PhD at the University of Strathclyde, UK.

Christopher Robert Hill is Lecturer in History at the University of South Wales, UK.

Jonathan Hogg is Senior Lecturer in twentieth-century history at the University of Liverpool, UK.

Martin Johnes is Professor of History at Swansea University, UK.

Claire Langhamer is Professor of Modern British History at the University of Sussex, UK.

Christophe Laucht is Senior Lecturer in Modern History at Swansea University, Wales, UK.

Christine Wall is Professor of Architectural and Construction History at the School of Architecture and Cities and the University of Westminster, UK.

Introduction: social and cultural histories of British nuclear mobilisation since 1945

Jonathan Hogg and Kate Brown

ABSTRACT
In the years after 1945, the British government mobilised money, scientific knowledge, people and military–industrial capacity to create both an independent nuclear deterrent and the generation of electricity through nuclear reactors. This expensive and vast 'technopolitical' project, mostly top-secret and run by small sub-committees within government, was central to broader Cold War strategy and policy. Recent attempts to map the resulting social and cultural history of these military–industrial policy decisions suggest that nuclear mobilisation had far-reaching consequences for British life. The guest editors of this special issue of *Contemporary British History* invited contributions that would explore aspects of the social or cultural history of nuclear Britain in the Cold War era, 1945–1991. We hope that this collection contributes to a more multivalent exploration of the consequences of nuclear choices which, we contend, are too often left unacknowledged by historians of post-war Britain.

The guest editors of this special issue of *Contemporary British History* invited contributions that would explore aspects of the social or cultural history of nuclear Britain in relation to the physical mobilisation of Cold War nuclear projects, in the years 1945–1991. We especially encouraged research that went beyond familiar sites, source-sets or personalities, and offered new ways of thinking about nuclear history in relation to broader trends in the historiography of contemporary Britain. The six articles in this special issue suggest that nuclear history can form an important contribution to more mainstream historiographical traditions such as selfhood, subjectivity and citizenship in post-war Britain, decolonisation, the cultural memory of World War II (WWII) and the politics of protest. Indeed, we argue that it is difficult to think of another aspect of contemporary British life that has fundamentally shaped government, military and political thinking, absorbed such a sizeable portion of public funds, and created such contested public discourse across decades, yet remains on the periphery of contemporary British historiography. In many ways, aspects of contemporary British history with richer and more unified historiographical traditions are shaped in some way by the structural shift that nuclear mobilisation represented, and the ideologies it enacted. The contributions to this special issue represent new approaches to the history of nuclear Britain, and offer new ways to think about the positioning of nuclear concerns in broader historical context. After all, how might we research and write nuclear history?

If we focus on just one year in British nuclear history, we are reminded that from the northernmost tip of the United Kingdom to its southernmost towns and villages, nuclear development structured social and political change, and shaped lives, in deeply ambiguous ways. In 1984, Shetland Island residents John Goodlad and Marjorie Flaws drafted the Declaration of Wyre. Handwritten using ornate calligraphy on a large parchment, and addressed to the King of Norway and the Queen of Denmark, the Declaration sought to 'reaffirm our strong historical ties with Norway and Denmark' in an attempt to forestall the 'proposed siting of the European Demonstration Reprocessing Plant at Dounreay', not far away on the north Scotland coast. The document, later delivered by Goodlad to Norway by hand after a trip across choppy seas, was a more general attempt to 'safeguard our laws, rights and traditions' from British intervention. Around the same time, 'Torness Alliance' activists were trying, unsuccessfully, to prevent the construction of Torness nuclear power station 30 miles east of Edinburgh. A few years earlier, the 'No Uranium' campaign briefly flourished on Orkney, off the north-east coast of Scotland, in opposition to plans to mine for uranium ore. Many of the same activists, a few years later, challenged plans to dump nuclear waste on Stormy Bank, a small island in the Orkneys.

Meanwhile in 1984, *Faslane: Diary of a Peace Camp* was published, which described how a peace camp had been created in 1982 as a permanent protest against the Trident nuclear submarines stationed at Faslane Naval Base, west of Glasgow. Further south, on the Wirral peninsula over the river Mersey from Liverpool, a peace camp was organised a year earlier against the proposed nuclear enrichment plant at Capenhurst. Only 30 miles south, near Nantwich, Hack Green bunker, appearing as a grey and stubby concrete box above ground, was being converted into one of seventeen regional government headquarters that would run the region in the event of nuclear war. In the heart of Wales, a train carrying spent nuclear fuel began its journey to Sellafield, Cumbria from Trawsfynydd nuclear power station. Tucked in a valley beneath the Snowdonia mountain range, the power station is still an imposing presence, a nuclear cathedral in the landscape. Now in the process of being decommissioned, it was designed by the architect Basil Spence in the late 1950s, who had re-designed Coventry cathedral following bomb damage from German air raids in 1940. In 1984, on large airfields such as Upper Heyford in Oxfordshire, or Greenham Common in Berkshire, planes, bombs and pilots were on constant standby to scramble towards Moscow with their nuclear payloads. On the front page of the *Daily Mirror* on 5 March of that year, readers were told about a group of mothers living near RAF Manston in Kent who were ready to kill their children in the event of nuclear war.[1]

Michael Foot, leader of the Labour Party in the early 1980s and a passionate anti-nuclear activist, had urged the British electorate to vote for unilateral disarmament in the 1983 General Election. Although this manifesto pledge became part of the 'longest suicide-note in history', by 1984, many city councils had become Nuclear Free, starting with Manchester in 1980. In 1984, the Sizewell B Inquiry, begun in 1982 at a concert hall in Snape Maltings, Suffolk, was nearing its conclusion. Resulting in a 3000-page report by Sir Frank Layfield, the Inquiry is an example of the contested nature of nuclear development, and of the huge paper-trail left in its wake. Meanwhile, as outlined by Dan Cordle and others, popular culture and the mass media narrated both the mundane and apocalyptic elements of the nuclear 1980s.[2] While the TV docudrama *Threads* (1984) is often touted as the dark pinnacle of the apocalyptic imaginary, the normalisation of nuclear mobilisation meant that the sight and sound of Vulcan nuclear bombers or F111 jets flying overhead, or high-stakes nuclear diplomacy reported in the news became a familiar backdrop to life.

Many more reverberations of nuclear mobilisation were happening in 1984, as they were at any other moment during the nuclear revolution. Whether working as part of the national nuclear project, attempting to resist some aspect of it or simply living with the knowledge of the possibility of nuclear war, all people were entwined in some way with processes of nuclearisation. From the production of nuclear fuel to the development of reactors and warheads and the disposal of nuclear waste, nuclearisation was at once remarkable in its scale and diversity, and notable for the way in which people from all walks of life were drawn into its mundane processes. The broad arc of nuclearisation was dependent on a supportive political and social base, on a range of formal sites and spaces—land was set aside to accommodate nuclear infrastructure—but also on a range of less formal social and cultural structures that legitimised and normalised the spread of nuclear development. In the years after 1945, the British government mobilised money, scientific knowledge, people and military–industrial capacity to create both an independent nuclear deterrent and the generation of electricity through nuclear reactors. This expensive and vast 'technopolitical' project, mostly top-secret and run by small sub-committees within government, was central to broader Cold War strategy and policy, and created significant social activism and political resistance.[3] This special issue continues work in recent years that has sought to place less emphasis on cultural production or elite culture, and more on the lives of individuals and histories of smaller communities below the 'national' lens of analysis.[4]

This comparative analysis of nuclear Britain builds on previous work that has tried to identify 'nuclear cultures' within British life. Perhaps most notably, the authors in this special issue are responding to the challenge set out by Jeff Hughes who, in 2012, wrote that:

> nuclear cultures were not an abstract parade of texts and representations [...] Nuclear science and technology and the political and ideological structures that spawned and sustained them shaped hundreds of millions of lives for more than half a century [...] Unpacking those structures, mapping the cultural politics of the nuclear, exploring the construction of the nuclear citizen in the past and today, should surely be the aim of any analysis of 'nuclear culture.'[5]

Moving away from identifying diverse 'nuclear cultures', the authors in this collection instead view British nuclear history as embedded within, rather than distinctive from, broader historical narratives of modern Britain.

Perhaps one reason for the traditional 'outsider status' of nuclear history within British historiography is the existence of 'nuclear exceptionalism' described by Gabrielle Hecht in *Being Nuclear* as a 'recurring theme in public discourse since 1945'. Hecht identified the 'insistence on an essential nuclear difference [...] manifested in political claims, technological systems, cultural forms, institutional infrastructures, and scientific knowledge [which] expressed the sense that an immutable ontology distinguished the nuclear from the non-nuclear.'[6] This phenomenon can help explain a historiographical trajectory that solidified the intellectual separation of the British nuclear project (understood as a scientific and technological one) from other histories of British society, culture, economics and politics. Traditionally, most major research projects on nuclear Britain have cleaved off into distinct silos: histories of science and technology, or Cold War diplomacy, which have not focused upon the social consequences of nuclearisation.[7] For years, and in part due to the secrecy surrounding British nuclear projects, the only nuclear histories were those written by historians working at the Atomic Weapons Establishment, based almost exclusively on policy, scientists and technological development.[8] This is one way that the genealogy of the term 'nuclear' has been strongly influenced by established Cold War interests and privileges, and one way that nuclear history was written to valorise nuclear science and technology. If we agree that nuclear exceptionalism does exist in some form, and acts to distort interpretations of nuclear history, then the epistemological and ontological foundations that support it need to be challenged.[9]

Recent attempts to map the social and cultural history of military–industrial policy decisions —especially resistance to them—suggest that nuclear mobilisation had far-reaching consequences for British life. The growth of cultural cold war studies in the 1990s led to Cold War historians focusing on cultural production in order to trace the discursive terrain that reinforced or resisted dominant policies and ideas.[10] This focus became more specialised in its focus on 'nuclear culture' as historians started to trace the social impact of nuclear development. Scholars have refined and broadened the term 'nuclear culture' and started to trace the ways that nuclear knowledge 'both embeds and is embedded in social practices, identities, norms, conventions, discourses, instruments and institutions—in short, in all the building blocks of what we term the social.'[11] The authors in this special issue identify and develop work that has offered novel ways to refine and deepen focus on the social experience of nuclearisation.

In order to achieve this, a range of under-utilised archives have been examined alongside oral histories and social memory in order to reveal subjective understandings of the nuclear age as it rolled into specific places in particular periods. In doing so, the particularities of the long-term visible and invisible pull of nuclear concerns inside the membrane of British political and cultural life are revealed. They have taken inspiration from other national historiographies of framing analysis on a local scale to see the repercussions of national and transnational nuclear programmes.[12] Several articles in this collection demonstrate unique epistemologies which historical actors used as a tool to understand and express the post-apocalyptic imaginary. Perhaps most vividly, our contributors teach us about the unique difficulties we face when thinking about analytical scale in relation to nuclear history.

Starting at the level of individual experience and subjectivity, the first two articles examine the inner lives of individuals living in the new atomic era, in the years after 1945. Claire Langhamer and then Jessica Douthwaite examine personal responses to the nuclear age and join the growing consensus that nuclear scholarship in the humanities should be focused on the subjective experience of nuclear technology, rather than the determinist idea that people's subjectivity was somehow irrevocably altered by the existence of nuclear technologies.[13] Through analysis of the Mass-Observation (MO) archives, Langhamer offers a systematic and elegant account of the emotional responses to the atomic bomb in 1945. After weaving previous interpretations of MO and WWII into an innovative emotions approach to nuclear culture, Langhamer analyses how people struggled with conflicting feelings in the process of making sense of atomic weapons in the months after Hiroshima. She argues that knowledge of the atomic bomb led to varied, powerful and self-conscious responses to it. Yet, MO is treated carefully as a source set, and Langhamer does not attempt to reconstruct emotions in pure and unadulterated form. Instead, the feelings expressed in responses to

MO are located within their social and cultural contexts, and the structuring role of MO is rightly acknowledged.

This impressive approach to source materials is continued by Jessica Douthwaite in her ambitious article on the subjective meanings of Civil Defence service from the point of view of volunteers. Building on the work of various scholars of nuclear civil defence, the article is an oral history that manages to highlight the contradictions and tensions inherent within the Civil Defence Corps (CDC) in the 1950s and 1960s.[14] Similarly to Langhamer, we are invited into the inner lives of individuals during the newly minted atomic age. Douthwaite unravels the emotions and attitudes of those who volunteered for the CDC. She shows that even the most committed CDC volunteers realised in the course of their training that nuclear war was not survivable. As volunteers trained to withstand a nuclear attack, the artistic imagination of nuclear apocalypse—in the form of catastrophic sets, make-up and theatrical role-playing—undermined the CDC premise that preparation would save the nation after an attack. Faced with this realisation, several subjects saved their faith in Civil Defence by calling up the heroism and can-do nature of an older generations' endurance of WWII bomb raids. Like Langhamer, the article notes how knowledge of the scale of nuclear destruction coincided with the symbolic use of the memory of the 1939–45 war. These sophisticated and multifaceted articles surely remind us of the urgent need for more oral histories of the Cold War era.

Also using oral history, Christine Wall is the only contributor in our special issue to focus on nuclear energy production. Her detailed and illuminating history of the planning and building of Sizewell A power station underscores the contested status of Britain's nuclear infrastructure. Wall recovers the conflicting attitudes of local residents to the Central Electricity Generating Board's construction of a nuclear power plant a mere one-and-a-half miles from the town of Leiston, Suffolk. Former construction workers remembered both the primitive and dangerous working conditions in building the high-tech plant and also their sense of accomplishment. Nuclear planners offered the usual 'nuclear village' benefits: jobs in a jobless area, increased revenue for business, a swimming pool and sports centre to emphasise a child-centred sense of safety and health alongside the ominously large and zoned off nuclear power plant.[15] The petitions of local fishing families, fearful that warm waters and radioactive emissions would swamp their business, were not recorded in meetings or archives, but recalled by interview subjects. The efforts of a locally active branch of the Communist Party of Great Britain had little effect in challenging the British state and in holding the 'consensus' institutions to account. Wall shows the limitations of democracy in the Cold War era. The lack of a democratic voice for local citizens and the long term, environmental implications of nuclear installations on local communities raises a question: did individual and collective experiences in the Cold War follow a pattern structured by geopolitics and national interest, or could a diversity of 'nuclear cultures' exist independently of these powerful influences?[16]

The next two articles continue this exploration of how broader Cold War policy was contested at a regional or local level, contributing to work that has shown how and why particular cities or regions responded differently to national nuclear policy.[17] It is now becoming clear that individuals within local and regional government could radically influence the ways in which nuclear information was devised and disseminated. Hazel Atashroo offers detailed analysis of the cultural politics of the Greater London Council (GLC) in the 1980s, and their exposure of government plans for abandoning London in case of a nuclear attack. The Civil Defence plan became a launching point for activists and the GLC to create a coherent peace message within a wider popular political frame. Like Douthwaite, Atashroo finds that her subjects turn to art to express the nuclear imaginary. The GLC embraced cultural work that was firmly embedded in a commitment to radical political positions, of which its commitment to peace was a central tenet. In contrast to national nuclear policy, the GLC funded anti-nuclear artists who used visual arts, performance and music to tap into an understanding of the strange, anti-urban anti-left fantasies that Civil Defence planners played out in envisioning a nuclear attack. Atashroo shows us how the existence of official nuclear policy and anti-nuclear activism altered the fabric of city life, and tapped into broader disagreements around the role and status of commemoration, local governance and democracy. Coverage in the mainstream press ensured that attempts to articulate local anti-nuclear (or anti-war) positions became amplified at the national level.

Christoph Laucht and Martin Johnes also focus upon the 1980s, examining Welsh anti-nuclear activism. Making the point that Welsh history is often marginalised within broader histories of Britain or the Cold War, Laucht and Johnes' close examination of nuclear culture in Wales greatly enhances our understanding of regional experiences of British nuclear mobilisation. The authors anchor their study in the early 1980s when people in deindustrialising Wales were resentful of both an influx of English migrants, and Thatcher administration policies that cut social welfare. As in Wall's account, plenty of people in Wales welcomed the employment opportunities the nuclear security state brought to their job-strapped communities. Anti-nuclear protestors, however, connected nuclear disarmament with concerns for Welsh economic and cultural autonomy. They understood that military expenses cut budgets for social welfare programmes and jobs, while military priorities threatened to make a smoking ruin of their homeland. Protestors linked a Nuclear Free Wales with the path to a better Welsh nation. Laucht and Johnes' richly researched article carries on the work of analysing how the nuclear threat was understood, and uncovers how a distinctive political culture could emerge that was squarely rooted in perceptions of the nuclear threat and connected to a wider context of political and social change.

As Christopher Hill's skilful article reminds us, Britain's nuclear story was intertwined with decolonisation and the global Cold War. Working at the intersection of imperial history and the history of nuclear weapons testing, Hill highlights the complex diplomatic and knowledge-producing manoeuvres that accompanied the detonation of nuclear weapons in the Algerian Sahara, a programme that commenced in 1960, two years prior to the end of the Algerian War of Independence. Hill shows how even in the midst of decolonisation, British diplomats successfully deployed colonial forms of cultural and technological power to erroneously assert the safety of nuclear bomb tests in North Africa. After outlining Britain's relationship with the French, Britain's relationship to both soon-to-be-independent colonies and the newly independent Ghana, and of course the domestic factors in West Africa, this rigorously researched article works as a corrective to the broad tendency to treat the histories of the Cold War and of the end of empire as different things.

These six contributions deepen and enrich our understanding of the ways in which nuclear policies, practices and narratives influenced British life. They help to erode the trend of 'nuclear exceptionalism' by reminding us that its powerful epistemological and ontological origins do not dovetail with social and cultural histories of the Cold War. People—as individuals or in groups—responded to the nuclearisation of the local, national and global community, yet a significant array of voices and opinions have been hidden or omitted from the nuclear history of Britain. We also understand more clearly how the nuclear condition could constrain democratic reflexes while, paradoxically, offer creative opportunities and the possibility of radical local governance. Uncovering these wide-ranging nuclear stories will continue to transform our appreciation of British 'nuclear culture', complimenting work that has focused on cultural production or representation.

The authors in this special issue have thought carefully about temporal, geographical and affective frames of analysis, and offered some original methodologies to assess new source materials. Making sense of the meanings of 'being nuclear' takes place in different registers, and requires careful calibration of analytical scale, alongside an appreciation of existing assumptions and imaginaries. The social and affective imprint left by the introduction and subsequent permanence of nuclear infrastructure and nuclear politics is too often relegated into broad contextual assumptions or journalistic metaphors, such as the 'shadow of the bomb' or the 'mushroom cloud of fear'. For too long, such phrases have been used to explain away the experiences and emotions of a generation. Perhaps then, this special issue will continue to challenge orthodoxies and suggest some new ways forward.

Notes

1. 'Mothers in A-War Death Pact', *Daily Mirror* 5 March, p.1.
2. Conze et al., eds. *Nuclear Threats, Nuclear Fear and the Cold War of the 1980s*. Hogg and Laucht, 'Introduction: British Nuclear Culture'; Cordle, *Late Cold War Literature and Culture*; and Hogg, *British Nuclear Culture*.
3. Hennessy, *The Secret State*, passim.
4. See Farish and Monteyne, 'Introduction: Histories of Cold War Cities.'
5. Hughes, 'What is British Nuclear Culture?,' 517–518.
6. Hecht, *Being Nuclear*, 6.
7. Barnaby and Holdstock, eds. *The British Nuclear Weapons Programme*; and Stoddart, *Losing an Empire and Finding a Role*.
8. Gowing, *Britain and Atomic Energy, 1939–1945*; and Arnold, with Pyne, *Britain and the H-Bomb*.
9. Work that approaches the place of nuclear knowledge in culture includes Middleton, *Physics Envy*; and van Munster and Sylvest, *Nuclear Realism*.
10. See Shaw, *British Cinema and the Cold War*; and Boyer, *By The Bomb's Early Light*.
11. Jasanoff, *States of Knowledge*, 3. For a working definition of nuclear culture, see Hogg, *British Nuclear Culture*, 7.
12. For some examples, see Brown, *Plutopia*; Natasha Zaretsky, *Radiation Nation*; Tompkins, *Better Active than Radioactive!*; Stawkowski, '"I Am a Radioactive Mutant": Emergent Biological Subjectivities at Kazakhstan's Semipalatinsk Nuclear Test Site'; Fox, *Downwind*: Pizzi and Hietala, eds. *Cold War Cities*; and Dodge et al., eds. *Cold War Cities*.
13. With thanks to Jessica Douthwaite for this idea.
14. Grant, *After the Bomb*.
15. See Blowers, *The Legacy of Nuclear Power* for more on nuclear peripheries and legacies.
16. A forthcoming article on uranium mining protests on Orkney argues that our standard conceptions of 'British' nuclear culture are limited and restrictive, and that responses to the nuclearisation of British life are far from fully researched. See Hogg, "Keep Orkney Active Not Radioactive".
17. See Farish and Monteyne, 'Introduction: Histories of Cold War Cities'.

Disclosure statement

No potential conflict of interest was reported by the authors.

ORCID

Jonathan Hogg http://orcid.org/0000-0002-6910-5308

Bibliography

Arnold, Lorna, with Katherine Pyne. *Britain and the H-Bomb*. Basingstoke: Palgrave, 2001.
Barnaby, F., and D. Holdstock, eds. *The British Nuclear Weapons Programme*. London: Cass, 2003.
Blowers, A. *The Legacy of Nuclear Power*. London: Routledge, 2016.
Brown, K. *Plutopia: Nuclear Families, Atomic Cities, and the Great Soviet and American Plutonium Disasters*. Oxford: Oxford University Press, 2013.
Boyer, P. *By the Bomb's Early Light: American Thought and Culture at the Dawn of the Atomic Age*. Chapel Hill, NC: University of North Carolina Press, 1995.
Conze, E., M. Klimke, and J. Varon, eds. *Nuclear Threats, Nuclear Fear and the Cold War of the 1980s*. Cambridge: Cambridge University Press, 2017.
Cordle, D. *Late Cold War Literature and Culture: The Nuclear 1980s*. Basingstoke: Palgrave Macmillan, 2017.
Dodge, M., R. Brook, and J. Hogg, eds. *Cold War Cities: Planning, Politics and Cultural Practices in the Age of Atomic Urbanism*. London: Routledge, forthcoming, 2019.
Farish, M., and D. Monteyne, 'Introduction: Histories of Cold War Cities.' *Urban History* 42, no. 4, November (2015): 543–546. doi:10.1017/S0963926815000607.
Fox, S. A. *Downwind: A People's History of the Nuclear West*. Lincoln: University of Nebraska Press, 2014.
Gowing, M. *Britain and Atomic Energy, 1939–1945*. London: Macmillan, 1964.
Grant, M. *After the Bomb: Civil Defence and Nuclear War in Cold War Britain, 1945–68*. Basingstoke: Palgrave Macmillan, 2010.
Hecht, G. *Being Nuclear: Africans and the Global Uranium Trade*. Cambridge, Mass.: MIT Press, 2012.
Hennessy, P. *The Secret State: Preparing for the Worst, 1945–2010*. 2nd ed. London: Penguin, 2010.
Hogg, J. *British Nuclear Culture: Official and Unofficial Narratives in the Long Twentieth Century*. London: Bloomsbury Academic, 2016.
Hogg, J. "'Keep Orkney Active Not Radioactive': Resistance to Uranium Mining on the Orkney Islands, 1971–1980." In *The Extractive Industries and Society*. Forthcoming, 2019.
Hogg, J., and C. Laucht, 'Introduction: British Nuclear Culture.' *British Journal for the History of Science* 45, no. 4, December (2012): 479–493.
Hughes, J. 'What is British Nuclear Culture? Understanding *Uranium 235*'. *The British Journal for the History of Science* 45, no. 4, December (2012): 495–518.
Jasanoff, S. *States of Knowledge: The Co-Production of Science and Social Order*. London: Routledge, 2006.

Middleton, P. *Physics Envy: American Poetry and Science in the Cold War and After*. Chicago: University of Chicago Press, 2015.

Pizzi, K., and M. Hietala, eds. *Cold War Cities: History, Culture and Memory*. Oxford: Peter Lang, 2016.

Proctor, R., and L. L. Schiebinger. *Agnotology: The Making and Unmaking of Ignorance*. Stanford, Calif: Stanford University Press, 2008.

Shaw, T. *British Cinema and the Cold War: The State, Propaganda and Consensus*. London: I. B. Tauris, 2001.

Stawkowski, M. E. "'I Am a Radioactive Mutant': Emergent Biological Subjectivities at Kazakhstan's Semipalatinsk Nuclear Test Site." *American Ethnologist* 43, no. 1, February (2016): 144–157. doi:10.1111/amet.12269.

Stoddart, K. *Losing an Empire and Finding a Role: Britain, the USA, NATO and Nuclear Weapons, 1964–70*. Basingstoke: Palgrave Macmillan, 2012.

Tompkins, A. S. *Better Active than Radioactive!: Anti-Nuclear Protest in 1970s France and West Germany*. Oxford: Oxford University Press, 2016.

van Munster, R., and C. Sylvest. *Nuclear Realism: Global Political Thought during the Thermonuclear Revolution*. Abingdon: Routledge, 2016.

Zaretsky, N. *Radiation Nation: Three Mile Island and the Political Transformation of the 1970s*. New York: Columbia University Press, 2018.

Weaponising peace: the Greater London Council, cultural policy and 'GLC peace year 1983'

Hazel A. Atashroo

ABSTRACT
This paper explores how the Greater London Council (1981–1986) deployed community focused cultural policy initiatives to disseminate cultural forms of nuclear scepticism during its 'GLC Peace Year 1983' campaign. Drawing upon archival sources and interviews, this paper will present an overview of Peace Year's cultural programme, which promoted London's 'nuclear-free zone' through arts commissions, poster campaigns, pop concerts, murals, documentary films and photography exhibitions. Focusing on two GLC funded projects aimed at promoting positive representations of women's peace activism, this paper will reflect upon the emotional and political impacts of the GLC's radical cultural strategy.

Introduction

Between 1981 and its abolition in April 1986, the final administration of the Greater London Council positioned itself as a vocal critic of the Thatcher government and its 'official narratives' about the British nuclear state.[1] The GLC's anti-nuclear campaign is exemplary of its defiant form of 'local socialism', in which the GLC acted in its 'official' capacity as an institution of the state to convey 'alternative' and 'unofficial' narratives about London's nuclear civil defence, actively contradicting central government.[2] There has been little recognition, however, of how the cultural policies of the GLC's Arts and Recreations Committee contributed to this anti-nuclear campaign through a year of arts sponsorship on the theme of 'Peace'. This paper will therefore present examples of the cultural production sponsored during 'GLC Peace Year 1983' as a facet of the GLC's broader radical cultural policy objectives. It will interrogate how the GLC's Arts Committees participated in a publicity war that sought to engage on the cultural front, deploying anti-nuclear artworks, festivals and community projects in London's public spaces to reach beyond peace activist networks. While this paper will consider how sponsored projects aimed to provoke emotional responses in rejection of central government's 'official' nuclear narratives, its case studies also evidence how those appeals to Londoners' nuclear anxieties were often contested and easily recuperated by those who opposed the GLC and its anti-nuclear stance.

London's nuclear-free zone: GLC peace year 1983 and cultural policy

The Labour GLC took office in April 1981 during a period described by Daniel Cordle as one in which 'people's sense of vulnerability' to nuclear dangers had significantly intensified. The announcement in 1979 that US nuclear missiles were to be stationed in the UK and Europe raised fears that growing international tensions between the US and the USSR could manifest themselves in a nuclear war on European territory.[3] As Cordle and Hogg have argued, this anxiety was magnified in March 1980 with the disclosure of the government's official nuclear strike response pamphlet, *Protect and Survive*—its emphasis on civilian self-reliance in the event of an attack inadvertently heightening the population's perceived vulnerability.[4] Unsurprisingly, this period saw a reinvigoration of peace activism and an increased attendance at CND's rallies, their renewed popularity presenting a threat to official narratives of deterrence that did not escape the notice of Thatcher's cabinet.[5] A civil defence rebellion in regional local government followed, with Manchester City Council the first to declare itself a 'Nuclear-Free Zone' and refuse to cooperate with civil defence exercises in November 1980, with 140 local councils, including the GLC, following suit in the coming years.[6]

With the arrival of the new GLC administration, officers in its secretive Civil Defence unit were unwilling to respond to enquiries about London's nuclear civil defence strategy posed by protagonists who were suspected to be CND sympathisers.[7] Such was the reticence to discuss matters of nuclear civil defence with incoming GLC officials that investigative journalist Duncan Campbell was employed by the Council to extract information and report back on current civil defence plans, culminating in his 1982 exposé, *War Plan UK*.[8] Campbell's revelations rendered the official advice of *Protect and Survive* farcical and propagandistic with the realisation that the government could not and would not protect the lives of Londoners in the aftermath of a nuclear attack. Defenceless urban populations were instructed to simply 'stay at home' and therefore wait to die passively in their millions.[9] Citing Campbell's findings that official response plans involved ring-fencing London with troops after the blast to prevent anyone from escaping, Ken Livingstone recounted government projections that 'within twelve weeks six million Londoners would be dead from blast, radiation and disease'.[10] Senior officials were, however, to be evacuated to safety in the event of a nuclear strike and yet as Livingstone wryly recounted,

> The thought of spending my last days locked in a bunker with Mrs Thatcher's Cabinet while all my friends died held little appeal [...] so we started working with CND and switched the government funds we received for war preparations into the campaign for unilateral nuclear disarmament. [...] we declared 1983 to be 'Peace Year' and organised a series of cultural events and posters throughout the city to reveal to Londoners the Government's secret plans for their sacrifice in the event of war.[11]

Following E. P. Thompson's call to *Protest and Survive*, the GLC refused to cooperate with the government's nuclear defence strategy and declared London a 'Nuclear-Free Zone' on 4 June 1982, reportedly finding new cultural uses for its considerable civil defence budget.[12] 'Nuclear-Free' London was inaugurated at an 'anti-nuclear weekend' with a reception for '500 peace representatives' at County Hall and an opening ceremony broadcast on LBC.[13] This began a sequence of cultural and community events that channelled resources into public activities centred upon raising anti-nuclear consciousness and publicising the GLC's rejection of central government strategy. Rather than comply with the government's planned 'Hard Rock' civil defence exercises scheduled that July, the Council opened three of London's 'wartime group control centres', communications bunkers reserved for officials in the event of an attack, inviting the public to 'judge for itself if London could survive the bomb'.[14] By the GLC's estimate, 4800 people visited these 'secret' control centres in six days.[15]

A fortnight after activists gathered to 'embrace the base' at RAF Greenham Common in December 1982, the GLC announced by press release that 1983 would be 'GLC Peace Year'. This would coincide with the twenty-fifth anniversary of CND and a General Election, in which Prime Minister Thatcher would be opposed by CND founding Labour leader Michael Foot. Inviting Londoners to participate in peace-themed activities, Chair of the GLC Arts and Recreation Committee Tony Banks announced that 'There can be no better way to convey this message through the length and breadth of London than through the arts'.[16] 'Peace Year' was an early indication of the Arts and Recreation Committee's recognition of the role cultural policy could play as vehicle for conveying a political message. This was by no means the first instance in which a State body in Britain sought to deploy artists and cultural producers in the service of the visual communication of nuclear narratives, as illustrated in Catherine Jolivette's account of the 1951 Festival of Britain and its exhibits on theme of atomic science.[17] However, Peace Year was more overtly focused on communicating anti-nuclear narratives that would contest central government's public reassurances regarding London's civil defence and official narratives promoting its strategy of nuclear deterrence.

Tony Banks's advisor Alan Tomkins was approached to organise the arts programme and invited artist and activist Peter Kennard to muster a group of activists and cultural producers to County Hall to draft proposals.[18] These were to be sponsored alongside the existing programme of public festivals, which were themselves to be incorporated into the overarching 'peace' theme. Arts commissions and cultural events would be complemented by an explosive public information campaign designed to communicate the dangers of nuclear war or accident in London and the inadequacy of Westminster's civil defence plans.[19] The GLC also recognised the importance of urban spaces for the delivery of its nuclear-free zone message, which were to become the sites of an ideological conflict regarding London's nuclear civil defence, through a series of billboard posters, promotional materials and public art projects that would play upon what Daniel Cordle has described as a 'politics of vulnerability'.[20] Focused on the unimaginable horrors that it was predicted nuclear war might unleash on the capital, these cultural interventions sought to bring nuclear annihilation into closer proximity to the population's everyday lived experience of the city, disrupting relatively peaceful streets and neighbourhoods.[21]

Renowned for his political photomontages, Peter Kennard's 'Dispatches from an Unofficial War Artist' exhibition was selected to launch Peace Year in January 1983. His visceral photomontages were later distributed in GLC-sponsored 'peace poster packs', which were sent to peace groups, schools and local authorities across the country.[22] Kennard was also selected to design the promotional materials for GLC Peace Year. His logo of two hands in silhouette snapping a nuclear missile in half was chosen in preference to the proposals of professional advertising agencies, which were largely confined to images of doves.[23] Over one weekend, Kennard made a doomsday-themed photomontage of London landmarks in the nuclear firing line for the iconic poster 'Keep London Out of the Killing Ground', which was plastered across London billboards only days later Figure 1. Subsequent GLC billboard posters alerted Londoners to civil defence plans to repurpose parks for mass graves in the event of a nuclear strike and a 'spot the nuclear train' series sought to inform Londoners about the dangers of nuclear waste transportation through London by rail. Another poster made a direct appeal to readers' sense of self-preservation, 'Only one in four people reading this poster would survive a nuclear strike on London (chances are it won't be you)'. Alongside Kennard, the work of various cultural producers was deployed to tour London venues and articulate the themes of GLC Peace Year. For instance, Edward Barber's 'Bomb Disposal: Peace Camps and Direct Action' exhibition at County Hall in March 1983 presented photographs of women peace activists at RAF Greenham and Molesworth. Unlike the sensationalised negative representations of peace activists found in right wing discourses and attendant press, Barber's photographs and statements from activists presented more positive images which aligned with the GLC's objectives.[24] Crucially, it was beyond the remit of the GLC Arts Committees to fund political demonstrations, however, they were able to sponsor sympathetic cultural production and recreational activities to entertain

Figure 1. Documentation photograph of billboard poster, designed by Peter Kennard for Greater London Council 'Peace Year' 1983. Text reads 'Keep London out of the Killing Ground. Give a peaceful lead to the world. Support GLC Peace Year 1983. GLC Working for London and Peace.' Copyright Peter Kennard.

the public.[25] Peace-themed music festivals were organised in London parks to coincide with the 1983 People's March for Jobs and major CND demonstrations. For example, the GLC funded a CND Youth pop festival in Brixton's Brockwell Park which was compered by John Peel and featured Madness, Style Council, The Damned and Clint Eastwood and General Saint, who were launching their fittingly titled single, 'Nuclear Crisis'.[26] Different tastes were also catered for at a classical music 'Proms for Peace' at the GLC's historic houses across London. Political street ensemble Fallout Marching Band were sponsored to purchase new instruments and perform public concerts, appearing at CND rallies and Peace Year festivals.[27] Touring theatre productions such as the 'GLC Peace Cabaret', 'GLC Nuclear Bunker Parties' and David Holman's play, 'Nineteen Eighty Three' took the anti-nuclear message to London's outer boroughs.[28] The GLC also employed contemporary artist John Dugger to produce a series of handmade peace banners at his *Banner Arts Studio* for the GLC in 1983 which were exhibited in County Hall and used at festivals and demonstrations.[29] These cultural events were perceived as an opportunity to communicate the GLC's alternative nuclear narratives to different audiences and reach beyond activist constituents and dominant media representations.

Films for peace

The independent film and video sector was a sponsorship priority for the GLC's Arts and Recreations Committee. GLC-sponsored video workshops provided technical skills to a more diverse range of users than the television industries admitted and often supported community documentary work that would otherwise not have been able to access professional facilities.[30] In support of independent producers, the GLC commissioned films for Peace Year, assisting financially in the production or completion of films presenting perspectives on nuclear issues that diverged from central government's 'official' narratives. These were promoted through a film hire catalogue, *Films For Peace 1983*, which listed tapes available to libraries, 'community workers, teachers, trade unions and church workers' and included instructions for holding screenings and discussion sessions. Prior to this GLC intervention, local peace groups had provided an informal forum for the private screening of censored films that dealt with politically sensitive nuclear issues and circulated 'unofficial' narratives about the nuclear state.[31] The GLC sought to participate in this arena to promote its own nuclear-free zone message to Londoners, using an approach to cultural policy that supported independent community video producers and distributors to act as a corrective to apparent media bias against peace activists.[32]

Under the new leadership of Tony Banks, the GLC's Arts and Recreation Committee undertook a radical redefinition of cultural policy, embarking on a programme of arts sponsorship that was to reach far beyond the remit of the Arts Council. As a quasi-autonomous non-governmental organisation, the Arts Council had long claimed to conduct the business of disbursing State arts grants at 'arm's length' from party political interference.[33] However, its claims to neutrality came under increased scrutiny during the 1980s, with Tony Banks as a particularly vocal critic. Redirecting the focus of sponsorship away from Arts Council funded 'elite' metropolitan venues, the GLC was in favour of a strategy in support of a rather loosely defined concept of 'popular' culture. The associated emphasis on popular community participation necessitated a more overt approach which, unlike the Arts Council's 'arm's length' claims, acknowledged the politics of arts sponsorship and cultural policy, a move described by Franco Bianchini as a shift from a cultural policy that sought to democratise 'elite' culture towards one intended to foster a 'cultural democracy'.[34] GLC arts sponsorship was expanded to include smaller community projects and training schemes targeting social groups that it acknowledged experienced discrimination under existing cultural provision, namely Londoners from ethnic minorities, lesbians and gay men, Londoners with disabilities, and more broadly, older people and women.[35]

The Livingstone GLC administration is often noted for its new personnel, many of whom had spent their formative years participating in activism or were at least sympathetic to ideas drawn from new social movements.[36] Significantly, the GLC's Women's Committee was formed to advocate for the needs of London's women and make their voices heard. In an attempt to ensure that gender disadvantage would not preclude women from cultural participation or securing employment in London's newly defined 'cultural industries', both the GLC's Arts and Recreations Committee and Women's Committees sought to promote women's cultural production, training and community projects.[37] These cultural initiatives and attendant cultural spaces were amongst a network of GLC funded 'material and emotional refuges for women' to which Stephen Brooke has recently referred. He notes,

> Space was fundamental to what the Labour GLC did between 1981 and 1986 […] The politics of space in 1980s London had particularly sharp edges because GLC funded centres were competing with an emerging neoliberal landscape […] space was a site of ideological conflict. [38]

The use of the rates to fund women's spaces, crèches and arts projects was an issue over which ideological conflict emerged in discourses on both the left and right. Public anger was sometimes directed towards these women's organisations, which were frequently held up in parliament and the press as examples of the GLC's so-called 'Loony Left' playing fast and loose with public money.[39]

The name of a women's peace group, 'Babies Against the Bomb' (BAB) had itself proven incendiary enough to provoke press outrage, providing journalists and politicians alike with a useful shorthand for narratives of GLC overspending on minority interests.[40] Indeed, its name appears in Hansard records on at least eight occasions between 1983 and 1993 with Baron Beloff stating in a 1984 Lords debate that,

> When one sees the babies against the bomb and the women of Greenham Common, and all these other well-meaning people led astray in this way, then one feels that to some extent our responsibility in giving a leadership has not been fully maintained. The CND and its associates—the whole of the so-called peace movement—are orchestrated from Moscow.[41]

Beloff's statement was an allusion characteristically disproportionate to the threat posed by a group of mothers who undertook sponsored pushchair walks, picketed embassies with prams, coordinated petitions and held informal coffee mornings in Kentish Town and Harlesden. Over coffee, the mothers planned their anti-nuclear consciousness-raising work and gained some relief from the daytime isolation of motherhood while their children played together. BAB attracted a variety of women, many of whom were completely new to politics, motherhood, and feminist ideas—hardly a dangerous faction 'orchestrated from Moscow'. As BAB founder Tamar Swade recalled, the women were brought together by their common nuclear anxiety, all recognising that the greatest threat to their new babies in 1983 was the very real prospect that the world was on the brink of nuclear war:

> One woman told me that the mention of nuclear war conjures up the waking nightmare of her children burning. Another pictures kissing her children goodbye for the last time. A third said her particular nightmare was that the four-minute warning would come while she was at work and she wouldn't be able to cross town in time to get to them.[42]

BAB was one of many women's organisations in receipt of modest financial support from the GLC's Women's Committee to hold their childcare-friendly meetings and undertake consciousness-raising work.[43] Despite their modest objectives and equally modest draw on public funds, Beloff's statement is illustrative of how BAB and small women's organisations became emblematic of a sensationalised, dangerous radicalism that the GLC were seen to promote. The misrepresentation of BAB was one factor in the GLC's sponsorship of *Born 1981: Babies Against The Bomb*, an independent film documentary produced by Joram Ten Brink and Jini Rawlings who were community video workers at the Moonshine Community Arts Workshop in Brent. Following extensive enquiries in the course of this research, a copy of a second edit of the film, entitled *Child's Play*, was located in the personal collection of BAB founder Tamar Swade, and the following description in based upon this copy.[44]

Presumably, GLC Peace Year organisers saw the proposal for the completion of a video documentary about BAB as an opportunity to set the record straight regarding the unwarranted attention that had been paid to a modest £800 Women's Committee grant in 1983/4 in support of a group of North London mothers running a crèche, albeit one with anti-nuclear leanings. The BAB documentary is itself an interesting case study in the sometimes uneasy relationship between feminist ideals, peace activism and motherhood, as BAB's focus on motherhood was not universally accepted by feminists, as Swade recounted,

> There are some feminists who frown upon this attitude and I would like to answer to them. [...] Does it make me any less of a person if my immediate, instinctive reaction to nuclear war is that of a mother? [...] Let's be tolerant, supportive, sisterly.[45]

The film records the mothers' activist group as they organise their consciousness-raising work while taking care of their children. It documents some of the non-violent direct actions they initiated, often with their children in tow. The testimonies in the film provide an insight into the role that emotions play in these womens' political commitment to anti-nuclear activism and exist as a valuable record of womens' activism beyond the Greenham and Molesworth epicentres. The mothers address the camera directly as they talk as a group and while they work on household chores, intermittently interrupted by their toddlers at play. These scenes of everyday domestic labour take place in their homes, but any suggestion of the insularity of their domestic lives is disrupted by the global reach of their discussions. One mother, while changing a nappy, explains clearly, 'The enemy to my child's future is the presence of nuclear weapons and the arms race. [...] Our country is going to have cruise missiles [...] It is a direct threat to his life to have those weapons here'.[46] This threat motivated BAB to organise a coach of London women to join the 'embrace the base' day at RAF Greenham Common in December

1982, where they are filmed forming part of the human chain around the base. One woman speaks of her elation on alighting from the coach at Greenham,

> There were just vast amounts of people there. And when we had the link up, to be linking hands with people that you don't know because they believe in what you believe in. I couldn't get over the feeling for days, I felt like a mother seeing her baby for the first time.[47]

She describes participating in a demonstration organised by BAB in London,

> We went to the Russian embassy and the American embassy, that was just off the top of our heads as there was a guy on the telly saying you should be protesting right outside the embassies rather than Greenham Common, so we said ok, we'll do it! And we done it! Which was a lot to do for just people, a small group of people.[48]

Others interviewed describe how joining this activist group had given them renewed confidence and purpose. One stated, 'I have become more energised in fighting for what I want, as before I was very timid. I was apathetic before'. Another suggested the group relieved the boredom of motherhood, '[The group is] essential for me […] It can get so lonely as a mother looking after one baby all day. It's really important to have some mind stimulus'. BAB gave these London women an opportunity to participate in a mode of disarmament activism that they perceived as being more sympathetic to their caring responsibilities than the demands of other activist groups while also providing a social space and an emotional support network for often isolated young mothers.

In the opening sequence of the BAB film, a group of women are seen staging a sombre march on Whitehall in October 1982, dressed in mourning black and wheeling empty pushchairs upon which rest makeshift tombstones bearing the names of children killed in the nuclear attacks on Hiroshima and Nagasaki.[49] This funereal group were followed by BAB's main organisers who passed police cordons with pushchairs decorated with colourful balloons to deliver a petition to Prime Minister Margaret Thatcher reportedly bearing 10,000 signatures BAB had collected from women's organisations across the country in support of disarmament.[50] In a speech to the Conservative Party Conference in October 1982, Thatcher had dismissed the views of unilateralist parents,

> I understand the anxieties of parents with children growing up in the nuclear age. But the question, the fundamental question for all of us is whether unilateral nuclear disarmament would make war *less likely*. I have to tell you it would not.[51]

Personal anxieties may have been an entry point for some BAB participants, but their statements in the film would suggest that their empathy clearly extended far beyond their personal fears. For these mothers, Hiroshima's child victims were *their* children, and children suffering in famines as countries wasted money on weapons were equally *their* children. In the film, Swade passionately reiterates,

> Millions of children in the Third World die of starvation, when billions of our money is being put into arms: what sort of a world is it! Even if we blow up tomorrow we must speak out against that. How can we stomach it? How can we live in that sort of world? […] There are children starving in the gutter […] The world is now a smaller place and those children starving—they are *our* children starving in *our* gutter.[52]

BAB activists claimed that in 1982 the world was becoming a smaller place, a perceived consequence of both globalisation and the international scale of nuclear capabilities, which not only brought the danger of nuclear war closer to their own homes, but also brought the suffering of mothers across the world to their doorsteps.[53]

The documentary films produced for Peace Year record various critical responses to the British nuclear state and London's civil defence in the early 1980s and the alliances that momentarily formed around those critical positions. BAB's film in particular indicates the GLC Women's Committee's support for alternative representations of women's peace activism in London. It is hard to ascertain the breadth of the distribution and public reception of the Peace Year films but it is likely that they may only have reached limited audiences at small activist screenings rather than the wider public consumption envisioned by the GLC policy makers. Nonetheless, as a community film production made in close collaboration with an activist group, BAB's film provides an interesting record of women's peace activism at a local level, presenting an alternative representation to those that more commonly reached mainstream broadcast media.

Wall and peace: nuclear narratives in public space

The GLC's promotion of London's 'nuclear-free zone' in 1983 also extended to the politicisation of public space through the sponsorship of anti-nuclear murals and the thematic designation of recreational areas as 'peace gardens'.[54] Six public murals were commissioned on anti-nuclear themes from London Muralists For Peace, a collective of mural teams working in consultation with the London CND.[55] Two remain intact, Ray Walker's recently restored 'Hackney Peace Carnival' which features lively portraits of local residents uniting in a carnival spirit against the bomb and Brian Barnes's 'Riders of the Apocalypse', a satirical depiction of mutually assured destruction painted on a housing cooperative building in New Cross.[56] Barnes's design features unflattering skeletal caricatures of Ronald Reagan, Margaret Thatcher, Michael Heseltine and Yuri Andropov as the horsemen of the apocalypse straddling nuclear missiles, in a manner reminiscent of the final scene of Kubrick's *Doctor Strangelove*. Notably, Reagan's golden missile is emblazoned with a portentous anamorphic skull, drawn from Hans Holbein the Younger's *The Ambassadors* (1533), rendering this mural a nuclear memento mori.[57]

However, these visceral images on public walls represented an incursion of a particular politics into London's public space and were not unproblematically received by its constituents. In July 1983, an application was presented to the GLC Women's Committee from London Wall, a four-woman community mural team from Brixton. Their struggle to find opportunities within a 'male-dominated art world' and their intention to design 'non-sexist' murals were important components of their application to the GLC. In their Peace Year proposal, they stated,

> As a result of our discussions with the women at Greenham Common, they would like us to paint a mural to celebrate their work for Peace [...] We have found what we consider to be a most suitable site, the side of a large building located on the corner of Kennington Rd. and Lambeth Rd., the building is directly overlooked by the Imperial War Museum. Our mural depicting women's struggle for peace and freedom will be seen by all who visit this monument to war. The implication is obvious. [58]

The Women's Committee noted with interest that the mural would portray women's peace activism positively, giving London women confidence to raise their own objections to nuclear weapons despite the dominant negative representation of women's peace activism. London Wall's chosen location, Surrey Lodge, was approved by the Women's Committee who proudly stated that 'every member of the public entering the Museum will see the women's peace mural and benefit from [...] an alternative view of warfare from that engendered by the Imperial War Museum'.[59] London Wall were granted £14,284 by the GLC in October 1983 and began public consultations. However, both their proposed subject matter and provocative choice of location was to cause immediate consternation and London Wall's proposal was to be, in the headline of one paper, 'torpedoed' by residents and the local and national press.[60]

Below sensationalist headlines, accounts in *South London Press*, the *Sun*, *Daily Telegraph*, *Daily Express* and the *Evening Standard* articulated a variety of local objections to the proposed mural, ranging from complaints about the political 'ban the bomb' message, the anticipation of vandalism, objections to ratepayers funding artists work, and local tenants simply not wanting any kind of mural at all.[61] In a rare moment of nuanced consideration, one letter printed in *Evening Standard* questioned the GLC's assumption that the Imperial War Museum's purpose was to glorify war.[62] The Museum itself refused to enter into the affray, its deputy director making a statement that he only hoped a 'good artist' would be chosen.[63] While London Wall muralist Louise Vines stated that she had garnered a hundred signatures in support of the project, the local press campaign had successfully amplified the negative responses, often drawing upon familiar anti-activist tropes to deride the project and its subject matter. In her defence of the project to GLC officers, Vines also noted that a negative leafletting campaign initiated by opposition Social Democratic Party Councillors in Labour-controlled Lambeth had made it almost impossible to make the local case for the artwork.[64]

London Wall's mural soon became part of familiar press narratives decrying the GLC's 'inappropriate spending' and support for radical causes with a third of the articles holding 'Red Ken' Livingstone personally responsible for this excess.[65] For instance, a *Daily Express* headline branded the mural 'An Insult To The Fallen' as commemorated by the Imperial War Museum, asserting that the funding of this project was indicative of the GLC Labour left's threat to the Labour Party's British values,

> What is unforgivable is the deliberate insult this represents to the dead of two terrible wars. Unless Neil Kinnock publicly repudiates the Labour leadership in London, Labour nationally will be fatally tainted as the anti-British party. [66]

In response to the local and national media outrage, the mural was relocated to a less prominent and less controversial site on the wall of a Community Service Volunteers building facing a petrol station on the Pentonville Road in Kings Cross. The final design featured three women wearing suffragette colours linking arms accompanied by a Japanese child in a dress patterned with cherries in reference to cherry trees planted in memorial to the victims of Hiroshima and Nagasaki. The central female figure holds a 'Sankofa bird', an emblem frequently used in African Diaspora contexts to denote reflection on the past. Eight symbolic images surround the four figures serving to link local women's centres with national peace activism and the international implications of nuclear war. These included a literal depiction of a 'telephone tree' indicating women's emergency communication at Greenham Common; a starving woman and child signifying the resources wasted on nuclear weapons; a woman imprisoned for her activism; a nuclear mushroom cloud over a destroyed Kings Cross station and women in overalls building two local women's centres.[67] However, by the time the mural was officially opened in its less contentious location in June 1984, the national press had lost interest in the story and its opening was only noted in the local *St Pancras Chronicle*, *Islington Gazette* and GLC-supported *City Limits*.

Stephen Brooke's suggestion that historians seek to identify to the 'work emotions do politically' within cultures of democracy may prove helpful when considering the public reception of Peace Year's cultural outputs.[68] Sponsored cultural projects such as the Women's Peace Mural were sited so as to be encountered as part of Londoners' everyday experience of the city, with the intention of reaching audiences beyond activist networks. This proliferation of what were often doomsday discourses writ large on bleak billboards and murals, pressing passers-by to confront the nuclear threat to their neighbourhoods, was a direct appeal to the city dweller's sense of vulnerability to nuclear attack, adding to and perhaps amplifying a pre-existing climate of concern regarding the effectiveness of urban nuclear civil defence in early 1980s London. While Peace Year's cultural production may well have had profound emotional impacts on some, as the case studies presented suggest, these impacts were felt unevenly—the GLC's appeal to London's nuclear anxieties could not reliably equate to wholesale support for disarmament as a means of allaying these fears. The GLC attempted to amplify and support women's expressions of anti-nuclear sentiment during Peace Year through the sponsorship of cultural projects, but the task of breaking through the dominant right wing press and central government narratives which were either acutely focused on belittling and discrediting women activists or ignoring them altogether was fraught with difficulty.

Conclusion

This paper has outlined the contribution made by the Greater London Council's Arts Committees to anti-nuclear discourses in early 1980s London, demonstrating how 'official' cultural policy could play a role in facilitating and circulating 'unofficial' narratives about the nuclear State. As recent accounts of 1980s Liverpool and Sheffield attest, nuclear narratives that were simultaneously 'alternative' and 'official', given their state-institutional origin, were emerging in some cases at the local level.[69] GLC Peace Year could be understood within this context, although it is important to acknowledge both the connections and distinctions between these local authorities.[70]

Tony Banks and others at the GLC had recognised that creative and participatory cultural expressions were already a component of the non-violent direct action repertoire of the rejuvenated peace movement in the early 1980s and sought to tap into this current. GLC endorsement added the official 'weight' of an elected body to cultural production presenting otherwise 'unofficial' narratives, in part aimed to attack central government's pro-nuclear position in the run up to the 1983 General Election. While GLC Peace Year's varied projects represent a useful record of some of the cultural expressions of nuclear scepticism in early 1980s London, as a sample, they are closely tied to their oppositional 'local socialist' state sponsors. GLC Peace Year therefore represents a useful case study in the task of 'mapping the cultural politics of the nuclear' as advocated by Jeff Hughes, identifying the political and ideological contexts within which varied cultural texts were produced, mediated, disseminated, and importantly, received within the public sphere.[71]

Beyond the political content of the various cultural initiatives, the GLC's use of ratepayers' money to fund any public art project was perceived as contentious by some, as evidenced in local newspaper responses to projects like the Women's Peace Mural.[72] Indeed, the GLC's perceived focus on arts and cultural activities in London may have unintentionally reinforced an unhelpful media characterisation of the anti-nuclear movement as a predominantly middle-class pursuit.[73] The attention that GLC-sponsored arts projects sometimes attracted had the added advantage of providing GLC politicians with a platform from which to challenge central government's official nuclear narratives and respond to criticism. However, some public controversies may have inadvertently invited discourses about Labour's weakness on defence issues, bolstering support for the nuclear deterrent.

As the case studies in this paper attest, the GLC's cultural policy approach to the dissemination of alternative nuclear narratives was easily 'weaponised' by those who disagreed with the GLC's agenda. These minor cultural insurrections and attendant localised disputes were to circulate nationally as part of sensationalist discourses centred on the indictment of peace activists, the Labour left in London and in effect, the Party as a whole.

Notes

1. Carvel, *Citizen Ken*, 1984.
2. For discussion of 'official' and 'unofficial' nuclear narratives see Hogg, *British Nuclear Culture*, 8–11. For discussion of varied 'local socialisms' see Payling, *Socialist Republic of South Yorkshire*, 2–4.
3. Ibid., 135; Hudson, *Now More Than Ever*, 114; Cordle, "Protect/Protest," 655; The nuclear accident in Pennsylvania in 1979 had also heightened fears about the safety of nuclear energy.
4. Anon, *Protect and Survive*, 137.
5. Ibid., 135; National Archives, CAB/128/70/12, 6.
6. Hudson, *Now More than Ever*, 134; and Stafford, "Stay at Home," 402–3.
7. Livingstone, *If Voting Changed Anything*, 231. The GLC's Civil Defence Unit at County Hall collaborated with the Ministry of Defence and the Home Office on a civil defence strategy for London tied to central government policy.
8. Ibid.; Livingstone, *You Can't Say That*, 214; Campbell, *War Plan UK*; and Hogg, *British Nuclear Culture*,139–40.
9. Stafford, "Stay at Home," 385.
10. Ibid., 232–233; Livingstone, *You Can't Say That*, 215; and Beckett, *Promised you a Miracle*, 90–91.
11. Livingstone, *If Voting Changed Anything*, 231–233. Archival evidence suggests that the GLC's collaboration with CND was not wholly uncritical. The GLC Ethnic Minorities Unit presented a report 'Peace Movement and Anti-Racist Initiatives' in 1983 highlighting concerns that CND was dominated by white middle-class interests, prompting CND to respond, see London Metropolitan Archive (LMA) LMA:GLC/DG/PRE/50/01.
12. Thompson, *Protest and Survive*.
13. "London Declared a Nuclear-Free Zone by GLC" *LBC*, 1982. BUFVC (Accessed 3 March 2016). http://bufvc.ac.uk/tvandradio/lbc/index.php/segment/0014300116001; "GLC to have Nuclear Weekend," *Times*, 3 June 1982.

14. LMA:GLC/DG/PRB/039/nos. 347, 430. Control centres including Pear Tree House in West Norwood, and others in North Cheam and Wanstead.
15. Ibid. no. 454.
16. Ibid. no. 635.
17. Jolivette, *British Art in the Nuclear Age*, 103–22.
18. Alan Tomkins, interview with the author, January 2016; LMA:GLC/RA/GR/02/102. Contributing peace groups included London Peace Action, Youth CND, Christian CND, International Fellowship for Reconciliation (Netherlands), Japanese Friendship Association, The Chile Solidarity Campaign, and The Quakers.
19. Clarke et.al. eds., *London under Attack*. The GLC also commissioned research including the Greater London Area War Risk Study (GLAWARS) which examined nuclear risks to London, research into nuclear waste transportation by rail and it also contributed to the Sizewell B inquiry.
20. Cordle, "Protect/Protest," 655.
21. Hogg, *British Nuclear Culture*, 7–8.
22. Kennard et al., *Dispatches*, 85–88; Kennard, *GLC Poster Pack*, V&A:E.1511-2004; LMA: GLC/RA/GR/02/102; Kennard and Slocombe, *Unofficial War Artist*. Around 2800 copies of Kennard's first GLC poster pack were made to meet demand. In 2016, Kennard's GLC work was exhibited at his Imperial War Museum retrospective.
23. Peter Kennard, interview with the author, London, 3 September 2015.
24. LMA:GLC/DG/PRB/35/040/no.123. Barber's exhibition toured a number of venues, on loan to peace groups. Images from Barber's exhibition at County Hall were amongst those included in his May 2016 retrospective at the Imperial War Museum.
25. Alan Tomkins, interview with the author, January 2016.
26. LMA:GLC/RA/GR/02/102. The CND Youth Rally's music 'Festival for Peace' on 7 May 1983 received a GLC grant of £21,500.
27. The Fallout Marching Band are credited with writing two songs from the 'Greenham Songbook', see 'Your Greenham' archive, accessed 30 March 2016, http://www.yourgreenham.co.uk/.
28. LMA:GLC/RA/GR/02/102.
29. John Dugger, interview with the author, February 2017.
30. GLC, *Campaign for a Popular Culture*, 87–90.
31. Cordle, "That's Going to Happen to us," 76.
32. GLC, *Films for Peace*; Young, *Femininity in Dissent*.
33. Bianchini, 'GLC – R.I.P', 103–17; Hewison, *Culture and Consensus*; Pearson, *State and the Visual Arts*; and Hesmondhalgh et. al. *Culture, Economy Politics*, 22–3.
34. Bianchini, "Cultural Policy and Political Strategy."
35. Terms of reference in use here reflect developments in policy and identity politics at the GLC between 1981 and 1986.
36. Curran et al., *Culture Wars*, 8; Gyford, *Politics Of Local Socialism*, 33–40; and Beckett, *Promised you a Miracle*, 358–9.
37. By the GLC's own admission, they achieved only limited success in this aim. See GLC, *Campaign for A Popular Culture*, 57–8. For "cultural industries," see GLC, *State of the Art*.
38. Brooke, "Spaces, Emotions and Bodies," 2015; and Brooke, "Space, Emotions and the Everyday," 1–33.
39. Curran et. al., *Culture Wars*. In some cases, such conflict resulted in the vandalism of premises run by GLC-sponsored women's organisations, for instance, Baines et al. See *Red Women's Workshop*, 25.
40. Carvel *Citizen Ken*, 208. John Carvel records Richard Brew, Tory leader of the GLC in 1982, listing '[…] feminists and the gay activists […] ethnic groups and the Irish […] CND, Babies Against the Bomb' as part of the roll call of 'nutters' whose votes Livingstone was seeking to attract, by way of grant aid. Curran, *Impacts and Influences*, 119. Curran noted that 'Babies Against the Bomb' was soon caricatured as 'Black Lesbians against the Bomb' in some press

reports. Hosken, *Ken: The Ups and Downs*, 151. Andrew Hosken asserted that Babies Against the Bomb was the most contentious of GLC grants.

41. Beloff, HL Deb 14 June 1984 vol. 452 cc1256-336, 1314. For other Hansard records of 'Babies Against the Bomb', see: HC Deb 26 April 1983 vol. 41 cc737-823, 770; HC Deb 23 July 1985 vol. 83 cc886-92; 887; HC Deb 27 July 1993 vol. 229 cc1051-8.
42. Swade, in Jones, *Keeping the Peace*, 64–67.
43. Swade, interview with the author, London 2016.
44. Ten Brink, Joram and Jini Rawlins, *Born 1981: Babies Against the Bomb/ Child's Play*, VHS, dir. Joram Ten Brink and Jini Rawlins, London: Moonshine Community Arts Workshop, 1983. Following unproductive enquiries at the BFI, Concord Films, and with the filmmakers, a copy of a second edit of the film, entitled 'Child's Play', was located at the home of Tamar Swade, founding member of 'Babies Against the Bomb'. 'Community video' productions distributed on obsolete formats have proven vulnerable to culling as tapes decay and archives transition to digital.
45. Swade in Jones, *Keeping The Peace*, 64–67.
46. See note 43 above.
47. Ibid.
48. Ibid.
49. 'Yesterday [...] 2,500 "Babies against the Bomb" marchers went from Hyde Park to Downing Street and County Hall. The march was headed by women wheeling empty push chairs representing children killed in Hiroshima and Nagasaki.' *Times*, 15 October 1982. This sequence in the film echoes the 'familial symbolism' and tropes of 'pre-emptive mourning' Alexandra Kokoli has identified in the work of women artist-activists at Greenham Common. Kokoli, 'Pre-Emptive Mourning Against the Bomb', 167–168.
50. Swade, interview with the author, February 2016.
51. Prime Minister Margaret Thatcher, 'Speech to the Conservative Party Conference', Brighton, 8 October 1982, Accessed January 2016. http://www.margaretthatcher.org/document/105032.
52. See note 43 above. This period also saw increasing media coverage of famines in Ethiopia.
53. Burkett, "Campaign for Nuclear Disarmament," 626. 'With nuclear weapons and their abilities to destroy large areas [...] perceptions of the Earth began to shrink.'
54. Gough, "Planting Peace," 21–41. This again exemplifies how space became a vital site of ideological conflict under the GLC.
55. Muralist Brian Barnes (O.B.E) commented that 'The best time for murals was under Thatcher. It reached a peak in 1983 when the GLC decided it would be "Peace Year" and they wanted anti-nuclear murals all over the city'. Barnes in Drew, *Reclaim the Mural*, 18.
56. For further images, see Atashroo, *Beyond The Campaign for a Popular Culture*, 146–162.
57. Thanks to Ben Wiedel-Kaufmann for drawing my attention to this detail.
58. Lambeth Archives (LA) LA:IV/288/2/3. GLC application statement by Louise Vines of London Wall.
59. LA:IV/288/2/3. Surrey Lodge was owned by the London Borough of Lambeth and leased to South Bank Polytechnic as a student residence.
60. "Fury over Red Ken's £14,000 Wall of Peace." *Sun*, 17 October 1983; "An Insult to the Fallen." *Daily Express*, 18 October 1983; "GLC, set to pay £14,000 for Mural." *Daily Telegraph*, 18 October 1983; "Women's £14,000 Wall of Peace." *Evening Standard*, 19 October 1983; "Brewing Up Trouble." *South London Press*, 21 October 1983; "A Better Argument for Peace." *Standard*, 21 October 1983; "War To Wall." *Evening Standard*, 26 October 1983; "Rebels Leave Ken with Back to the Wall." *Standard*, 8 November 1983; "It's War! Tenants Slam Peace Mural: We Will Burn Down Painting." *South London Press*, 22 October 1983; "Wall Mural Plan is Knocked Down: Residents Halt Missile Protest." *South London Press*, 20 January 1984; "Peace Mural is Torpedoed by Residents." *Standard*, 25 January 1984.
61. LA:IV/288/2/3. One resident of Lambeth Towers, adjacent to the proposed site, was reported to have stated 'I wouldn't care if it were Mickey Mouse or Snow White they were painting.

We do not want any mural whatsoever'. Anon., "It's War!" *South London Press*, 22 October 1983.
62. "A Better Argument for Peace." *Evening Standard*, 21 October 1983.
63. Robert Crawford, in "GLC set to pay £14,000 for Mural." *Telegraph*, 18 October 1983.
64. Steyn, "Women's Peace Mural," 1–3. Steyn recorded that an "SDP-Liberal alliance" leafleted the area, in an attempt to discredit both the mural and the GLC. This account is indebted to Juliet Steyn's 1986 review though utilises materials subsequently deposited in Lambeth Archives.
65. Ibid.; Curran et. al, *Culture Wars*. Typical of the tone of press narratives about the GLC.
66. "An Insult to the Fallen." *Daily Express*, 18 October 1983. These accusations were made in the months following Labour's General Election defeat in June 1983.
67. LA:IV/288/2/4; Steyn, "Women's Peace Mural."
68. Brooke, "Spaces, Emotions and Bodies," 2015.
69. Hogg, "Nuclear Resistance in 1980s Liverpool," 602; and Payling, "Socialist Republic of South Yorkshire."
70. The GLC were involved in national critique of nuclear policy and civil defence, and some of the GLC Peace Year's output such as poster packs and films are likely to have circulated beyond London.
71. Hughes, "Understanding Uranium 235," 518.
72. Anon., "It's War!" *South London Press*, 22 October 1983.
73. O'Farrell, "Things Can Only Get Better," 41. In his humorous memoir, O'Farrell judged that 'circus arts' participants at peace demonstrations created an image problem, 'They get shown on the news, and everyone says, "CND—what a bunch of middle-class twats!".'

Acknowledgements

I wish to thank the editors and reviewers of this special issue of CBH and Professor Jonathan Harris and Dr Oliver Peterson Gilbert whose helpful comments improved this paper. I am also grateful to Dr Alan Tomkins, Dr Loraine Leeson, Professor Joram Ten Brink, Frankie Armstrong, Tamar Swade, Peter Kennard, John Dugger, Ben Wiedel-Kaufmann and the archivists at London Metropolitan Archive and Lambeth Archives for their generous assistance.

Disclosure statement

No potential conflict of interest was reported by the author.

Funding

This work is supported by the AHRC under grant no. 1513414.

ORCID

Hazel A. Atashroo http://orcid.org/0000-0002-4276-1065

Bibliography

Anon. *Protect and Survive*. London: Central Office of Information, 1980.
Atashroo, H. "Beyond the 'Campaign for a Popular Culture': Community Art, Activism and Cultural Democracy in 1980s London." PhD diss., 2017.
Baines, J., Mackie, S., Robinson, A. and Stevenson, P., *See Red Women's Workshop: Feminist Posters 1974–1990*. London: Four Corners Books, 2016.
Beckett, A. *Promised You a Miracle: UK 80-82*. London: Allen Lane, 2015.
Bianchini, F. "GLC-RIP: Cultural Policies in London 1981–1986." *New Formations* 1, no. 1 (1987): 103–116.
Bianchini, F. "Cultural Policy And Political Strategy: The British Labour Party's Approach To Arts Policy with Particular Reference To The 1981–86 GLC Experiment." PhD diss., University of Manchester, 1995.
Brooke, S. "Spaces Emotions and Bodies: The Everyday Culture of Politics in 1980s London.", University of Birmingham Modern British Studies Conference, July 2015.
Brooke, S. "Space, Emotions and the Everyday: The Affective Ecology of 1980s London." *Twentieth Century British History* 28, no. 1 (2017): 110–142. doi:10.1093/tcbh/hww055.
Burkett, J. "The Campaign For Nuclear Disarmament And Changing Attitudes Towards The Earth In The Nuclear Age." *The British Journal for the History of Science* 45, no. 4 (2012): 625–639. doi:10.1017/S0007087412001094.
Campbell, D. *War Plan UK: The Truth about Civil Defence in Britain*. London: Burnett, 1982.
Carvel, J. *Citizen Ken*. London: Chatto and Windus, 1984.
Clarke, R., and A. H. Ehrlich, eds. *London under Attack: The Report of the Greater London Area War Risk Study Commission*, Oxford: Basil Blackwell, 1986.
Cordle, D. "Protect/Protest: British Nuclear Fiction of the 1980s." *The British Journal for the History of Science* 45 (2012): 653–669. doi:10.1017/S0007087412001112.
Cordle, D. "'That's Going to Happen to Us. It Is': Threads and the Imagination of Nuclear Disaster on 1980s Television." *Journal of British Cinema and Television* 10 (2013): 71–92. doi:10.3366/jbctv.2013.0122.
Curran, J., J. Petley, and I. Gaber. *Culture Wars: The Media and the British Left*. Edinburgh: Edinburgh University Press, 2005.
Curran, J., A. Smith, and P. Wingate, eds. *Impacts and Influences: Media Power in the Twentieth Century*. London: Routledge, 1987.
Hatherley, O. and Work In Progress (Art collective), *Reclaim the Mural: The Politics of London Murals*. London: Whitechapel Gallery, 2013.
GLC. *Films for Peace 1983*. London: GLC, 1983.
GLC. *The State of the Art or the Art of the State? Strategies for the Cultural Industries in London*. London: GLC Industry and Employment Branch, 1985.
GLC. *Campaign for A Popular Culture: A Record of Struggle and Achievement: The G.L.C.'s Community Arts Programme 1981–86*. London: GLC Arts and Recreations, 1986.
Gough, P. "Planting Peace: The Greater London Council and the Community Gardens of Central London." *International Journal of Heritage Studies* 13, no. 1 (2007): 22–40. doi:10.1080/13527250601010844.
Gyford, J. *The Politics of Local Socialism*. London: Allen & Unwin, 1985.
Hesmondhalgh, D., K. Oakley, D. Lee, and M. Nisbett. *Culture, Economy and Politics: The Case of New Labour*. Houndmills, Basingstoke Hampshire: Palgrave Macmillan, 2015.
Hewison, R. *Culture and Consensus: England, Art and Politics since 1940*. London: Methuen, 1995.
Hogg, J. "'The Family that Feared Tomorrow': British Nuclear Culture and Individual Experience in the Late 1950s." *The British Journal for the History of Science* 45, no. 4 (2012): 535–549. doi:10.1017/S0007087412001045.
Hogg, J. "Cultures of Nuclear Resistance in 1980s Liverpool." *Urban History* 42 (2015): 584–602. doi:10.1017/S0963926815000590.
Hogg, J. *British Nuclear Culture: Official and Unofficial Narratives in the Long 20th Century*. London: Bloomsbury, 2016.
Hogg, J., and C. Laucht. "Introduction: British Nuclear Culture." *British Journal for the History of Science* 45, no. 4 (2012): 479–493. doi:10.1017/S0007087412001008.

Hosken, A. *Ken: The Ups and Downs of Ken Livingstone*. London: Arcadia Books, 2008.
Hudson, K. *CND – Now More than Ever: The Story of a Peace Movement*. London: Vision Paperbacks, 2005.
Hughes, J. "What Is British Nuclear Culture? Understanding *Uranium 235*." *The British Journal for the History of Science* 45, no. 4 (2012): 495–518. doi:10.1017/S0007087412001021.
Jolivette, C., ed. *British Art in the Nuclear Age*. Farnham: Ashgate, 2014.
Jones, L. *Keeping the Peace*. London: Women's Press, 1983.
Kennard, P., A. Hopkins, and P. Brawne. *Dispatches from an Unofficial War Artist*. Hampshire: Lund Humphries, 2000.
Kennard, P., and R. Slocombe. *Unofficial War Artist*. London: Imperial War Museum, 2015.
Kokoli, A. M. "Pre-Emptive Mourning against the Bomb: Exploded Domesticities in Art Informed by Feminism and Anti-Nuclear Activism." *Oxford Art Journal* 40, no. 1 (2017): 153–168. doi:10.1093/oxartj/kcx004.
Livingstone, K. *If Voting Changed Anything, They'd Abolish It*. New ed. London: Fontana, 1988.
Livingstone, K. *You Can't Say That: Memoirs*. London: Faber and Faber, 2011.
Lobb, S. *The Murals of Brian Barnes*. London: Creekside Press, 2013.
O'Farrell, J. *Things Can Only Get Better*. London: Black Swan, 1999.
Payling, D. "Socialist Republic of South Yorkshire: Activism in Sheffield in the 1970s and 1980s." PhD diss., 2015.
Pearson, Nicholas. *The State and the Visual Arts: A Discussion of State Intervention in the Visual Arts in Britain, 1760–1981*. Milton Keynes: Open University Press, 1982.
Shaw, T. "The BBC, the State and Cold War Culture: The Case of the War Game." *English Historical Review* 494 (2006): 1351–1384. doi:10.1093/ehr/cel282.
Stafford, J. "Stay at Home: The Politics of Nuclear Civil Defence, 1968–83." *Twentieth Century British History* 23 (2012): 383–407. doi:http://dx.doi.org/10.1093/tcbh/hwr034.
Steyn, J. *The Women's Peace Mural (The Sankofa Bird)*. Aspects, Spring, 1986.
Taylor, B. C. "Nuclear Pictures and Metapictures." *American Literary History* 9 (1997): 567–597. doi:10.1093/alh/9.3.567.
Ten Brink, J., and J. Rawlins. *Born 1981: Babies against the Bomb/Child's Play*, VHS, dir. Joram Ten Brink and Jini Rawlins. London: Moonshine Community Arts Workshop, 1983.
Thatcher, M. "Speech to the Conservative Party Conference." Brighton, October 8, 1982. Accessed January 2016. http://www.margaretthatcher.org/document/105032.
Thompson, E. P. *Protest and Survive*. 2nd ed. London: Bertrand Russell Peace Foundation, 1980.
Wiedel-Kaufmann, B. "To The Wall: London's Murals and 'the Left', 1975-1986", PhD diss., Plymouth University, forthcoming.
Young, A. *Femininity in Dissent*. London: Routledge, 1990.

'... what in the hell's this?' Rehearsing nuclear war in Britain's Civil Defence Corps

Jessica Douthwaite

ABSTRACT
Between 1948 and 1968, Civil Defence Corps recruits trained to protect local communities in the event of nuclear war in Britain. Across that period, the policies that governed civil defence were also reformed to support the development of Britain's nuclear deterrent. In that context, an imagined nuclear war gradually came to inform defence strategies that sought to deter, rather than prepare for, armed conflict. The nuclear deterrent determined a new era of security in which the original purpose of civil defence was increasingly viewed as redundant in official and everyday opinion. By the mid-1960s, nuclear deterrence was an accepted tool of Cold War peace and CDC was discontinued. This article uses the original oral history testimonies of civil defence volunteers to investigate experiences of nuclear war according to people engaged directly in official projections of war. The article engages with scholarship on the imagined and discursive Cold War to argue that recruits experienced nuclear training through personal conceptualisation processes extending far beyond official versions of nuclear attack. The article argues that oral history narratives provide an unrivalled source through which to profile the fragile and ambiguous interior processes that underpinned official and unofficial interpretations of nuclear security at the time.

Colin 'played' in his first Civil Defence Corps [CDC] training exercise – a simulation of rescue operations in nuclear warfare – in Orpington, Kent, in 1954.[1] Exercises like this were designed by government defence planners on the basis that through training performances, CDC recruits would be conditioned for real attack.[2] During our oral history interview, Colin evocatively described the surprising experience that day of encountering volunteers from the Casualties Union [CU] wearing full make-up and acting as dead and injured victims.[3] In the interview, his experience was expressed by the refrain: 'what in the hell's this?'[4] Quickly identifying his role in the event, to 'act the part', Colin directed his St. John's Ambulance First Aid staff as if the exercise was a real emergency.[5] Colin corroborated the official exercise interpretation by engaging with the plot; his memory suggested that training did indeed condition participants' expectations for future wars. Yet, in the act of conforming to the performance contained in the exercise, Colin necessarily recognised the fictitious nature of training for nuclear war. As Colin reminded me, there were 'no explosions.'[6] His comment echoed drama studies scholar Tracy Davis, who refers to nuclear attack in civil defence as the 'deferred event'; 'no bombs were dropped,' she argues, thus exercise recruits, 'rehearsed nuclear war, they did not live it'.[7]

In this article, original oral history interviews with civilians recruited to civil defence services between 1949 and 1968 provide a unique window onto the experience of training for a 'deferred' nuclear event.[8] Drawing on oral history approaches that privilege the importance of imagination, narrative and subjectivities, the article applies an innovative methodology to new evidence, investigating everyday exposure to Cold War, nuclear mentalities in the CDC.[9] The article argues that interview testimonies contain hidden narratives that reveal the interior processes by which official projections of nuclear weapons were simultaneously internalised and subverted. While Davis notes that recruits themselves 'envisioned ways to identify and resolve anxious problems', this article contends that civilian visions of Britain's nuclear future were not always resolved, but co-existed alongside multiple experiences and feelings inspired by civil defence.[10] The article contributes to histories of civil defence cultures by emphasising the symbolic, as well as material, influence of nuclear weapons on civilian experiences of the Cold War.[11] It demonstrates that a more nuanced history of Britain's Cold War must include a focus on individuals and the way in which complex assessments of nuclear war operated to sustain nuclear structures.

The article begins with the historical context in which civil defence was established, introducing the purpose and implementation of theoretical training in the CDC. The first section discusses the ways in which, against the backdrop of increasingly discordant public nuclear debates, recruits' internal assessments of nuclear attack differed from outward engagement with training. The article then moves on to consider the significance of generational memory and post-war cultures in shaping recruits' expectations and behaviours during training, analysing the extent to which such experiences counted as 'nuclear'. In contextualising the imaginative and personal frameworks through which these recruits accessed early Cold War state structures, oral history analysis is discussed throughout the article as an apt, undervalued approach to uncovering how multiple concepts, meanings and symbols inform individual experience in the past.

Civil defence training in the 1950s: policy and theory

During the Second World War, the Air Raid Precaution Act, 1937, obliged local authorities to organise civil defence for communities.[12] The CDC was stepped down at the close of the war, but in 1949, was re-formed and based on the same organisational model.[13] Implicitly, the voluntary organisation was a Cold War entity. Labour, and subsequently Conservative, governments sought to protect British vulnerabilities from Soviet aggression in the context of increasingly tense economic and military events in post-war Europe.[14] In the words of Sir John Hodsall, Director-General of civil defence training in 1949, the CDC was intended to, 'build-up in peacetime, on a voluntary basis, a good, strong, well-trained, efficient nucleus on which rapid expansion could take place at time of emergency'.[15] CDC headquarters were based in each local authority and recruitment was directed by nationwide and local initiatives.[16]

Many early CDC recruits were former members of the Home Guard and ex-service personnel; however, by 1952 over half the volunteers recruited to civil defence had no former experience of service in war.[17] The interview participants in this article were all children during the war, except for Colin, and Matilda (a CDC officer discussed below). By 1954, 160,000 recruits, in a Corps roughly 300,000 strong, were female (though duties remained largely gendered).[18] The recruits interviewed for this article straddled two generations, not old enough to be fully immersed in the experience of the Second World War, for the most part, they were also too old to participate in the permissive youth cultures of 1960s Britain.[19] However, as a younger generation they were engaged in changing modes of cultural consumption, leisure habits, and access to education and media, all of which was contributing to increased individualism in post-war Britain.[20] The age at which recruits joined the CDC, and their gender, influenced participants' experiences of rehearsing war and the way that memories were expressed in the interview.[21] The article will explore this in the most pertinent instances of analysis.

The training models used in the CDC evoked conventional expectations of air raid bombings, as witnessed in the Second World War. Despite the awareness that atomic warfare posed a new challenge to national defences, civil defence theory endorsed the lesson that atomic attack would be massive but not 'extraordinary'.[22] Civil defence literature, lectures and demonstrations aimed to debunk sensationalist public opinion on the atom bomb by emphasising that its nuclear effects were akin to those seen in 'ordinary bombings'.[23] As the introduction to a training pamphlet stated in 1951, '[A]nyone who thinks that there is no defence against the atom bomb is wrong [...] in the city of Hiroshima, over half the people who were within a mile from the atomic explosion are still alive.'[24] In paper-based training, recruits were taught calculations, procedures and hypotheses intended to inform survival skills in conventional and atomic war.[25] This was augmented by specialist information depending on volunteers' roles in first aid, navigation, transport, evacuation, communications or fire rescue.[26]

Gradually, however, debates about the role of the atom bomb in Britain's broader defensive strategies fed into the training materials disseminated to civil defence recruits.[27] As Grant uncovers, while the Home Office [HO], administratively responsible for civil defence, was committed to fortifying defence procedures for atomic war, the Ministry of Defence [MoD] favoured developing nuclear weapons as a strong and modern deterrent suited, they said, to avoiding war in the nuclear age.[28] Deterrence did not supplant conventional defence straightaway; it required an emotional and intellectual exertion of belief across society to be established in material terms.[29] Thus, as Jonathan Hogg argues, the vocabulary of logic and permanence described by the nuclear deterrent was 'loaded with meaning amassed over years of repeated assumptions and assertions'.[30] In their interviews, these CDC recruits voiced an internalised process of meaning-making on nuclear issues that occurred across a period of time during which nuclear 'knowledge' was unstable.[31]

In 1955, a secret report by official government scientists concluded that Britain's civil defence resources required radical improvement, at high costs, to mitigate the predicted consequences of radiation in nuclear war.[32] The suggestion that nuclear attack would unleash destruction on an unimaginable scale, took hold in cultural and official terms, while increased spending on Britain's nuclear weapons development programme signalled the government's favour for deterrent-based security.[33] At this juncture, official support for the CDC diminished. Simultaneously, in order to ensure the deterrent remained unused, politicians publically deployed visions of nuclear apocalypse.[34] Winston Churchill, for example, said, there was 'no absolute defence against the hydrogen bomb', nor guarantee against 'devastating injury' from its use, to avoid such terrifying consequences Britain needed 'defence through "deterrents"'.[35] However, mindful of its potential as a popular morale booster, and in some views as a realistic facet of the deterrent, ministers did not withdraw the CDC.[36] Henceforth, as Grant argues, the 'worth' of civil defence was 'left ambiguous' and there was 'no agreement over what civil defence was actually for'.[37] In this transitionary period, government debated the existence of CDC not because it was outdated in an era of nuclear weapons, but because it was a derivative itself of nuclear deterrence. This paradox was written into the training CDC recruits received and, the article will argue, threaded interview narratives with contradiction and dissonance.[38]

Historians are turning to study the conceptual, discursive and psychosocial environment in which civilians and experts alike formed assumptions about nuclear security in the Cold War.[39] Grant argues that by supporting the 'façade' of readiness, which 'bolstered the deterrent' CDC recruits became a 'real part of Britain's *overall* defence strategy'.[40] This article is the first in histories of civil defence to demonstrate that oral history methodology is a valuable tool in investigating the lived experience of this ambiguous and malleable discursive context. Agreeing with Raphael Samuel and Paul Thompson that 'oral memory offers a double validity in understanding a past in which, as still today, myth was embedded in real experience' these testimonies highlight the mythological dimension to Britain's nuclear regime.[41] The article will now move on to investigate how participants' 'encounters' with nuclear weapons in civil defence training were gradually informed by, in Hogg's words, 'underlying assumptions on nuclear danger'.[42] Britain's post-war context inspired personal interactions with multiple sources of information on nuclear danger via various interpretational models. These testimonies provide an opportunity to hear how this experience occurred amongst one set of civilians whose 'nuclearity', can be viewed as an indicator of broader civilian experience in post-war British society.[43]

Civil defence training: assumptions and ambivalence

CDC recruits learned about the effects of nuclear bomb blasts through state-endorsed science that was employed in episodically updated training manuals.[44] However, across the 1950s, as stories of the effects of weapons testing and radioactive fallout reached the public, civilians were also exposed to multiplying and contradictory public sources of information on nuclear health issues.[45] Christophe Laucht shows that widespread public consternation at the effects of fallout from nuclear testing undermined the credibility of civil defence, yet was not incompatible with a sustained positive public reception of Britain's nuclear weapons development programme.[46] By volunteering for civil defence, interview participants actively implicated themselves in the state's nuclear deterrent, yet their memories reflected what Laucht describes as, 'considerable ambivalence in public opinion on atomic arms'.[47] Through training lectures, tests and exams, recruits learnt calculations, skills and procedures intended to provide confidence in any rescue situation.[48] The nuclear science discussed in these paper-based exercises was often secondary to conventional guidance on practical skills, such as first aid procedures.[49] The conjectural presence of nuclear radiation was a backdrop to training, yet also a constant, unforgettable responsibility.

In his role as the St Andrews' Ambulance first aid coordinator for civil defence training in Scotland, George was well acquainted with paper-based hypotheses: the plans, as he put it, 'for what would happen.'[50] To the extent that they 'thought about it,' recruits were 'theoretically [...] prepared,' but in truth, he said, 'we never thought that these plans would have to be put into action'.[51] As George asserted, 'it was all theory as far as we were concerned'.[52] Yet, George was also partly responsible for large-scale exercise operations around Glasgow in the late 1950s. Setting the scene for an inter-organisation practice, he said:

> '... we would put casualties into the buildings and the rescue service of the civil defence had to rescue them, and the first aid service had to deal with them, and the ambulance service had to move them, and the nursing auxiliary also had what were called forward medical lead units where they set up [...] makeshift hospitals...'[53]

Throughout his interview, George emphasised that though lifelike, civil defence training did not give him the impression that war was imminent. The language that he used to describe his experience was procedural, suggestive of the routinized practices that civil defence recruits experienced in the classroom. His tone implied there was a lack of variety in the nuclear rehearsal scenarios provided by the authorities.[54] For example, in this somewhat bald description of 'all the exercises', George remembered:

> 'There was always a period afterwards where radiation [was] spreading in the country, people having to be evacuated and where they would go... how they'd be fed and what would be done with them [...] the premise was always that if there was an atomic bomb on Scotland it would fall near Glasgow [...] Glasgow was virtually destroyed and [...] survivors from Glasgow were evacuated to other areas of the city [...] the radiation would be spreading with the prevailing wind south, north eastwards across Scotland and where would people be going and how would people be cared for?'[55]

By suggesting that rehearsals were almost identical, George implied that exercises for nuclear war were predictable. Of course, training was dependent on repetitively testing skills and knowledge. Yet, as Davis argues, the nuclear attack was a non-event, unpredictable because it had never happened.[56] Thus, in some cases, like George's, civil defence practices did not excite an engagement with plot, script and performance but dulled the imagination through the hypothetical, abstracted concepts written into rehearsals materials. However, beyond civil defence training, and remembering back to the context of the 'development from atomic into nuclear weapons', George admitted that, '... we were all concerned then, yes, that the weapons were getting more and more destructive and what, would happen [...] it did concern us.'[57]

Asked if he felt prepared to face a possible crisis, George laughed and replied 'we would have survived somehow [...] we got through one war'.[58] The uncertainty contained in more than one instance like this in the interview posed an incongruous challenge to the matter-of-fact tone in which George remembered civil defence training. By referring frequently to the nuclear disquiet inspired by information in press and public sphere, while denying personal fear and discussing training with little emotion, George evoked an impression of the ambivalent public atmosphere in which his memories originally took shape. Indeed, his reference to surviving the Second World War, employed as a comparison for nuclear survival in many other interviews, indicated that the fragility of life in the nuclear age had a historical precedent to be reluctantly accepted.

As George suggested, one of the biggest difficulties facing civil defence recruits was that in the public sphere official knowledge on nuclear science was contested to the extent of being discredited.[59] As anti-nuclear criticism increased, the CDC's reputation diminished, particularly given that a lack of funding left it inadequately equipped and poorly accommodated.[60] Several participants revealed the narrative discord initiated by an experience in which CDC members were spokespeople for nuclear survival, while also being as vulnerable to the imagined nightmares contained in the public sphere as the rest of society.[61] Even committed recruits, like Colin, began to question unimaginative and outdated training materials.

Colin was 29 years old in 1954 on his first civil defence exercise.[62] Recruited to a voluntary position training St John's Ambulance recruits via his employment as a junior doctor at the local hospital, he became a passionate advocate of training civilians in first aid across organisations, including the CDC and CU.[63] Colin suggested that his authority as a medical practitioner, with real experience of injury, validated his belief that the performance of casualties in civil defence training practices was highly realistic. Nevertheless, even Colin, when he paused to reflect on the theoretical training that underpinned rehearsals, remembered the dissonance that unbelievable nuclear narratives caused him:

> '... an atom bomb falling on Charing Cross station [laughing] it never dropped anywhere else but always Charing Cross station, every exercise we had... in this period of time... we had an atom bomb on Charing Cross station, priceless... It would've... knocked us down to bits...'[64]

One memory in particular revealed the implicit uncertainty caused by training narratives.[65] Colin recalled a moment, driving home from a training event, when he paused to doubt his role towards civil defence recruits because 'if the bombs drop[ped]' then what he had 'taught them would be completely inadequate.'[66] This memory was indicative of a conceptual struggle that many interviewees echoed: a belief in nuclear survival was only possible as long as the lessons acquired in training remained hypothetical.[67] In many cases, this discord was resolved by rationalising themselves as an element of the deterrent.

Matilda was 101 when I interviewed her, in the company of her son.[68] After referring to archived civil defence documents that originally belonged to her, I was delighted to discover that their owner was alive.[69] Matilda's interview must be considered, therefore, in the context of her age, the development of our relationship, and the specific interview environment; in many ways, it was similar to a reminiscence session.[70] Matilda had a purpose beyond my presence, and still being energetic, she carved out her own path in answer to my questions.[71] At the same time, in responding to me, she referred 'out to more public, structural, determinants' of change in her lifetime and as a result those references bore weight in my analysis.[72] Civil defence in the 1950s, she said, was part of a façade created by the government 'to make it look as if we were keyed up ready to press the button'.[73] In effect, Matilda believed she played a part in deterrence, and like

Colin, corroborated the official aims for civil defence by colloquially paraphrasing the directives contained in one of her pocket books.[74] However, her comment contradicted several other moments in the interview, which revealed that her experiences of nuclear weapons were unresolved.

Matilda became a CDC officer aged 43 in 1958.[75] However, her story of civil defence began in the Second World War, when, as a midwife, she lived in various regions of bombed and evacuated England, delivering babies and caring for mothers pre- and post-delivery.[76] In the interview, she deployed an attitude of Second World War spirit and stoicism to defend the rationale on which the CDC was based. Defiant and frequently humorous, Matilda suggested that anxiety or fear in the face of nuclear attack was futile and ridiculous. For example, describing her reaction to other female CDC colleague's nerves, she said, 'some of them ended up not coming because they were so frightened, but I said 'look dear, be prepared, don't take it so seriously but be prepared.'[77] She followed this by listing the types of civil defence procedures that ensured civilian readiness. Training upheld her conviction that going through 'the motions' prepared recruits to withstand the worst wartime scenarios.[78]

In defending her survivalist views, Matilda vocalised an emotional culture of the Second World War, which many historians have examined for its continued impact on British society in the 1950s.[79] For example, referring to memories of cycling through air raids on midwife duty she suggested that a precedent of selflessness and bravery, established on the Home Front, informed her courage in the face of nuclear threat.[80] In Matilda's case, this culture assisted her acceptance of fatality in the nuclear age, because, conventional or nuclear, she said: 'if my name is on it I shall get it, if it isn't on it I won't'.[81] Yet, paradoxically, aware of the complex and fatal new concerns raised by radiation, Matilda acknowledged that training did not provide 'a very rosy view' of survival. She remembered that even senior staff disbelieved nuclear survival, explaining that the 'whole place' would be 'infected, polluted' so 'you hadn't a cat's chance in hell' of living.[82] 'A mask wouldn't withstand' radiation, she emphasised, and death would be 'lingering'.[83] In reality, Matilda recognised that nuclear attack was hopeless because, 'had the button been pressed the whole world would've been gone... you'd be dead as a dodo'.[84]

As a lecturer and officer, senior positions in the Middlesex County CDC Ambulance division, Matilda would have been more rigorously acquainted with the lessons contained in nuclear training for civil defence. Memories and cultural representations of the Home Front in the Second World War informed the style and tone of official civil defence guidance. Mailda's pocketbook, for example, presented a range of common sense advice, from conventional activities such as the, 'do's and don'ts on field cable laying,' to detailed and candid sections on coping with the effects of radiation poisoning.[85] Its language dramatically changed in tone in those sections on how to cope with severe nuclear medical problems, with one section ending: '[D]eath is inevitable in the most severe cases. YOUR JOB is to get your casualty to hospital quietly, gently and quickly.'[86] Descriptions of severe nuclear conditions and the gravity of civil defence responsibilities in nuclear war, were presented alongside jovial commentary on less shocking topics, such as best methods for cooking potatoes at mass feeding stations.[87] Thus, Matilda's interview narrative was representative of collective approaches to coping with nuclear vulnerability in the 1950s; Matilda coped via similar emotional and cultural languages to her pocketbook. Without initiating a dialogue in the oral history interview, delineated by, in Alessandro Portelli's words, 'culturally shared symbolic structures and narrative devices', these connections could not have been made.[88]

Civil defence rehearsals: props and performance

In order to create a space in which to test recruits' coping mechanisms – technical and emotional – in war, civil defence planners carefully stage-managed exercise plots, roles, injuries, fatalities, sets, landscapes, timings, weather conditions and props.[89] Training sets provided a cost-saving and efficient means by which to enable multiple organisations to practice different tasks in one place, including: reconnaissance, rescue, trapped casualties searches, rescuing from upper floors, basements and craters, and using ropes and ladders and clearing debris.[90] Local authorities encouraged civil defence groups to use existing derelict buildings and empty lots of land as authentic training 'sets' or purpose-built buildings that replicated bomb damage. These sites might be disused properties damaged by air raids in the Second World War.[91] In Glasgow, for example, George explained:

> '… civil defence took advantage of areas of redevelopment… these years following the war there were a lot of old houses in in Glasgow, rundown areas that were being knocked down and new housing built, so as any area was being knocked down, the civil defence sort of took it over for a week or two and used the sort of houses that were being demolished as areas of destruction…'[92]

Sally Alexander argues that generational memory is affective, relational, and deliberate, communicated by the same means it was acquired: through a sensory and 'psychic dimension'.[93] In many cases, while the material trauma of the recent past was present in the bomb damage on which they trained, the affective presence of war did not influence recruits' experiences during practices for nuclear attack. In 1952, Malcolm was recruited from the National Service to the Civil Defence Experimental Mobile Column [EMC] aged 18 years old.[94] This now largely forgotten organisation was specifically created to travel the length and breadth of the United Kingdom publicising civil defence initiatives and testing civil defence techniques.[95] In the EMC, Malcolm completed some of the most authentically staged exercises conducted by civil defence authorities to test recruits' responses to fire, casualty, debris obstruction and equipment handling under the conditions of nuclear attack.

Malcolm was aged four when the Second World War began in 1939. In his interview, he remembered air raids in his hometown of Torquay, where sometimes, he found the bombing 'quite scary'.[96] After the demolition of his grandparents family home on one serious occasion, he described being 'shocked' by the distress of his grandmother and seeing 'the end of the road… cordoned off where several people had been killed'.[97] In our interview, he indicated that it was impossible, in replicated landscapes of Second World War destruction, to bring childhood memories of real anxiety to bear on nuclear spaces. For example, describing the impressive construction and design of one practice site, he said:

> … the hotel was called the Spread Eagle and half of it was missing, it was purposely built as a wreck you see, so the Epsom unit had a bomb site that'd been deliberately built as a bomb site […] it was very clever… how they managed to build a hotel with half of it missing, you know, fallen off, I would've thought that would've been more difficult than building a hotel…[98]

However, asked if it was 'ever scary to imagine' that kind of destruction, while engaged in realistic practices at the same location, Malcolm replied 'not really... I'd seen bomb sites before'.[99] In effect, in bomb-scarred post-war Britain, the quality of reproduction might be judged impressive, but authenticity did not impress realistically on emotions.

Instead, Malcolm suggested that he approached realistic exercises as assault courses. He remembered feeling tested by sites that 'were a little difficult'; 'different set-ups' he said, such as those at the docks, presented new challenges.[100] Malcolm related one memory of practicing an underground rescue while wearing 'breathing apparatus' with particular amusement:

'it was a hell of a way [down], and oh there were posts, and anyway I crawled through and you couldn't see that much, and eventually I found a body and I picked it up [...] obviously a dummy [laughs] and I brought it back, and I got halfway back and I'd gone round the post so that [laughs] my apparatus had run out of length so I had to go all the way back again [laughing] and come back the way I had [gone].'[101]

Comments in CDC exercise evaluation reports suggest that many recruits behaved similarly during training rehearsals – with less respect for physical realism than rehearsal plans intended. In one report, a stern voice reminded recruits that 'speed in releasing a casualty is nullified if the casualty is killed in the process.'[102] Malcolm was a believer in civil defence, yet he also remembered being sceptical about the efficacy of advice given by public civil defence guidance to 'draw your curtains' against nuclear attack.[103] The realities of nuclear radioactivity were written into civil defence exercises; however, though recruits acted a part to the extent that they followed the plot – physicalized by script and setting – they did not always fulfil the invisible nuclear roles contained in that narrative.

One way in which to convey the effects of radiation was through live casualties, trained to emulate the medical and psychological reactions appropriate to different characters and injuries; this could be anything from quality and frequency of breath, to the inability to complete full sentences.[104] In the introduction to this article, Colin described his first encounter with a little known, yet crucial group in the civil defence structure, the CU.[105] Established in the Second World War, the organisation drew on theatrical and medical expertise to simulate human casualties for realistic civil defence, emergency and military exercises in emergencies.[106] In Colin's case, he soon 'cottoned on' to the aims demanded of him and his team to conduct 'initial first aid' on casualties, followed by 'sending ... them... on a stretcher' to 'the centre where they would be better looked after'.[107] In effect, Colin began improvising in tandem with the narrative embedded in the rehearsal. Although the CU actively promoted acting techniques in civil defence rehearsals, civil defence planners did not prioritise this as a means to instil useful attitudes and behaviours in CDC recruits themselves. Improvisation depended on individual preferences to adapt to the performative expectation set by civil defence rehearsal.

David, three years older than Malcolm, also joined the EMC in 1952.[108] During the interview, he used many of his own photographs to illustrate the drama of his training rehearsal experiences. Pointing to one such contemporary photograph taken during a rope rescue operation in 'a burnt out cotton mill,' David described himself standing on a seventy-foot ladder with an unconscious woman in a fireman's lift over his shoulder.[109] 'We weren't playing games', he said, 'I picked her up and put her over my shoulder and brought her down three 70 foot ladders [...] which was dangerous for her and for me, but I mean for her in particular perched on my back.'[110] Recognising that in reality there was 'nothing wrong with that lady,' David visualised a situation that, regardless of the rehearsal, was authentically life-threatening.[111]

David used his photographic evidence to prove the risk involved in civil defence rehearsals, and yet, at no point during his interview did he link this experience of danger with the gravity of nuclear attack. Instead, David suggested that he normalised risk by imitating and honouring the cultural codes of the Second World War:

> '... it's what you've been trained to do and you just got on with it, and I'm sure it was probably the same thing with civil defence people during the Blitz, you didn't think well I might get hurt, somebody's got to be rescued, I got to go and rescue them, and we did, we did.'[112]

As Davis argues, rehearsals are imitative in technique – 'an embodied mimetic methodology... inherently and crucially theatrical.'[113] David's recourse to the Second World War was reflective of his exposure to particular cultural expectations of young men in military roles, in an era of National Service.[114] Despite the opportunity, David hardly developed his memory of nuclear issues in the interview. His most telling comment came in answer to a question about the Cuban Missile Crisis, 1962, an event popularly known to have inspired global nuclear fear.[115] According to David though, it was, 'another phase you had to accept and get on with, I mean you can't run away from it'.[116] David's attitude represented a 'Blitz spirit' approach to nuclear war, experienced across generations, throughout society. This contributed to the impression that in rehearsing war in civil defence David imitated the behaviours of earlier wartime cultures, and in the process, nuclear issues were silenced.

In oral histories, a 'cultural circuit' envelops the interview space with layers of cultural meaning and experience that are invested with significance in new and inventive ways depending on its context.[117] Alistair Thomson summarises the way in which this lifelong process might transpire in the interview narrative, which is, 'an effort in the first instance to make a story and to make sense of significant war or post-war experience; drawing upon (and sometimes silenced by) available and changing cultural meanings and expressive forms.'[118] The physical setting in which David practiced civil defence, accompanied by the presence of casualties with conventional injury contributed to an ability to perform known behaviours while omitting to acknowledge the new issues created by nuclear attack. In effect, the hypothetical nuclear narrative contained in that exercise was unpractised, while cultural behaviours inscribed collectively through previous wars were enlivened so as to bring meaning to David's performance.[119]

Not all recruits were intent on rehearsing any official or conventional script during training. Grant shows that in responding to recruitment propaganda that incentivised material and personal gain through the CDC, younger recruits were not necessarily initiating a duty to the state by volunteering.[120] Judith, Barbara and Heather made a joint decision to join a local branch of CDC together in 1955.[121] In individual interviews with each friend, they warmly remembered life in mid-1950s Birmingham as young, employed, sociable, single women. Each woman explained their decision to join civil defence by emphasising it as an opportunity to be involved in a more serious pursuit, useful to the local community that was also sociable. Importantly, they also emphasised that civil defence training represented a free and accessible source of practical education. In that context, all three suggested that, the diligence they applied to learning nuclear theories was only equal to their approach to any other training gained in the CDC: arising from an interest in learning real and applicable lessons. Heather made this particularly clear when she laughingly remembered that, 'the reason we joined was because we thought, '"[W]e can learn to drive if we join civil defence," and that was the whole reason we joined.'[122]

Barbara could not remember the word for 'radiation' in her interview, yet it was evident from her descriptions of the impact of bomb blasts that she had absorbed the detail provided in training.[123] For example, she said:

> '... you knew that if you were anywhere near [the impact zone] that there would be nothing left, and if you were, I can't remember the mileage now, but if you were sort of in the area but not hit by the blast [...] you know when the nuclear fallout, if you were hit by that, your chances of living were not very good, I can remember that [...] all that was in the training [...] it gave you the distances, but I can't remember the distances now.'[124]

All three women remembered more information about civil defence for nuclear attack than they thought they would, an interview trait particularly observed amongst female participants across oral history research.[125] Despite learning a great deal in classroom training however, Barbara, Judith and Heather each emphasised how little the make-up and casualty simulation portrayed in civil defence exercises affected them. Judith reflected that she 'didn't really take [exercises] seriously...'[126] Barbara echoed Judith, explaining:

> '[CU] used to have make-up and it was so realistic and it, you know you'd look at it and you'd think 'oooh' [let's out a gasp] but it was very good, oh we learnt a lot I think [...] well I don't think I took it very seriously...'[127]

The three women joined the CDC with objectives that reflected the social constraints imposed on women in post-war Britain; learning skills, particularly practical skills, was unfeminine.[128] However, given its special emphasis on the role of voluntary women in civil defence, the CDC offered an opportunity to gain further education acceptably.[129] Yet in interviews, the use of humour to describe civil defence rehearsals trivialised their contributions to training. Fond and amusing memories reflected the other objective in joining the CDC: sociability. In effect, each woman's motivations to acquire new skills and be purposeful resulted in a serious education in skills for nuclear attack. Yet, though diligent in civil defence classes, such commitment did not transfer to civil defence rehearsals where the nuclear narrative was overruled by the enjoyable and social atmosphere of group activities.

Some civil defence recruits practiced specific skills acquired in training, in spite of, and not because of, the nuclear objectives written into exercise rehearsals. For example, Sue joined CDC in 1961 because she, 'really just wanted to learn first aid' and repeated this personal aim throughout her interview.[130] Descriptions of detailed realistic exercise scenarios in the interview demonstrated that Sue engaged seriously with training for nuclear attack:

> '[...] I remember somebody chalking on somebody's head that... that they'd got [...] radiation [...] those that you could help or put a tourniquet on, or you know those that

were bleeding heavily [...] wrapping them up [in] whatever was available whether it be a scarf or piece of sheeting or towelling or something like that, and we were learning to actually prioritise, and also you know those that'd had heart attacks and things like that...'[131]

However, though Sue's memory of nuclear training was clear, she remembered those experiences in order to highlight the first aid skills that she practiced during training rehearsals. The irony of her civil defence training was that, in learning about survival skills, Sue also learned theories that exposed her to the, 'complete devastation' of real nuclear attack. Watching films and hearing lectures on real nuclear war, Sue realised that, in her words, 'you would be... everyone would be dead, complete devastation and that concerned me and that stuck in my mind.'[132]

Sue demonstrated that though recruits recognised nuclear issues in learning new skills, such learning did not necessarily support the official narrative of civil defences survival in nuclear attack. Sue's theoretical training lectures were intended to provide basic knowledge that would enable her to cope in attack settings, but as she said, 'I just remember these films about the poison gas and complete devastation [...] obviously there was a slight chance of [survival...] but I did feel that it was very serious.'[133] The paradox of civil defence training was that for Sue, as she said, 'it wasn't until I went into the civil defence that I realised the severity of it'.[134] Sue's detailed descriptions of first aid in the interview, coupled with her reflective memories on the 'frightening' nature of the lessons she learned about the Cold War and nuclear weapons in training, developed a rich narrative that profiled how nuclear meanings were individualised in an era of competing experiences of nuclear danger.

By the early 1960s, a large proportion of British society was highly sceptical that civil defence had a role to play at all in a world in which nuclear weapons dominated defence systems.[135] An acceptance of deterrence strategy had largely placated anxieties about nuclear war, while overground nuclear testing had been banned and thus its hazards eradicated from public view. Tim joined the CDC in 1963.[136] In the interview, he repeatedly justified the value of civil defence, in war and peace. He maintained that:

'... *yes*, the casualties would be much worse than they had been as a proportion of the population in World War Two [...] but there would be a [...] a significant number of survivors and [...] those were the ones that we wanted to help, yes there would be great tragedy but there would be great hope.'[137]

Tim over-emphasised nuclear survival during his interview, echoing perhaps, the arguments he was obliged to defend when he joined the CDC. However, he also argued for the CDC as a central element in Britain's policies of nuclear deterrence because, he said, 'if you are ready [...] you are less likely to be attacked.'[138]

Tim was a loyal, committed civil defence advocate and therefore recognised the peaceful value of a nuclear deterrent, yet the Labour government's line that the CDC 'wasn't needed', because there was 'not going to be a nuclear war' was a bit, in Tim's opinion, 'pushing your luck'.[139] In effect, the struggle to fully explain whether the CDC role was to protect the community in real nuclear war, to deter attack by embodying the nuclear deterrence strategy, or to perish with the nation at large was at the surface of Tim's interview narrative. The presence of nuclear danger justified Tim's reflections on CDC as an invaluable source of protection, but it also confirmed that the notion of peace through completely deterred war was unrealistic. By 1968, Tim's view was in a minority, the CDC was deemed redundant in the nuclear age of deterrence because it was neither a realistic method to protect civilians in nuclear attack, nor a realistic means to contribute to a developing technological system based on deterrence. Tim's experience illustrated how a knowledge of many different perspectives on war and nuclear issues could be unsettling. That experience demanded a personal effort to rank and rationalise civil defence in a nuclear age, before being able to outwardly voice the dimensions of an individual worldview with confidence.

Conclusions

Interviews with civil defence recruits revealed the inherent dysfunction entailed in training for a weapon that was culturally and militarily, unimaginable. The CDC recruits interviewed for this article presented multiple understandings and experiences of nuclear weapons that mirrored the discursive political context in which civil defence also acquired the symbolism of deterrence that underpinned security in the Cold War era. The interview setting created an atmosphere ripe for reflection and interpretation, profiling the lived dimensions of those military and political developments. First, by analysing recruits' memories of theoretical training lessons and experiences of the contemporary information environment, the article demonstrates that even amongst the most committed of recruits the pressures of nuclear debates penetrated civil defence experiences. The way in which those pressures were understood by recruits in practice, the final section of the article shows, depended on a myriad of cultural, generational and social responses to the activities and environments in which they trained as individuals. Interview participants ignored, reinforced, undermined and rejected civil defence training through the concepts and cultures contained in the training itself. The physical and performative approach taken to rehearsing war only provided another outlet for the same problems society faced believing in, and conceptualising security and survival in the nuclear age.

'Nuclearity' in the 1950s, depended on individual attachments to inter-generational, cultural, social or emotional influences at any one time. Most importantly, just as these influences were never static, neither were experiences of the nuclear Cold War. Nuclear weapons redrew the military boundaries that governed war strategies in the post-war world. These interview participants showed that, despite endorsing the state's prerogatives, recruits did not passively internalise official versions of war. Equally, participants invested morally in official narratives of nuclear deterrence strategy. Thus, the interviews highlighted the internal processes that governed the growth of public support for nuclear weapons as a peaceful deterrent against a backdrop of uncertainty. The everchanging, imagined visions of the 'deferred' attack contained in nuclear rehearsal narratives invoked a constant interaction between civilians and the permanent, yet uncertain moral and military boundaries of nuclear warfare. The state's nuclear regime, though expressing confidence in its resilience, was also dependent on the development of nuclear myths to sustain itself. The 'myth and memory' exposed in these oral histories contributed to a historical understanding of mediated consciousness in which, as described by Samuel and Thompson, 'fact and fantasy, past and present,' played a role in underpinning uncertain British nuclear myths with realism.[140]

Notes

1. Circa 1954, date cross-referenced in: Interview with Esmond Colin Dawson (2015); Museum of the Order of St. John, London (hereafter MOSJ) *Dr Dawson collection*; Wellcome Library, London, (hereafter WL) SA-CAS Acc 1185.
2. Davis, *Stages of Emergency*.
3. Claxton, *The Struggle for Peace*; Claxton, *More Ways than One*; Davis, "Between History and Event."
4. Interview, Dawson (2015).
5. Ibid.
6. Ibid.
7. Davis, *Stages of Emergency*, 85.
8. All oral history interviews referenced in this article were conducted by Jessica Douthwaite during Collaborative Doctoral Partnership PhD research at Imperial War Museum, London (hereafter IWM) and University of Strathclyde.
9. Abrams, "Liberating the Female Self"; Abrams, *Oral History Theory*; Andrews, *Narrative Imagination*; Bornat, "Remembering and reworking emotions"; Clifford, "Emotions and gender in oral history"; Portelli, *The Battle of Valle Giulia*; Roper, "Slipping Out of View"; Sheftel and Zembrzycki, *Oral History Off the Record*; Summerfield, *Reconstructing Women's Wartime Lives*; Thomson, "Anzac Memories Revisited."
10. Davis, *Stages of Emergency*, 4.
11. Biess, "'Everybody Has a Chance'"; Brown, *Plutopia*; Cronqvist, 'Survivalism in the Welfare Cocoon'; McEnaney, *Civil defense begins at home*; Major and Mitter, *Across the Blocs*; Nehring, *Politics of Security*; Oakes, *The Imaginary War*.
12. Essex-Lopresti, *A Brief History of Civil Defence*; Noakes, 'Serve to Save', 742–43.
13. Grant, *After the Bomb*.
14. Kent 'British policy and the origins of the cold war'; Deighton, *The impossible peace*; Deighton, 'Britain and the Cold War, 1945–55'; Reynolds, *From World War To Cold War*.
15. John Hodsall, 'Permanent Defence', in *The facts about civil defence: fourteen vital articles reprinted from the 'Municipal Journal'* (c. 1950) in IWM LBY CD 511.
16. Grant, "Civil Defence gives meaning to your leisure."
17. Grant, *After the Bomb*, 73.
18. See note 16 above.
19. On this 'in-between' generation, see: Abrams, "Liberating the female self"; Grant, "Civil Defence gives meaning to your leisure"; Vinen, *National Service*.
20. Jackson with Bartie, *Policing Youth*; King, *Family men*; Osgerby, *Youth in Britain since 1945*.
21. On age and gender in oral history, see: Andrews, *Narrative Imagination*; Bornat, "Reminiscence and Oral History"; Pattinson, 'The thing that made me hesitate …'.
22. Pavey, "Atomic Weapons," 6, in MOSJ, Civil Defence.
23. Ibid., 6.
24. "Civil Defence and the Atom Bomb," 1, in MOSJ, Civil Defence.
25. See for example, Home Office civil defence basic training pamphlets on atomic warfare, chemical warfare, and high explosive missiles, in MOSJ, Civil Defence.
26. See for example Her Majesty's Stationery Office [HMSO] handbooks on civil defence, in IWM, LBY K. 16 / 263; 4' LBY K. 16 / 265. Also, civil defence training correspondence, in Transport for London Corporate archives (hereafter TfL) LT000668/430; LT000014/159.
27. Grant, *After the Bomb*; Smith, "What to Do If It Happens."
28. See note 13 above.
29. Baylis, *Ambiguity and Deterrence*; Barnett, "No protection against the H-bomb"; Bingham, "The Monster?"; Gorry, *Cold War Christians*; Grant and Ziemann (eds.), *Understanding the Imaginary War*; Hennessy, *The secret state*; Maguire, "Never a Credible Weapon"; Smith, "What to Do If It Happens."
30. Hogg, *British Nuclear Cultures*, 7.

31. Hogg, *British Nuclear Cultures*, 8. See also, Hogg, "The Family That Feared Tomorrow"; Hogg, "Cultures of Nuclear Resistance."
32. Smith, "What to Do If It Happens."
33. Grant, "The Imaginative Landscape of Nuclear War."
34. Barnett, "No protection against the H-bomb"; Bingham, "The Monster?"; Grant, Grant, "Images of Survival"; Grant, "The Imaginative Landscape of Nuclear War"; Hogg, *British Nuclear Cultures*.
35. Churchill, "The Hydrogen Bomb," 1895.
36. See note 13 above.
37. Ibid., 122.
38. On dissonance see for example: Abrams, *Oral History Theory*; Bourke, *Fear*; Stearns, *American Fear*; Weart, *Nuclear Fear*.
39. Baylis and Stoddart, "The British Nuclear Experience"; Bennett, *In the ruins of the Cold War bunker*; Bennett, "Cold War Ruralism"; Grant and Ziemann, *Understanding the Imaginary War*; Grant, "Images of Survival"; Hammond, *British fiction and the Cold War*; Hogg, *British Nuclear Cultures*; Hogg and Laucht, "Introduction: British Nuclear Culture"; Nehring, *Politics of Security*.
40. Grant, *After the Bomb*, 198.
41. Samuel and Thompson, *The Myths We Live by*, 6.
42. Hogg, "Cultures of Nuclear Resistance," 537.
43. On 'nuclearity': Hogg, *British Nuclear Cultures*; Hogg, "The Family That Feared Tomorrow"; Hogg, "Cultures of Nuclear Resistance."
44. For example, *Collection of civil defence material collected by Mr and Mrs Liles 1958–68*, in IWM LBY 08 / 1045; *Civil defence and nuclear attack course notes*, (1960) in IWM LBY 79 / 3220; E.E. Massey, "Thermonuclear weapons, radioactivity and fallout," 1958, in IWM LBY K.16/268.
45. Barnett, "No protection against the H-bomb"; Bingham, "The Monster?"; Hogg, *British Nuclear Cultures*.
46. Laucht, "Scientists, the Public, the State."
47. Ibid., 231.
48. For example, *Collection of civil defence material collected by Mr and Mrs Liles 1958–68*, in IWM LBY 08 / 1045; *Civil defence and nuclear attack course notes*, (1960) in IWM LBY 79 / 3220; *Certificates issued to Matilda Morris on civil defence training*, (1958–1961) in IWM LBY K. 16 / 270–274.
49. For example, see: MOSJ, Civil Defence.
50. Interview with George Watt (2015).
51. Interview, Watt (2015).
52. Ibid.
53. Ibid.
54. On language and tone in oral history interviews see: Riessman, "Analysis of Personal Narratives."
55. See note 51 above.
56. Davis, *Stages of Emergency*; Davis, "Between History and Event."
57. See note 51 above.
58. Ibid.
59. Hogg, *British Nuclear Cultures*; Laucht, "Scientists, the Public, the State."
60. Grant, *After the Bomb*; Bennett, *In the ruins of the Cold War bunker*; Bennett, "Cold War Ruralism."
61. In addition to those cited in the article this was also suggested in: Interview with Kevin Knight (2015) Interview with Patricia Murray (2016) and Interview with Pat Andrews, (2015). On narrative structure in life stories, see for example: Abrams, *Oral History*; Molly Andrews, *Narrative Imagination*; Portelli, *The Battle of Valle Giulia*.
62. See note 4 above.
63. See: *Dr Dawson collection*, in MOSJ; and, WL, SA-CAS Acc 1185.

64. See note 4 above.
65. On memory as an interview 'moment' see: Abrams, "Liberating the Female Self."
66. See note 4 above.
67. In addition to those cited in the article this was also suggested in: Interview, Andrews (2015); Interview with Anne Hirons (2015); Interview with Lawrence Holmes, (2015).
68. Interview with Matilda Morris (2017).
69. Certificates and documents; IWM LBY K. 16 / 263–274.
70. Bornat, "Reminiscence and Oral History."
71. Ibid.
72. Ibid., 228.
73. Interview, Morris (2017).
74. *Civil Defence Volunteers Pocket Book; West Sussex Division* (1959/60), IWM LBY K.16/264.
75. See note 73 above.
76. Ibid.
77. Ibid.
78. Ibid.
79. Francis, "Tears, Tantrums, and Bared Teeth"; Dixon, *Weeping Britannia*; Summerfield and Peniston-Bird, *Contesting Home Defence*; Summerfield, "Dad's Army, the Home Guard"; Summerfield, "Film and the Popular Memory."
80. Francis, *The Flyer*; Grayzel, *At Home and under Fire*; Levine and Grayzel, (eds.), *Gender, Labour, War and Empire*; Summerfield, *Reconstructing Women's Wartime Lives*.
81. See note 73 above.
82. Ibid.
83. Ibid.
84. Ibid.
85. *Civil Defence Volunteers Pocket Book*, IWM LBY K.16/264.
86. Ibid., 52.
87. Ibid., 54.
88. Portelli, *The Battle of Valle Giulia*, 83.
89. For example exercise narratives, see: London Transport Executive Industrial Civil Defence Report, Exercise 'Quad', (24 March 1962) 1–4; London Transport Executive Industrial Civil Defence Report, Exercise 'Double', (18 March 1961) 1–5, in TfL civil defence collection, LT000014/158.
90. Travers, "Realistic sets aid the task of rescue training" in *The facts about civil defence*, in IWM: LBY CD 511.
91. Ibid.
92. See note 51 above.
93. Alexander, "Do Grandmas Have Husbands?," 163.
94. Interview with Malcolm Bidder (2015).
95. Reid and Bidder, (eds.), *We Blazed the Trail*.
96. Interview, Bidder (2015).
97. Ibid.
98. Ibid.
99. Ibid.
100. Ibid.
101. Ibid.
102. Report, Exercise 'Quad', 2, in TfL civil defence collection, LT000014/158.
103. See note 96 above.
104. See for example: "Schedule of Casualties" in *Exercise Six*, 1–4 in TfL civil defence collection, LT000014/158.
105. Claxton, *The Struggle for Peace*; Claxton, *More Ways than One*.
106. This was discussed in popular culture as much as it was civil defence, see for example: 'Spare time Casualty' in *The Lady*, (2 February 1961); 'Look, I'm a Concussion!' in *Punch*, (8 February 1961), in WL Acc SA-CAS 1185.

107. See note 4 above.
108. Interview with David Chivers (2015).
109. Interview, Chivers (2015); newspaper clipping, 'After the Raider's Had gone', (c. 1954).
110. Interview, Chivers (2015).
111. Ibid.
112. Ibid.
113. Davis, *Stages of Emergency*, 4.
114. Vinen, *National Service*.
115. David Lowe and Tony Joel, *Remembering the Cold war*.
116. See note 110 above.
117. Abrams, "Liberating the Female Self"; Summerfield, *Reconstructing Women's Wartime Lives*; Thomson, "Anzac Memories Revisited."
118. Thomson, "Anzac Memories Revisited," 25.
119. Roper, "Slipping Out of View"; Roper and Tosh, *Manful Assertions*.
120. See note 16 above.
121. Interview with Heather Howell (2015); Interview with Barbara Leather (2015); Interview with Judith Essex-Lopresti (2015).
122. Interview, Howell (2015).
123. On silences or omissions in oral history interviews see essays in, Sheftel and Zembrzycki (eds.), *Oral History Off the Record*.
124. Interview, Leather, (2015).
125. Leydersdorff, Passerini, Thomson, "Introduction"; Pattinson, "The thing that made me hesitate …".
126. Interview, J. Essex-Lopresti interview (2015).
127. See note 124 above.
128. Beaumont, *Housewives and citizens*; Hilton and McKay, (eds.) *The Ages of Voluntarism*; Simonton, ed., *The Routledge History of Women*.
129. See note 16 above.
130. Interview with Sue Dexter (2015).
131. Interview, Dexter (2015).
132. Ibid.
133. Ibid.
134. Ibid.
135. Nehring, *Politics of Security*.
136. Interview with Tim Essex-Lopresti (2015).
137. Interview, T. Essex-Lopresti (2015).
138. Essex-Lopresti interview; (2015).
139. Ibid.
140. Samuel and Thompson, *The Myths We Live by*, 21.

Acknowledgements

I am extremely grateful to Jonathan Hogg and Matthew Grant for their conscientious and thought-provoking comments on previous drafts of this article. Thanks also to James Southern and Anna Maguire for reading first drafts and giving me supportive and useful feedback. Without my enthusiastic and untiring archives contact at the Museum of the Order of St. John, Abigail Cornick, much of my primary research would be less developed. I am grateful to her and the staff at MOSJ for their assistance.

Disclosure statement

No potential conflict of interest was reported by the author.

Bibliography

Abrams, L. *Oral History Theory*. London: Routledge, 2010.

Abrams, L. "Liberating the Female Self: Epiphanies, Conflict and Coherence in the Life Stories of Post-War British Women." *Social History* 39, no. 1 (2014): 14–35. doi:10.1080/03071022.2013.872904.

Alexander, S. ""Do Grandmas Have Husbands?" Generational Memory and Twentieth-Century Women's Lives." *The Oral History Review* 36, no. 2 (2009): 159–176. doi:10.1093/ohr/ohp078.

Alexander, S., and B. Taylor, eds. *History and Psyche: Culture, Psychoanalysis, and the Past*. New York: Palgrave Macmillan, 2012.

Alley, E. "Civil Defence Corps, 1949–68." In *A Brief History of Civil Defence Association*, edited by T. Essex-Lopresti, 35-45. Derbyshire: Higham Press, 2005.

Andrews, M. *Narrative Imagination and Everyday Life*. Oxford: Oxford University Press, 2014.

Barnett, N. ""No Protection against the H-Bomb": Press and Popular Reactions to the Coventry Civil Defence Controversy, 1954." *Cold War History* 15, no. 3 (2015): 277–300. doi:10.1080/14682745.2014.968558.

Baylis, J. *Ambiguity and Deterrence: British Nuclear Strategy, 1945–1964*. Oxford: Oxford University Press, 1995.

Baylis, J., and K. Stoddart. "The British Nuclear Experience: The Role of Ideas and Beliefs (Part One)." *Diplomacy & Statecraft* 23, no. 2 (2012): 331–346. doi:10.1080/09592296.2012.679488.

Beaumont, C. *Housewives and Citizens: Domesticity and the Women's Movement in England, 1928–64*. Manchester: Manchester University Press, 2014.

Bennett, L., ed. *In the Ruins of the Cold War Bunker: Affect, Materiality and Meaning Making, Place, Memory, Affect*. London: Rowman & Littlefield International, 2017.

Bennett, L. ed.. "Cold War Ruralism: Civil Defense Planning, Country Ways, and the Founding of the UK's Royal Observer Corps' Fallout Monitoring Posts Network." *Journal of Planning History* 17, no. 3 (2017): 205–225.

Bessell, R., and D. Schumann, eds. *Life after Death: Approaches to a Cultural and Social History of Europe during the 1940s and 1950s*. Cambridge: Cambridge University Press, 2003.

Biess, F. "'Everybody Has a Chance': Nuclear Angst, Civil Defence, and the History of Emotions in Postwar West Germany." *German History* 27, no. 2 (2009): 215–243. doi:10.1093/gerhis/ghp003.

Bingham, A. "The Monster'? the British Popular Press and Nuclear Culture, 1945–Early 1960s." *The British Journal for the History of Science* 45, no. 4 (2012): 609–624. doi:10.1017/S0007087412001082.

Bornat, J. "Reminiscence and Oral History: Parallel Universes or Shared Endeavour?" *Ageing and Society* 21, no. 02, March (2001): 219–241. doi:10.1017/S0144686X01008157.

Bornat, J. "Remembering and Reworking Emotions: The Reanalysis of Emotion in an Interview." *Oral History* 38, no. 2 (2010): 43–52.

Bourke, J. *Fear: A Cultural History*. London: Virago, 2006.

Burke, P. "Performing History: The Importance of Occasions." *Rethinking History* 9, no. 1 (2005): 35–52. doi:10.1080/1364252042000329241.

Chamberlain, M., and P. Thompson, eds. *Narrative and Genre*. London: Routledge, 1998.

Claxton, E. C. *More Ways than One of Fighting a War: The Story of a Battle School for Civil Defence and the Creation of Casualties Union*. Sussex, England: Book Guild, 1990.

Claxton, E. C. *The Struggle for Peace: The Story of Casualties Union in the Years following the Second World War*. Lewes: Book Guild, 1992.

Clifford, R. "Emotions and Gender in Oral History: Narrating Italy's 1968." *Modern Italy* 17, no. 2 (2012): 209–221. doi:10.1080/13532944.2012.665284.

Cronqvist, M. "Survivalism in the Welfare Cocoon: The Culture of Civil Defense in Cold War Sweden." In *Cold War Cultures: Perspectives on Eastern and Western European Societies*, edited by A. Vowinckel, M. M. Payk, and T. Lindenberger, 191–210. New York: Berghahn Books, 2012.

Cull, N. J. "Reading, Viewing and Tuning in to the Cold War." In *The Cambridge History of the Cold War, Volume II*, edited by M. P. Leffler and O. A. Westad, 438-459. Cambridge: Cambridge University Press, 2010.

Davis, T. C. "Between History and Event: Rehearsing Nuclear War Survival." *The Drama Review* 46, no. 4 (2002): 11–45. doi:10.1162/105420402320907001.

Davis, T. C. *Stages of Emergency: Cold War Nuclear Civil Defense*. Durham, N.C: Duke University Press, 2007.

Deighton, A. *The Impossible Peace: Britain, the Division of Germany and the Origins of the Cold War*. Oxford: Oxford University Press, 1990.

Deighton, A. "Britain and the Cold War, 1945–1955." In *The Cambridge History of the Cold War, Volume I*, edited by M. P. Leffler and O. A. Westad, 112-132. Cambridge: Cambridge University Press, 2010.

Dixon, T. *Weeping Britannia: Portrait of a Nation in Tears*. Oxford: Oxford University Press, 2015.

Eustace, N., E. Lean, J. Livingston, J. Plamper, W. M. Reddy, and B. H. Rosenwein. "AHR Conversation: The Historical Study of Emotions." *The American Historical Review* 117, no. 5 (2012): 1487–1531. doi:10.1093/ahr/117.5.1487.

Francis, M. "Tears, Tantrums, and Bared Teeth: The Emotional Economy of Three Conservative Prime Ministers, 1951–1963." *The Journal of British Studies* 41, no. 3, July (2002): 354–387. doi:10.1086/341153.

Francis, M. *The Flyer: British Culture and the Royal Air Force, 1939–1945*. Oxford: Oxford University Press, 2008.

Gorry, J. *Cold War Christians and the Spectre of Nuclear Deterrence, 1945–1959*. Houndmills, Basingstoke, Hampshire: Palgrave Macmillan, 2013.

Grant, M. *After the Bomb: Civil Defence and Nuclear War in Britain, 1945–68*. Basingstoke, UK: Palgrave Macmillan, 2010.

Grant, M. "'Civil Defence Gives Meaning to Your Leisure': Citizenship, Participation, and Cultural Change in Cold War Recruitment Propaganda, 1949–54." *Twentieth Century British History* 22, no. 1 (2011): 52–78. doi:10.1093/tcbh/hwq040.

Grant, M. "Images of Survival, Stories of Destruction: Nuclear War on British Screens from 1945 to the Early 1960s." *Journal of British Cinema and Television* 10, no. 1 (2013): 7–26. doi:10.3366/jbctv.2013.0119.

Grant, M. "The Imaginative Landscape of Nuclear War in Britain, 1945–65." In *Understanding the Imaginary War: Culture, Thought and Nuclear Conflict, 1945–90*, edited by M. Grant and B. Ziemann, 92-115. Manchester: Manchester University Press, 2016.

Grayzel, S. R. *At Home and under Fire: Air Raids and Culture in Britain from the Great War to the Blitz*. New York: Cambridge University Press, 2012.

Grayzel, S. R., and P. Levine, eds. *Gender, Labour, War and Empire: Essays on Modern Britain*. Basingstoke: Palgrave Macmillan, 2009.

Haggett, A. *Desperate Housewives, Neuroses and the Domestic Environment, 1945–1970*. London: Pickering & Chatto, 2012.

Hammond, A. *British Fiction and the Cold War*. Basingstoke, Hampshire: Palgrave Macmillan, 2013.

Hennessy, P. *The Secret State: Whitehall and the Cold War*. London: Penguin Books, 2003.

Hilton, M., and J. McKay, eds. *The Ages of Voluntarism: How We Got to the Big Society*, British Academy original paperback. Oxford: Published for the British Academy by Oxford University Press, 2011.

HMSO & Scottish Home Department. Manual of Civil Defence. Volume 1, Pamphlet No. 1 : Nuclear Weapons 1956.

HMSO & Scottish Home Department. Manual of Civil Defence. Volume 1, Pamphlet No. 2 : Radioactive Fall-out : Provisional Scheme of Public Control 1956.

HMSO & Scottish Home Department. Manual of Civil Defence. Volume 1 Pamphlet No. 1 : Nuclear Weapons 1959.

Hogg, J. "'The Family that Feared Tomorrow': British Nuclear Culture and Individual Experience in the Late 1950s." *The British Journal for the History of Science* 45, no. 4 (2012): 535–549. doi:10.1017/S0007087412001045.

Hogg, J. "Cultures of Nuclear Resistance in 1980s Liverpool." *Urban History* 42, no. 4 (2015): 584–602. doi:10.1017/S0963926815000590.

Hogg, J. *British Nuclear Culture: Official and Unofficial Narratives in the Long 20th Century*. London: Bloomsbury Academic, 2016.

Hogg, J., and C. Laucht. "Introduction: British Nuclear Culture." *The British Journal for the History of Science* 45, no. 4 (2012): 479–493. doi:10.1017/S0007087412001008.

Home Office. Civil Defence Manual of Basic Training Volume II, Basic Chemical Warfare (1949).

Home Office. Civil Defence Manual of Basic Training Volume II, Basic Methods of Protection Against High Explosive Missiles (1949).

Home Office. Civil Defence Manual of Basic Training Volume II, Atomic Warfare (1950).

Hughes, J. "What Is British Nuclear Culture? Understanding Uranium 235." *The British Journal for the History of Science* 45, no. 4 (2012): 495–518. doi:10.1017/S0007087412001021.

IWM Collections. Collection of Civil Defence Material Collected by Mr and Mrs Liles 1958–68 LBY 08 / 1045.

IWM Collections. Collection of Civil Defence Material issued to Matilda Morris, 1958–1962 LBY K. 16 / 263 – 272.

IWM Film archive. BBC television. 'Civil Defence Makes Sense' *Panorama*, (1 October 1956).

Jackson, L. A., and A. Bartie. *Policing Youth: Britain, 1945–70*. Manchester: Manchester University Press, 2014.

Jackson, M. *The Age of Stress: Science and the Search for Stability*. Oxford: Oxford University Press, 2013.

Kent, J. "British Policy and the Origins of the Cold War." In *Origins of the Cold War: An International History*, edited by M. P. Leffler and D. S. Painter, 155-167. New York: Routledge, 2005. (Rewriting Histories).

King, L. *Family Men: Fatherhood and Masculinity in Britain, C.1914–1960*. Oxford: Oxford University Press, 2015.

Laucht, C. "Scientists, the Public, the State, and the Debate over the Environmental and Human Health Effects of Nuclear Testing in Britain, 1950–1958." *The Historical Journal* 59, no. 1 (2016): 221–251. doi:10.1017/S0018246X15000096.

Lowe, D., and T. Joel. *Remembering the Cold War: Global Contest and National Stories, Remembering the Modern World*. London: Routledge Taylor & Francis Group, 2013.

Maguire, R. ""Never a Credible Weapon": Nuclear Cultures in British Government during the Era of the H-Bomb." *The British Journal for the History of Science* 45, no. 4 (2012): 519–533. doi:10.1017/S0007087412001033.

Major, P., and R. Mitter, eds. *Across the Blocs: Cold War Cultural and Social History*. London: Taylor & Francis, 2004.

Malin, B. J. "Media, Messages and Emotion." In *Doing Emotions History*, edited by S. J. Matt and P. N. Stearns, 184-204. Urbana: University of Illinois Press, 2013.

Malin, B. J. "The Path to the Machine: Affect Studies, Technology, and the Question of Ineffability." *Communication and Critical/Cultural Studies* 13, no. 1 (2016): 40–57. doi:10.1080/14791420.2015.1110246.

Matt, S. J. "Current Emotion Research in History: Or, Doing History from the inside Out." *Emotion Review* 3, no. 1 (2011): 117–124. doi:10.1177/1754073910384416.

McEnaney, L. *Civil Defense Begins at Home: Militarization Meets Everyday Life in the Fifties*. Princeton, N.J. : Princeton University Press, 2000.

Museum of the Order of St John. Dr Dawson Collection OSJ/2.

Nehring, H. *Politics of Security: British and West German Protest Movements and the Early Cold War, 1945–1970*. Oxford: Oxford University Press, 2013.

Oakes, G. *The Imaginary War: Civil Defense and American Cold War Culture*. New York: Oxford University Press, 1994.

Osgerby, B. *Youth in Britain since 1945*. Oxford, UK: Blackwell Publishers, 1998.

Pattinson, J. "The Thing that Made Me Hesitate …': Re-Examining Gendered Intersubjectivities in Interviews with British Secret War Veterans." *Women's History Review* 20, no. 2 (2011): 245–263. doi:10.1080/09612025.2011.556322.

Pavey, A. E. "Atomic Weapons." *First Aid & Nursing* LVIII, no. 680, February, 1951. 6-7.

Portelli, A. *The Battle of Valle Giulia: Oral History and the Art of Dialogue*. Madison, Wisconsin: University of Wisconsin Press, 1997.

Preston, J. "Protect and Survive: 'Whiteness' and the Middle-Class Family in Civil Defence Pedagogies." *Journal of Education Policy* 23, no. 5 (2008): 469–482. doi:10.1080/02680930802054412.

Reddy, W. M. "Historical Research on the Self and Emotions." *Emotion Review* 1, no. 4 (2009): 302–315. doi:10.1177/1754073909338306.

Reid, R. G., and M. Bidder, eds. *We Blazed the Trail: An Illustrated History of the Civil Defence Experimental Mobile Column, 1953/4*. Bognor Regis, West Sussex, England: Woodfield, 2008.

Reynolds, D. *From World War to Cold War: Churchill, Roosevelt, and the International History of the 1940s*. Oxford: Oxford University Press, 2006.

Roper, M. "Slipping Out of View: Subjectivity and Emotion in Gender History." *History Workshop Journal* 59 (2005): 57–72. doi:10.1093/hwj/dbi006.

Roper, M., and J. Tosh, eds. *Manful Assertions: Masculinities in Britain since 1800*. London: Routledge, 1991.

Samuel, R., and P. Thompson, eds. *The Myths We Live By, History Workshop Series*. London: Routledge, 1990.

Scottish Oral History Sound Archives. *Voices of the Cold War in Britain, 1945–1962*. Interview collection by Jessica Douthwaite (2015–2017).

Sheftel, A., and Z. Stacey, eds. *Oral History off the Record: Toward an Ethnography of Practice*. New York: Palgrave Macmillan, 2013.

Smith, M. "'What to Do if It Happens': Planners, Pamphlets and Propaganda in the Age of the H-Bomb." *Endeavour* 33, no. 2 (2009): 60–64. doi:10.1016/j.endeavour.2009.04.007.

Stearns, P. N. *American Fear: The Causes and Consequences of High Anxiety*. London: Routledge, 2006.

Summerfield, P. *Reconstructing Women's Wartime Lives: Discourse and Subjectivity in Oral Histories of the Second World War*. Manchester: Manchester University Press, 1998.

Summerfield, P. "Dad's Army, the Home Guard, and the Memory of the British War Effort." In *The Lasting War: Society and Identity in Britain, France and Germany after 1945*, edited by M. Riera and G. Schaffer, 86-99. Basingstoke: Palgrave MacMillan, 2008.

Summerfield, P. "Film and the Popular Memory of the Second World War in Britain 1950–1959." In *Gender, Labour, War and Empire: Essays on Modern Britain*, edited by S. R. Grayzel and L. Philippa, 157–75. Basingstoke: Palgrave Macmillan, 2009.

Summerfield, P., and C. M. Peniston-Bird. *Contesting Home Defence: Men, Women and the Home Guard in the Second World War*. Manchester: Manchester University Press, 2007.

Thomson, A. "Anzac Memories Revisited: Trauma, Memory and Oral History." *Oral History Review* 42, no. 1 (2015): 1–29. doi:10.1093/ohr/ohv010.

Transport for London Corporate Archives. Civil Defence files. 668/430; 14/158; 14/159; 346/055

Vinen, R. *National Service: A Generation in Uniform 1945–1963*. London: Penguin Books, 2015.

Weart, S. R. *Nuclear Fear: A History of Images*. Cambridge, MA: Harvard University Press, 1989.

Wellcome Library, Casualties Union papers, SA/CAS, boxes 1–3 acquisition number 1185

Mass observing the atom bomb: the emotional politics of August 1945

Claire Langhamer

ABSTRACT

In August 1945, the social investigative organisation, Mass-Observation, asked its panel of volunteer writers to 'Describe in detail your own feelings and views about the atom bomb, and those of the people you meet'. This article uses the responses to explore the emotional politics of 'nuclearity' in the immediate aftermath of the bombing of Hiroshima and Nagasaki. First it examines the impact that the atomic explosions had upon ways of narrating, and managing, the emotional self. Second it explores the influence of nuclear knowledge on felt social relations. The article argues that first use of the atom bomb had a profound impact upon British people's understandings of the past, the present and the political future; and that the responses of ordinary people in turn helped to shape a messy and contradictory popular nuclear culture within which feeling operated as a way of knowing, and intervening in, the world.

Introduction

On 1 September 1945, a 32-year-old housewife composed her thoughts on the latest questionnaire sent to her by the British social investigative organisation, Mass-Observation. The 'Directive' for August 1945 posed a series of questions on the peace in Europe and on the new Labour government.[1] That the volunteer writers who received this directive were expected to detail their emotions, as well as their opinions and experiences, was established from the outset. The first question asked that they 'Describe in detail your own feelings and views about the atom bomb, and those of the people you meet'.[2]

In writing her *own feelings* about the atom bomb, this particular woman was mindful of recent events in her life—she had just given birth to a daughter. We see the complex interplay of past experience, present feeling and future thinking in her response. We can also identify a personal, notably visceral, emotional politics of 'nuclearity'[3]:

> My feelings about the Atom bomb? Hard to describe—a sort of primal shudder and at once the thought 'then if this can happen what is the good of anything?' I see the earth like an ant-heap about to be crushed by a field-boot—casually, just like that—and I can neither deflect the blow nor warn the ants. I know I am one of them but I feel detached from it all

though I feel my children cannot escape annihilation, and understand for the first time the mothers who poisoned their children in the face of the enemy advance...My feelings are so overwhelming that I have no views—whatever we think about who should handle the thing and who should not be admitted to the fellowship it is only a matter of time until some damn fool goes too far. As sensible to trust men of today—or of any day—with such power as to leave a baby alone with a man-eating tiger. We shall destroy ourselves entirely...I can't talk about it—so I have no friends views to add. I am afraid. I AM AFRAID. And where will it get me? We are impotent.[4]

The emotional power of this response was not out of place amongst replies to the August Directive. While the dropping of the atomic bomb on two Japanese cities provoked diverse feelings amongst Mass-Observation's volunteer panel of writers, few denied the historical and personal significance of these final acts of the Second World War. Regardless of whether they vehemently opposed the action, actively supported it, or inhabited a position of moral and strategic uncertainty, the Mass-Observers believed that the world had changed decisively; or more precisely they *felt* they had entered a new 'atomic age'.

***

In recent years, historians have sought to move nuclear history beyond a 'top-down' focus on personalities and high politics.[5] Opening up, and problematising, concepts such as 'nuclear culture' and 'nuclearity', scholars increasingly engage with the broader themes of postwar social, cultural and political history. Some—including contributors to this special issue—have taken the so-called 'emotional turn', responding in part to Joseph Masco's declaration that 'Reclaiming the emotional history of the atomic bomb is crucial today'.[6] Masco has used mass circulation images of nuclear damage in the United States to explore 'the affective coordinates of the nuclear security state', showing how citizens were emotionally managed through 'civil defence' programmes which sought to transform paralysing nuclear terror into productive nuclear fear.[7] The goal, he argues, was 'The microregulation of a nation community at the emotional level'.[8] And yet, as Frank Beiss shows for West Germany, state attempts to manage nuclear fear could have unforeseen outcomes: 'The perception and articulation of popular fears regarding civil defence stood in uneasy tension with the dominant emotional regime in West Germany and ultimately helped to transform it'.[9] This sense of emotion as a driver of nuclear change is further developed by Friederike Brühöfener in her study of the West German Peace Movement: 'Articulating "my fear of nuclear war" was not only the expression of a person's immediate feelings—it could also function as a useful method to foreground the individual as an important political factor'.[10] Brühöfener identifies this as a late twentieth-century phenomenon rooted in the social psychological currents of the 1970s, but I will suggest that we see it in an earlier period too.[11]

Building on these approaches, and on Jonathan Hogg's work on 'nuclear anxiety' in Britain, this article considers what the emotional politics of the atom bomb looked like in 1945.[12] It uses 'ordinary'—or at least non-elite—people's writing for Mass-Observation to explore first, the impact that the atomic explosions had upon ways of narrating, and managing, the emotional self, and second, the influence of nuclear knowledge on felt social relations.[13] I will argue that use of the atom bomb by the United States had a profound impact upon British people's understandings of the past, the present and the political future; and that the responses of ordinary people in turn helped to shape a messy and contradictory popular nuclear culture within which feeling operated as a way of knowing, and intervening in, the world.

As is well known, Mass-Observation recruited paid and unpaid observers to conduct 'anthropology of ourselves...a scientific study of human social behaviour'.[14] Its methods included the solicitation of diaries, received from 474 people across the mid-century period, the discursive questionnaires the organisation referred to as Directives, essay competitions, social surveys and various other ethnographic practices.[15] A consistent, and perhaps surprising, interest in feeling is evident across all of these research practices. Mass-Observation sought out individual and collective feeling—rarely 'emotion'—not as a proxy for attitude, but as something of interest in its own right. As its then Director—Bob Willcock—put it in 1942, 'Mass-Observation is particularly concerned with people's behaviour, their subjective feelings, their worries, frustrations, hopes, desires, expectations and fears'.[16] This interest was notably apparent in the Directives sent to its 'National Panel' of volunteer writers. Feeling-requests were an important element within these texts and the word 'feel' or 'feelings' was sometimes underlined to emphasise the specificity of what was required. These questions were often rooted in the themes of everyday life; they could also spin around the experience of particular emotions such as fear and hope. In October 1942, for example, the panellists were asked 'What are your main personal fears now? Divide your answer into (a) Present everyday fears and (b) Fears about the future. At other times the questions were wilfully open-ended: 'How do you feel about 1944?'[17]

Mass-Observation's interest in its panel's feelings was not, however, restricted to the realm of the 'personal' or everyday. Feeling was also mobilised as a research category when enquiring about current and future world affairs; and in ways that actively blurred the boundaries between the personal, the national, the international and the political. Mass-Observation was an early measurer of civilian morale and of what it termed 'mass-mentality and mass reaction'.[18] In a 1940 publication, *War Begins at Home*, co-creators of Mass-Observation Tom Harrisson and Charles Madge noted that 'For the civilian, war is above all a process of anxiety' suggesting that:

> In order to conduct a war thoroughly, we must then turn certain passive feelings into active feelings, and externalise violent hatreds which are ordinarily turned inwards within civilised individuals in this country. Similarly, personal, private ethics and desires have to be transformed, elevated and merged into a general pattern of the whole community. The private interest has to become the public interest.[19]

If Mass-Observation was not sure—at least initially—what morale actually was, this did not stop it engaging in an expansive programme of data collection.[20] As Dibley and Kelly have more recently suggested, Mass-Observation did, in fact, play a significant role both in establishing morale as an area of research and in suggesting strategies through which the state might manage it.[21]

But Mass-Observation's interest in the national mood was not limited to the immediate concerns of everyday home front life. Feelings about the world were regularly solicited. Panellists were asked to compose their feelings about India (August 1942 and May 1943), the bombing of Germany (December 1943) and about the situation in Greece (December 1944–January 1945).[22] In February 1942, they were asked to reflect on their 'present feelings' about the British Empire: 'Have they changed since war began?' Here, as elsewhere, individual Mass-Observers were asked to reflect on the processes through which their feelings—and sometimes, other people's feelings—had changed over time.

The material generated by Mass-Observation provides ways of getting at individual emotional expression within a self-consciously collective wartime context. The self-declared motivations of those who wrote for it included creativity, self-improvement, historical-mindedness and curiosity. A belief that wartime writing for the organisation was a form of active citizenship drove the involvement of some and Mass-Observation encouraged this perspective. Writing to its volunteer writers in May 1940 it declared that

> the increased tension of the war ought to make the whole of M-O more determined than ever to carry on its work, because we believe that it is important work and that we should be inconsistent and unscientific if we gave it up just because there's a war on.[23]

In August of the same year the panel was reassured that 'The stuff that observers have been sending in is quite definitely going to prove of first class importance when the time comes to write a history of this war'.[24]

Writing for Mass-Observation was, then, an act of citizenship with future, as well as present, significance. Encouraged by a distinctive mode of questioning, writing for Mass-Observation was also an avowedly emotional citizenship practice.[25] Indeed Mass-Observers might be understood as members of a loose 'emotional community' to use Barbara Rosenwein's much deployed formulation, or to borrow from Benno Gammerl, they might be seen as manifesting particular 'emotional styles' within a specific emotional space.[26] Their writing also demonstrates what cultural theorist Sara Ahmed terms, the 'sociality of emotion'.[27]

The wartime directives have been used by a number of historians for varied purposes. Both Jennifer Purcell and James Hinton—with different emphases—have used them biographically, in tandem with diary material, to reconstruct the mid-century lives of individual Mass-Observers.[28] Others have approached them more thematically as a lens through which to explore attitudes towards 'race' and ethnicity, love and sex, and gender and national identity.[29] The two approaches can, of course, be combined. A substantial core of volunteers maintained their relationship with Mass-Observation across the war years, and they were not infrequently asked repeat questions. The Directives therefore offer a unique longitudinal autobiographical data source allowing for the charting of the changing views of individuals on specific topics over time. They also facilitate the contextualisation of one specific response through recourse to the writer's other contributions. The woman cited at the beginning of this article was not the most prolific of Mass-Observers, but she nonetheless responded to Directives in January and February 1939, April 1944, January, August and November 1945 and submitted an extensive diary entry in May 1944.[30]

Here, however, I want to use the Directive material as 'a sort of documentary cross-section' rather than as a way of reconstructing individual lives or even individual attitudes across time.[31] A total of 178 members of the panel answered the Directive of August 1945: 85 of these were women and 93 were men. The numbers responding to Mass-Observation's questionnaires fluctuated sharply across the war. For example, in May 1942 there were 496 responses but numbers declined in 1945 and only once in that year did they exceed the 200 mark.[32] In its early stages younger men dominated the panel, but by 1945 it was more representative of the age and gender, if not social class, distribution of the population more broadly.[33] I approach their responses as offering a snapshot view—a slice of feeling—in order to interrogate the emotional complexity of a particular moment in time. The article explores feelings about the atom bomb in the immediate aftermath of the destruction of Hiroshima and Nagasaki and assesses the epistemological resources that individuals drew upon in framing their responses to these cataclysmic world events. Fundamentally I ask what knowledge of the atom bomb felt like to those who wrote to Mass-Observation in 1945; a moment when nuclear anxiety was not yet part of the fabric of everyday life, even if a 'nuclear imagination' was already established.[34] It was, in fact, a moment when individuals were thrown upon their own resources to actively work out for themselves what 'nuclearity' might mean for themselves and for the world.

Writing feeling

Historians of modern Britain have become increasingly interested in the management of wartime feeling. Amy Bell has explored the 'repressed fears and dark emotions' that haunted those who endured the London blitz, demonstrating that both the control and the expression of feeling characterised wartime citizenship.[35] Lucy Noakes identifies restrained self-management as the expected wartime response to bereavement and yet notes that 'an emotional reticence should not be read as evidence that grief was not deeply felt'.[36] Charting the social and political work of mid-century psychoanalysis, Michal Shapira argues that 'Total war, waged against civilians as much as soldiers incited advanced discussions about emotional and mental well-being' while James Hinton suggests that total war also encouraged individuals to interrogate 'the meaning of their own lives'.[37] William Reddy has argued that periods of crisis effect transformations in emotional style.[38] The dropping of the atom bomb in August 1945 appears to have been one such moment.

Those who wrote their feelings about the atom bomb were, as we have seen, well versed in offering an emotional response; many chose a narrativised form, writing in detail about where and how they heard the news. 'When I heard the news on the wireless one night I think I was as horrified as if this had happened to an allied city; the sheer enormity of the thing was chilling' wrote a 34-year-old farm worker.[39] A woman serving in the WAAF 'first heard about the atomic bomb on the nine o'clock news in a Bournemouth hotel. The lounge was full of old ladies and retired Indian army colonels, which made it seem even more unreal…'[40] The context of first knowledge was emphasised within these structured accounts; so too was the physicality of the initial response. Mass-Observation's language of 'feeling', rather than 'emotion', encouraged responses that transcended any distinction between cognition and embodiment.[41] For this group of writers—men and women alike—consideration of their own embodied reaction offered an initial way of reflecting on events that defied easy conceptualisation. A teacher recorded that she 'felt sick at heart that a civilised nation could use such a weapon. My sister and I heard it while at breakfast, we looked at each other, I could see her face quite white'.[42] A writer recalled 'a sinking (or should I say a "shrinking"?) feeling inside me'.[43] A London social worker simply stated that 'The idea of the atomic bomb gives me the "creeps"'.[44] As Joanna Bourke reminds us, 'The emotion of fear is fundamentally about the body—its fleshiness and its precariousness'.[45]

In writing their feelings about the atom bomb, Mass-Observers frequently deployed a narrative of emotional reappraisal, reflecting on shifts in their response over time and according to a fast changing context. This should not surprise us. Mass-Observation had long encouraged its volunteer writers to be reflexive in their self-narration: a question from the May–June 1945 Directive had asked, for example, 'How do you feel now the war's over in Europe, and how does this compare with how you expected to feel?'[46] Individuals recorded their journey through various stages of horror, fear, awe, jubilation, and pity; others expressed 'relief', and some even felt curious. Above all, feelings were messy and difficult to pin down: 'wonder, anticipation, fear all blend in the spontaneous emotion'.[47] Sara Ahmed has suggested that 'Messiness is a good starting point for thinking with feelings: …they often come at us, surprise us, leaving us cautious and bewildered'.[48] Her twenty-first century description has particular traction within the 1945 context as individuals were faced with events that they struggled to process.

Mass-Observers reported shifting responses over the days and weeks following the explosions. This could make it tricky for them to 'feel' their initial feelings. A soldier recorded that 'First feelings of people I met were of horror and fear. So much has happened since that I'm afraid the first wave of feeling has been overlaid…'[49] For some the passage of time brought clarification and greater hopefulness. A Glasgow secretary explained her own journey from consternation through rejoicing to hope:

> My first reaction to the atomic bomb was one of complete consternation—a feeling of having lost any sense of security at all, that within a few years we would all be killed and mankind would vanish from the face of the earth. At the same time I had a slight feeling of rejoicing that this must surely bring the end of the Japanese war very soon, but this was a very minor triumph compared with the staggering effect of the news. Then gradually I began to hope that the atomic bomb would mean the end of all wars, that no nation would ever have the stupidity to risk war that would mean complete extinction…[50]

For others, feelings evaded clarification or shifted back and forth between extremes of fear and hope. Feelings of horror increased, as the after effects of the atomic blasts became widely known. A civil servant was particularly reflexive in her consideration of the development of her feelings and views:

> My first feelings about the atom bomb were of utter horror combined with fear—horror at the ghastly effects—even as first described—and also that we should use this awful weapon. Fear that the war was at last entering on [sic] the phase anticipated at its beginning,—of utter destruction of all civilisation and mutual extermination. Fear, that even if this worst did not happen, the disintegration started by the bomb would spread and spread uncontrollably until it eventually engulfed the whole world. Statements made in the next few days were reassuring on this last point, as it was said that the effects were not spreading or continuing; and of course events have proved the first fear unjustified.

After this initial stage of horror and fear—according to her narrative—she found herself reassured by allied claims that the bomb had ultimately saved both allied and Japanese lives by shortening the war. And yet this feeling of surety did not last:

> …the last two day's reports rather over rule this reassurance. In the first place the story of the first reporters to enter Hiroshima—of the poisonous air and of people dying now who seemed to have been uninjured, show that the effects of the bomb do continue—perhaps

indefinitely—long after the original explosion and who can say how they will spread. Secondly reports now show that the Japanese 'were at the end of their tether'—so it would appear that the use of the bomb did not shorten the war to such an extent as we suppose… it has marred the joy of victory and made it almost impossible to give thanks in sincerity to God for victory and peace because they have been claimed by what seems more like a gift from the devil than from God.[51]

While some Mass-Observers attended to the shifting texture of their emotional response, others considered the broader possibilities and utility of feeling, or sought to distinguish between what they felt and what they thought, as Mass-Observation's question had indicated that they should. A Sussex teacher made a sharp distinction between the two forms of response: 'I feel disgust, I think it was right to use our maximum means against the enemy and finish the war quickly'.[52] Others spoke to the longer term impact of war on their emotional register: 'Horror and fear have limits and we've long ago reached them' wrote one woman, 'I only feel cold about the atom bomb'.[53] A sergeant in the Royal Air Force whose 'most conscious feeling about the atomic bomb is one of resignation', admitted that 'war has stunted much tenderness'[54] while a former Royal Navy Volunteer Reservist noted that, 'Feelings—either I have few, or the only feeling I have is relief that it ended the war'.[55] Some actively rejected the utility of an emotional response to the atom bomb: 'We have to be very careful when assessing any scientific achievement in not getting emotional about it'.[56] As I have argued elsewhere, the relationship between 'reason' and 'emotion', or at least constructions of these, became a matter for debate within postwar British politics—'emotion' was castigated by politicians and the press as an inferior and implicitly feminine way of knowing.[57] And yet amongst Mass-Observers writing in 1945, the emotional response was only infrequently rejected.

Some of the correspondents reflected on the epistemological materials upon which their response drew. 'You ask me for my feelings and views, as well as those of the people I meet', wrote one, 'The following are a few random notes, by no means a considered opinion, but reflecting partly what I have read, partly what I have heard from others, and to a small degree my own original thoughts'.[58] Mass-Observation had long encouraged such reflection, periodically asking their volunteer writers the same set of questions on opinion formation. Panellists were asked to rank 12 factors influencing their 'activities and opinion', including books, newspapers and personal experience—each of which was consistently highly ranked.[59] The value of experience as the basis for knowledge claims rose particularly dramatically over the course of the war: from fifth place amongst the ranked factors in 1940 to first place when the questions were asked in September 1946.[60]

Indeed the panellists drew upon their own experience and knowledge of warfare in crafting their responses to the atom bomb. The poison gas of the First World War was one such point of reference: 'I don't believe that this bomb will frighten people out of war; the ghastly tales of poison gas didn't do so…', despaired a 65-year-old man.[61] Others drew upon their own experiences of aerial bombing to try to make sense of this new form of warfare, suggesting that the atom bomb was a more merciful—because, they claimed, speedier—way to die. 'They at least would be spared the fear of wondering and of hearing the noise. Most people are more worried by the noise of near misses than anything and here the actual victims would be spared this, and one could imagine death was instantaneous', claimed a chartered electrical engineer.[62] A Kent housewife suggested that

> perhaps it is a good thing because now war will be different, shorter, and one will be snuffed out quickly; there will probably be no forces, thus saving much waste of time and money. No long endurance of years of raids, terror and blackout.[63]

Those who crafted their responses later in September, as the on-going effects of the atom bomb became apparent, were less likely to advance this position.

As well as marshalling their own experiences, Mass-Observers referenced cultural resources in writing their feelings about the atom bomb. Jeff Hughes has rightly pointed to the 'diversity of cultures of the nuclear' but here I am interested in the resources that individual Mass-Observers explicitly cited.[64] The press was a target of particular criticism; portrayed as a source of anxiety or as a mouthpiece of scientists. 'Newspapers [are] to blame for general alarm' declared one woman.[65] Another claimed that 'opinion is led by the newspapers, and particularly by articles by scientists, to an amazing extent'.[66] Some preferred to ignore newspaper coverage entirely—'I like others didn't read or even scan *Picture Post* last week to avoid the subject' wrote one man.[67] Science fiction writing apparently offered more useful scripts and terminology. A clerk in the RAF wrote that:

> My personal feeling as soon as I heard the first bomb was 'Well! That's the end of it!'—and a sense of relief that the Jap war had finished months ahead of expectations. At the same instant I recollected reading a story in an American magazine a long time ago, describing the end of the war being brought about by a powerful bomb, and thought that once more fiction had become fact![68]

Atomic weapons were deployed by a number of science fiction writers from the late nineteenth century onwards, but it was the work of H. G. Wells that Mass-Observers most often referenced.[69] A woman in the forces explained that:

> In November 1940 I read a book by H G Wells, in which he described an atom bomb raid on Paris. The description was vivid—how the earth was churned to black liquid, how the devastated city glowed red with flames. I shuddered with horror to think that the Luftwaffe raids experienced at the time could ever be so horrible. Then I was comforted, thinking to myself that such bombs would never be invented in my lifetime: when the news of the first atom bomb raid on Japan was announced, my first thoughts were off the gory description in that book by HG Wells. I was again shaken with horror. Such bombs had been invented in my lifetime![70]

The concept of a 'Wellsian nightmare', or 'Wellsian affair', had popular purchase.[71] As a government draftswoman put it: 'we were being whirled into a Wellsian future against our will. I always believed in a Wellsian future, but I never expected to be in on it and have never had any wish to be'.[72] In fact as a 20-year-old secretary put it, 'the possibilities surpassed anything H. G. Wells ever wrote'.[73]

The sociality of feeling

In crafting their responses to the atom bomb, Mass-Observers actively constructed distinct, although sometimes overlapping, emotional communities that span around their own particular position.[74] These self-made communities demonstrate the 'sociality of feeling' and the ways in which feeling tied the individual to the world. As Goodwin,

Jasper and Polletta argue, 'Emotions are part of the "stuff" connecting human beings to each other and the world around them, like the unseen lens that colours all our thoughts, actions, perceptions and judgements'.[75]

Most panellists claimed that their own views were widely shared across place, and space. Indeed this assertion provided evidence for the veracity of their position. 'Above all I have noticed how unanimous people are in their feelings about the atom bomb' wrote a 20-year-old, 'Everyone thinks it is terrible—but beyond that they don't quite know what to feel'.[76] A 17-year-old shorthand typist who thought it 'frightful' and 'quite shocking', stated that 'All the people with whom I have discussed the atomic bomb seem to feel pretty much the same as I, about it'.[77] Those who supported its use similarly cited the ubiquity of their view.

> I don't look on it as any different from an ordinary bomb except that it is more to be feared because of its greater power. I'd say this is how most folks look at it just as a bigger and better bomb,

wrote a man in his thirties.[78] A farmer's wife whose bomb enthusiasm stemmed from her belief that it had shortened the war, claimed that 'the simple folk around here seem to take more or less a like view. I have not heard the other line expressed at all'.[79]

There were, nonetheless, a minority of Mass-Observers who saw themselves as sitting outside of any community of feeling—who felt isolated and emotionally 'out of place' and at the jagged edges of shared feeling. An aero-examiner living in Newport, for example, recorded that 'the people I meet don't seem the least perturbed, they are daft or I am barmy—an immediate world round table conference seems imperative to me'.[80] In fact it was those that supported use of the bomb—women as well as men, writing from diverse locations—who were more likely to paint themselves as outsiders.[81] An army vicar admitted to being 'rather shocked at the amount of "Sob-stuff" I am hearing from people about the bomb and atomic energy as a whole. People, at least 75% of those with whom I've spoken, are muddle headed or cowards or both'.[82]

Beyond this positioning of the self in relation to the collective, the sociality of feeling—and its boundaries—was apparent in writing about specific categories of other people; notably so in relation to other nations. After years of wartime mobilisation, the national 'we' wielded significant discursive power. 'Generally speaking the view seems to be 'It's a damn bad thing but thank God we got it first!' noted one man.[83] A teacher recorded that 'Nearly everyone expressed horror and fear, but thought the A Bomb was justifiable, because Germans were trying to make it to use against us', while a secretary felt 'positive that if the Japanese had had the atom bomb first, they would have used it to exterminate white races. If Germans had had it they would have exterminated Britons, and used the other European nationals as slave races'.[84]

For some writers national feelings—and the wartime processes through which they had been fermented—framed their responses to those killed in the attacks. One man admitted that he 'could not feel any pity or sorrow for the Japanese dead and dying, partly because of the imperceptible hardening of my perceptives [sic] by the cumulative horrors of war, and also because distance deadens feeling'.[85] While one Mass-Observer was sure that 'no one said 'they deserved it', some of his fellow Mass-Observers actually did.[86] A housewife suggested that 'we didn't drop enough and it's a thousand pities that Germany caved in too soon'.[87] An electrical engineer living in Blackburn reported that 'the general opinion of the people I have met is that we should have dropped more of them on Japan. Very few stated why or what would have been gained other than wiping out the Japanese'.[88]

Others, however, expressed a sense of shame and likened the attacks to Nazi atrocities. For a young agricultural worker 'its indiscriminate use on the two Japanese towns proves that for barbarism the Nazis "have nothing on us"'.[89] A head teacher concurred,

> My own attitude is clear: I cannot think of any definition of "atrocity" or of "war criminal" which rules out this bomb and the people who gave orders for its use (including Churchill and Truman and the pilots who dropped them).[90]

Mass-Observers articulated powerful emotional responses that spoke to transnational emotional ties. A London teacher, for example, confided that 'Even at the time of the announcement I began to feel that I should not be able to lift up my head in the presence of a Japanese'.[91] Objections to the bombing of densely populated areas without warning, and condemnation of the second bombing, were widespread.[92] One of the most prolific of female Mass-Observers admitted that she was:

> Too horrified to want to think or speak of it and yet it is seldom out of my mind. It casts a gloom over everything and its horrifying possibilities make nothing worth while doing. As few people speak to me about it, and as those who do only express horror briefly, I think most of my friends feel the same. My next door neighbour wrote to the local paper and said that after the elimination camps in Germany the bombing of Hiroshima and Nagasaki were the most horrible acts ever perpetuated by man.[93]

Even as early as the summer of August 1945 individuals were, then, trying to weigh up the moral equivalence of acts of war.

They were beginning to weigh international relations in a postwar world too, increasingly unsure as to whom Britain's future allies and enemies would be. Global anxieties focused upon knowledge of the atomic secret. There was a clear distrust of the United States, exacerbated by the ending of the lend-lease programme: 'they may use it against Britain and do us another dirty trick', wrote one Mass Observer.[94] There was also 'some annoyance that although a British invention it had to be made in America and dropped by an American plane'. Acknowledging the contingency of his feelings on the subject, this writer added that 'The debt settlement seems to have affected my feelings towards the US'.[95] A number of people advocated sharing atomic knowledge with the Russians or with the Council of the United Nations in an effort to foster world peace and dilute the global power of the United States.

If former allies could not necessarily be trusted then nor too could scientists. While the status of the scientist-expert was complex, scientific discovery provoked more fear than optimism. 'The ingenuity of science is wonderful and admirable' admitted a Norwich-based schoolteacher, 'that it should be directed to such ends is worse than prostitution and a kind of blasphemy'.[96] According to a particularly animated Mass-Observer, 'the "scientists" who told us there was no God, and then sold their great intelligence to the highest military bidders, should have been blown up with their own devilish invention'.[97] Others argued that science should be harnessed for more positive purposes, writing from a subject position of 'ordinariness' that wielded considerable affective and political power coming out of a 'peoples war'.[98] A coal miner asked why science was 'so horribly successful in weapons of destruction' but had not yet cured the common cold or cancer: 'I am only an ordinary man, but if I can see such a misdirection of scientific research, surely those who have been trained and educated to view these problems with a keener intellect than I can see it'.[99]

A minority stood in defence of science sometimes invoking a dichotomy between 'reason' and 'emotion' to do so. One young man asserted that the popular response had confirmed a feeling 'that people are emotionally afraid of science: afraid, because it is a product of the brain, and their own brains are not trained to minimise the emotional aspect in favour of an outlook that would enable them'.[100] A Sussex teacher railed against what she perceived to be widespread hypocrisy:

> I despise the attitude of mind which shouts against "scientists"—no doubt while opening a tin of meat from the other side of the world, or using some other of the million and one products of science and without any intention of foregoing them.[101]

Some went further in their defence. A member of the WAAF reported on an operation room cartoon drawn by one of the pilots. Entitled 'Public Hero No 1. 1945 type' it apparently depicted 'a Professor (holding up a test-tube) with a huge brain, and decorated with an enormous "gong"'.[102]

The scientist/non-scientist cleavage was not the only fracture in the imagined community of feeling. Mass-Observers also cited gender, occupation and religiosity as important delineators of feeling and perspective. A Brighton woman wrote that 'all war in future will be so terrible. I do wish that all the nations would resolve never to have another! Perhaps when women have more power, this happy state of things will come to pass!'[103] A housewife asserted that 'Women—ordinary ones I mean—are life givers—not destroyers. Any bombs therefore are deplorable, even if in the world of today a necessity'.[104] Both suggest a link between masculinity and militarism; an association that would again be voiced in the Campaign for Nuclear Disarmament marches of the late 1950s and at Greenham Common in the 1980s.[105] There was certainly a perception amongst some male Mass-Observers that reaction to the atom bomb was gendered and that women were more likely to exhibit an 'emotional' response to the subject. Analysis of the panel responses as a whole suggests that this was not actually the case. Mass-Observation had explicitly requested that its panellists narrate their feelings on the topic and men, as well as women, responded in emotional terms.

A cleavage was, however, identified between civilian and service responses:

> Service chaps to whom I speak and correspond think the bomb wasn't used enough on Japan. No one has the slightest sympathy for the dirty little yellow creatures and everyone feels we shouldn't be getting that so-called 'loss of face' attitude there even if we'd killed off a few more...The civilian attitude however, seems altogether different. Civvies appear to be under the impression that use of the bomb is inhumane and don't take into consideration the fact that at least quarter of a million lives have been saved. Casualties would have been extremely heavy in the invasion of Japan and after all, it is allied soldiers lives we're worried about. No one should care a twopenny cuss whether 200,000 Japs have been killed so long as our own chap's lives are saved. I've seen enough young, intelligent and decent chaps killed on the battlefield and I don't want to see or hear any more.[106]

Here we see a sharp distinction drawn between the armed forces and those at home; a weighing up of the relative value of life; explicitly racist attitudes towards the Japanese people and, ultimately, the use of lived experience as an evidential base. A 29-year-old shared some of these sentiments admitting that 'my feelings, as a soldier, are purely relief. It means that thousands of good men's lives, perhaps including my own have been spared', so too did a Bradford housewife who explained that 'my son's life is infinitely more precious to me than those of a million Japs'.[107]

Perhaps the most significant dividing line—and the one that generated the strongest feelings of inclusion and exclusion—concerned broad questions of morality. Such questions haunted almost all of the responses even where they were not explicitly addressed. Was the atom bomb morally different to other weapons? Was the targeting of civilians justified if it had indeed hastened the end of the war? What were, in fact, the ethical parameters within which Total War could be conducted and what role should the churches take in mapping those parameters. According to a Leicester music teacher:

> Of the people I meet I find that the intensely religious ones are definitely against the use of the atom bomb as they are also against all scientific inventions used against us by our enemies. They seem to regard them as the special work of devils operating through human beings. The more secular and usually broader minded people take into consideration the fact that the atom bomb, by shortening the war, saved the lives of hundreds of our men.[108]

In contrast one young woman believed that as a result of the action, 'Britain and America now have no right to call themselves Christian or civilised. They have no right to condemn the SS of Belsen'; other Mass-Observers also deployed Christianity as a tool of condemnation.[109] But in the heightened emotional climate of 1945, the public pronouncements of church leaders could provoke strong feelings too.[110] A science teacher had 'no patience with those clerics and others who protest against its use while condoning the use of other bombs. They should have protested earlier or not at all', whilst a particularly frustrated Mass-Observer was

> ...irritated by the stupidity of the people who persisted in writing to the papers, saying it was an-Christian, and brutal, and like German methods. Total War has shown us that civilians are as much a military target as frontline soldiers, and since the Japanese at home are compelled to make munitions etc. they were not to be exempted from our attacks.[111]

Conclusion

The Mass-Observers who replied to the August 1945 Directive believed themselves to have entered a new age. It was a moment of such significance that some struggled to articulate their feelings. As one man put it,

> I have often wondered what it was like to live at one of the turning points of man's evolution; now I have experienced it I wish I could capture in words the emotion that has pervaded me as a result of the BBC announcers calm announcement.[112]

Others engaged with the new world at some length. A soldier sent Mass-Observation a personal 'manifesto' entitled 'New World or No World?' in which he argued that:

> Rightly developed, for the people and by the people, atomic energy can become the people's prize; the prize for which they have worked and suffered and died so often. In the hands of the

people of the world, it can clothe them, feed them, give them shelter; it can enable the resources of this globe—indeed, of the whole universe—to be harnessed and utilised for their benefit; it can bring us all in our lifetime undreamt-of wonders and treasures; it can make the world not only safe for our children, but a veritable paradise in life.

The use of a 'people's war' rhetoric here is striking, as is the commitment to a truly global 'people's peace'. And there certainly *were* Mass-Observers who approached the atomic age with hope and optimism, envisaging a world without warfare, with enhanced international cooperation and worldwide prosperity.

However the majority of correspondents were less optimistic about the future, providing a first glimpse of the nuclear anxiety that would haunt British lives over subsequent decades. A 46-year-old housewife recorded that 'I do not view the future use of atomic energy with any degree of enthusiasm—I hope to be dead by then anyway'.[113] In fact three out of five panellists told Mass-Observation that they felt depressed about the peace.[114] A significant proportion believed that world destruction was imminent—there were references to 'world suicide', and a 'sword of Damocles hanging over civilisation'.[115] An electrical engineer explained that

> Most people we have talked to have had a feeling of dread, wondering if it is possible to control such a force for good and not for evil intent. This same feeling seems almost universal and applies to all classes. There is a fear that this is the end.[116]

A farm worker put it more succinctly: 'We are in for the Age of Fear'.[117]

Indeed when Mass-Observation published its study of *Peace and the Public* in 1947, it pointed to an overwhelming mood of pessimism about the future and a, sometimes paralysing, fear of imminent war amongst those it surveyed.[118] When it had interviewed a cross-section of Hammersmith residents in June 1946, seven out of every ten suggested that there would be another war within 25 years.[119] As the *Newcastle Journal* explained, 'Investigations by Mass-Observation during 1946 show that the war transformed Britain from a nation of wishful-thinkers into one of pessimists, largely convinced of the inevitability of another conflict'.[120] According to Mass-Observation, the emotional culture of Britain had been transformed.

Underpinning this emotional shift lay knowledge of the atom bomb and its almost unimaginable destructive powers. 'Nuclearity' exercised an increasingly powerful influence upon the feelings and experiences of 'ordinary' British people in the years after 1945, as multiple nuclear narratives unfurled. Those who responded to Mass-Observation's August 1945 Directive had fewer cultural scripts to draw upon, but the impact of the atom bomb on feelings about the present, and the future, was no less powerful. As one man put it: 'I have three children and we have all along planned to have four. My wife revived the question: I hesitated and thought of the future in terms of the atom bomb'.[121]

Notes

1. Mass Observation Archive (MOA) Directive, August 1945.
2. Ibid.
3. Hogg defines 'nuclearity' as 'a shifting set of assumptions held by individual citizens on the danger of nuclear technology, assumptions that were rooted firmly in context and which circulated in, and were shaped by, national discourse'. Hogg, "The Family that Feared Tomorrow," 535.

4. MOA Directive, August 1945, DR 1022.
5. See, for example, the special issue of *The British Journal for the History of Science* on "British Nuclear Culture," 2012.
6. Masco, "Survival is your Business," 387.
7. Ibid., 372, 368.
8. Ibid., 368.
9. Beiss, "Everybody has a Chance," 218.
10. Brühöfener, "Politics of Emotions," 103.
11. Ibid., 102.
12. Hogg, *British Nuclear Culture*.
13. James Hinton has suggested that 'many of the panel members did not think of themselves as "ordinary". They tended to see themselves as unusual people, distinguished by their desire to self-fashion their lives free from the conventions of their social milieu'. Hinton, *The Mass Observers*, 374.
14. Madge and Harrisson, *Mass-Observation*, 10.
15. For more on Mass-Observation's research methods see Hinton, *The Mass-Observers*, 260–93. On Mass-Observation in its intellectual context see Hubble, *Mass Observation and Everyday Life*.
16. MOA, FR 1415, 21.
17. MOA, Directive, December 1943.
18. Harrisson and Madge, *War Begins at Home*, v.
19. Ibid., 424.
20. Beaven and Griffiths, "The Blitz, Civilian Morale and the City," 73.
21. Dibley and Kelly, "Morale and Mass Observation."
22. For an analysis of responses to this last Directive see Hassiotis, "British Military Opinion."
23. MOA, Directive, May 1940.
24. MOA, Directive, August 1940.
25. On different models of citizenship see Grant, "Historicizing Citizenship in Post-war Britain." On citizenship during the war see Rose, *Which People's War*.
26. Rosenwein, *Emotional Communities*; and Gammerl, "Emotional Styles."
27. Ahmed, *The Cultural Politics of Emotion*, 9.
28. Hinton, *Nine Wartime Lives*; and Purcell, *Domestic Soldiers*.
29. Kushner, *We Europeans?*; Rose, *Which People's War?*; Langhamer, *The English in Love*; and Noakes, *War and the British*.
30. MOA, Diary, D5389.
31. MOA, FR 2278A, 4.
32. Numbers taken from *Mass Observation Online*. In the years after 1945 the numbers participating in the project rose with a peak number of responses—704—reached in February 1949.
33. Hinton, *The Mass-Observers*, 268–9.
34. Hogg, *British Nuclear Culture*, 26.
35. Bell, "Landscapes of Fear," 154. See also Bell, *London Was Ours*.
36. Noakes, "Gender, Grief and Bereavement," 84.
37. Shapira, *The War Inside*; and Hinton, "Middle-Class Socialism," 116–7.
38. Reddy, "Historical Research," 312.
39. MOA, Directive, August 1945, DR 1093, male, born 1912.
40. Ibid., DR 1651, female, born 1909.
41. Hera Cook defines feeling as 'the subjective experience resulting from the combination of embodied emotions and cognitions'. Cook, 'From controlling Emotion to Expressing Feelings," 630.
42. MOA, Directive, August 1945, DR 1313, female, born 1891.
43. Ibid., DR 3479, male, born 1923.
44. Ibid., DR 1563, female, born 1898.
45. Bourke, "Fear and Anxiety," 123. See also Bourke, *Fear*.
46. MOA, Directive, May-June 1945.

47. MOA, Directive, August 1945, DR 3090, male, born 1911.
48. Ahmed, *The Cultural Politics of Emotion*, 210.
49. MOA, Directive, August 1945, DR 1680, male, born 1917.
50. Ibid., DR 3545, female, born 1917.
51. Ibid., DR 2675, female, born 1892.
52. Ibid., DR 1078, female, born 1900.
53. Ibid., DR 1974, female, born 1904.
54. Ibid., DR 3630, male, born 1908.
55. Ibid., DR 2568, male, born 1903.
56. Ibid., DR 2684, male, born 1908.
57. Langhamer, "The Live Dynamic Whole," 420–1.
58. MOA, Directive, August 1945, DR 1679, male, born 1890.
59. MOA, FR 2250, "Opinion Forming," May 1944.
60. MOA, Directive, September 1946.
61. MOA, Directive, August 1945, DR 1098, male, born 1880.
62. Ibid., DR 1165, male, born 1906.
63. Ibid., DR 2892, female, born 1893.
64. Hughes, "What is British Nuclear Culture?"
65. MOA Directive, August 1945, DR 3368, female, born 1909.
66. Ibid., DR 3119, female, born 1924.
67. Ibid., DR 1345, male, born 1917. *Picture Post* dedicated a whole issue to the subject entitled 'Man Enters The Atom Age'. *Picture Post*, 25 August 1945. For a study of nuclear representations in *Picture Post* between August 1945 and June 1957 see Laucht, "Dawn—or Dusk?"
68. MOA, Directive, August 1945, DR 2512, male, born 1907.
69. Hogg, *British Nuclear Culture*, 34–7.
70. MOA, Directive, August 1945, DR 3642, female, no date of birth given.
71. Ibid., DR 1061, female, born 1889; and DR 3603, male, born 1916.
72. Ibid., DR 3669, female, born 1918.
73. Ibid., DR 3119, female, born 1924.
74. Rosenwein defines emotional communities as 'groups—usually but not always social groups—that have their own particular values, modes of feeling and ways to express those feelings'. Rosenwein, *Generations of Feeling*, 3.
75. Goodwin, Jasper and Polletta, *Passionate Politics*, 10.
76. MOA, Directive, August 1945, DR 3119, female, born 1924.
77. Ibid., DR 3454, female, born 1928.
78. Ibid., DR 1393, male, born 1909.
79. Ibid., DR 3371, female, born 1894.
80. Ibid., DR 2697, male, born 1903.
81. Ibid., DR 1490, female, born 1914.
82. Ibid., DR 3187, male, born 1900.
83. Ibid., DR 2512, male, born 1907.
84. Ibid., DR 1313, female, born 1891; DR 3474, female, born 1898.
85. Ibid., DR 3679, male, no date of birth given.
86. Ibid., DR 1345, male, born 1917.
87. Ibid., DR 2254, female, born 1901.
88. Ibid., DR 2399, male, born 1901.
89. Ibid., DR 3650, male, born 1921.
90. Ibid., DR 2567, male, born 1893.
91. Ibid., DR 2984, female, born 1980.
92. Ibid., DR 1688, male, born 1911.
93. Ibid., DR 1014, female, born 1885.
94. Ibid., DR 3120, female, borm 1869.
95. Ibid., DR 3674, male, no date of birth given.
96. Ibid., DR 2795, male, born 1914.

97. Ibid., DR 3642, female, no date of birth given.
98. I explore the affective and political power of the claim to be ordinary in '"Who the Hell are Ordinary People?"'.
99. MOA, Directive, August 1945, DR 1226, male, born 1893.
100. Ibid., DR 3479, male, born 1923.
101. Ibid., DR 1078, female, born 1900.
102. Ibid., DR 1651, female, born 1909.
103. Ibid., DR 2463, female, born 1890.
104. Ibid., DR 1061, female, born 1889.
105. See for example some of the interviews in *March to Aldermaston*. On Greenham Common see Roseneil, *Disarming Patriarchy*.
106. MOA, Directive, August 1945, DR 2090, male, born 1923.
107. Ibid., DR 2635, male, born 1916; DR 2903, female, born 1896.
108. Ibid., DR 3022, female, born 1904.
109. Ibid., DR 3642, female, no date of birth given.
110. On letters to the press see Grant, *After the Bomb*, 14–17.
111. MOA, Directive, August 1945, DR 2992, female, born 1913; DR 3683, male, no date of birth given.
112. Ibid., DR 3090, male, born 1911.
113. Ibid., DR 3034, female, born 1899.
114. Mass-Observation, *Peace and the Public*, 9–10. The question, 'How do you feel about the peace now?' was the second question put to the panel in August 1945.
115. MOA, Directive, August 1945, DR 3636, male, born 1918; DR 3119, female, born 1924.
116. Ibid., DR 1165, male, born 1906.
117. Ibid., DR 1093, male, born 1912.
118. Mass-Observation, *Peace and the Public*.
119. Ibid., 15.
120. *Newcastle Journal*, 12 May 1947.
121. MOA, Directive, August 1945, DR 3054, male, no date of birth given.

Disclosure statement

No potential conflict of interest was reported by the author.

Bibliography

Ahmed, S. *The Cultural Politics of Emotion*. Edinburgh: Edinburgh University Press, 2004.
Anderson, L., K. Reisz, and C. Menges. *March to Aldermaston*. 1959. In *Free Cinema*, BFI. London: BFI video, 2006.
Beaven, B., and J. Griffiths. "The Blitz, Civilian Morale and the City: Mass-Observation and Working-Class Culture in Britain, 1940–41." *Urban History* 26, no. 1 (1999): 71–88.
Beiss, F. "'Everybody Has a Chance': Nuclear Angst, Civil Defence, and the History of Emotions in Postwar West Germany." *German History* 27, no. 2 (2009): 215–243. doi:10.1093/gerhis/ghp003.
Bell, A. *London Was Ours: Diaries and Memoirs of the London Blitz*. London: I B Tauris, 2007.

Bell, A. "Landscapes of Fear: Wartime London, 1939–1945." *Journal of British Studies* 48, no. 1 (2009): 153–175. doi:10.1086/592386.

Bingham, A. "'The Monster'? The British Popular Press and Nuclear Culture, 1945-Early 1960s." *The British Journal for the History of Science* 45, no. 4 (2012): 609–624. doi:10.1017/S0007087412001082.

Bourke, J. "Fear and Anxiety: Writing about Emotion in Modern History." *History Workshop Journal* 55 (2003): 111–133. doi:10.1093/hwj/55.1.111.

Bourke, J. *Fear. A Cultural History*. London: Virago, 2005.

Brühöfener, F. "Politics of Emotions. Journalistic Reflections on the Emotionality of the West German Peace Movement, 1979–1984." *German Politics and Society* 33, no. 4 (2015): 97–111.

Cook, H. "From Controlling Emotion to Expressing Feelings in Mid-Twentieth-Century England." *Journal of Social History* 47, no. 3 (2014): 627–646. doi:10.1093/jsh/sht107.

Dibley, B., and M. Kelly. "Morale and Mass Observation: Governing the Affective Atmosphere on the Home-Front ." *Museum and Society* 13, no. 1 (2015): 22–41.

Gammerl, B. "Emotional Styles – Concepts and Challenges." *Rethinking History. The Journal of Theory and Practice* 16, no. 2 (2012): 161–175. doi:10.1080/13642529.2012.681189.

Goodwin, J., J. M. Jasper, and F. Polletta, eds. *Passionate Politics. Emotions and Social Movements*. Chicago: University of Chicago Press, 2001.

Grant, M. *After the Bomb. Civil Defence and Nuclear War in Britain, 1945–68*. London: Palgrave Macmillan, 2016.

Grant, M. "Historicizing Citizenship in Post-War Britain." *Historical Journal* 59, no. 4 (2016): 1187–1206. doi:10.1017/S0018246X16000388.

Harrisson, T., and C. Madge, eds. *War Begins at Home by Mass Observation*. London: Chatto and Windus, 1940.

Hassiotis, L. "British Military Opinion and Military Intervention in Greece, December 1944-January 1945: Stories from Mass-Observation." *Journal of Contemporary History* 50, no. 2 (2015): 296–317. doi:10.1177/0022009414552870.

Hinton, J. "Middle-Class Socialism: Selfhood, Democracy and Distinction in Wartime County Durham." *History Workshop Journal* 62 (2006): 116–141. doi:10.1093/hwj/dbl002.

Hinton, J. *Nine Wartime Lives: Mass Observation and the Making of the Modern Self*. Oxford: Oxford University Press, 2010.

Hinton, J. *The Mass Observers. A History, 1937–1949*. Oxford: Oxford University Press, 2013.

Hogg, J. "'The Family that Feared Tomorrow': British Nuclear Culture and Individual Experience in the Late 1950s." *The British Journal for the History of Science* 45, no. 4 (2012): 535–549. doi:10.1017/S0007087412001045.

Hogg, J. *British Nuclear Culture. Official and Unofficial Narratives in the Long 20th Century*. London: Bloomsbury, 2016.

Hogg, J., and C. Laucht. "British Nuclear Culture." *The British Journal for the History of Science* 45 (2012): 479–493. doi:10.1017/S0007087412001008.

Hubble, N. *Mass Observation and Everyday Life: Culture, History, Theory*. London: Palgrave, 2006.

Hughes, J. "What Is British Nuclear Culture? Understanding *Uranium 235*." *The British Journal for the History of Science* 45, no. 4 (2012): 495–518. doi:10.1017/S0007087412001021.

Kushner, T. *We Europeans? Mass-Observation, Race and British Identity in the Twentieth Century*. London: Ashgate, 2004.

Langhamer, C. "The Live Dynamic Whole of Feeling and Behavior: Capital Punishment and the Politics of Emotion, 1945–1957." *Journal of British Studies* 51, no. 2 (2012): 416–441. doi:10.1086/663841.

Langhamer, C. *The English in Love: The Intimate Story of an Emotional Revolution*. Oxford: Oxford University Press, 2013.

Langhamer, C. "'Who the Hell are Ordinary People?' Ordinariness as a Category of Historical Analysis." *Transactions of the Royal Historical Society* 28(December 2018).

Laucht, C. "'Dawn – Or Dusk?': Britain's *Picture Post* Confronts Nuclear Energy." In *The Nuclear Age in Popular Media. A Transnational History, 1945–1965*, edited by D. Van Lente, 117–148. London: Palgrave, 2012.

Madge, C., and T. Harrisson. *Mass-Observation*. London: Frederick Muller, 1937.

Masco, J. "'Survival Is Your Business': Engineering Ruins and Affect in Nuclear America." *Cultural Anthropology* 23, no. 2 (2008): 361–398. doi:10.1111/cuan.2008.23.issue-2.

Mass Observation Archive. Directive. May 1940

Mass Observation Archive. Directive. August 1940.

Mass Observation Archive. File Report 1415. "Mass-Observation." 2nd September 1942.

Mass Observation Archive. Directive Responses. August 1945.

Mass-Observation Archive. Directive Responses. December 1943.

Mass Observation Archive. File Report 2278A. "August Newsletter 1945 from Mass-Observation."

Mass-Observation. *Peace and the Public. A Study by Mass-Observation*. London: Longmans, 1947.

Newcastle Journal, 12th May 1947. Clipping in Mass Observation Archive. 50/1/G.

Noakes, L. *War and the British: Gender and National Identity 1939–91*. London: I. B. Tauris, 1998.

Noakes, L. "Gender, Grief and Bereavement in Second World War Britain." *Journal of War and Culture Studies* 8, no. 1 (2015): 72–85. doi:10.1179/1752628014Y.0000000016.

Picture Post 28, no. 8, 25 August 1945.

Purcell, J. *Domestic Soldiers: Six Women's Lives in the Second World War*. London: Constable, 2010.

Reddy, W. "Historical Research on the Self and Emotions." *Emotion Review* 1, no. 4 (2009): 302–315. doi:10.1177/1754073909338306.

Rose, S. O. *Which People's War: National Identity and Citizenship in Wartime Britain 1939–1945*. Oxford: Oxford University Press, 2004.

Roseneil, S. *Disarming Patriarchy: Feminism and Political Action at Greenham*. Buckingham: Open University Press, 1995.

Rosenwein, B. H. *Emotional Communities in the Early Modern Ages*. Ithaca: Cornell Press, 2006.

Rosenwein, B. H. *Generations of Feeling: A History of Emotions, 600-1700*. Cambridge: Cambridge University Press, 2015.

Shapira, M. *The War Inside. Psychoanalysis, Total War, and the Making of the Democratic Self in Postwar Britain*. Cambridge: Cambridge University Press, 2013.

Resist and survive: Welsh protests and the British nuclear state in the 1980s

Christophe Laucht and Martin Johnes

ABSTRACT
This article explores Welsh protests against chief policies of the British nuclear state, especially nuclear deterrence, civil defence and its close relationship with the USA. It contributes to the social, cultural and political histories of the post-war British nuclear state by further demonstrating the plural character of protests across and within the British nations. It shows that, while local authorities, individuals and extra-parliamentary groups certainly dreaded the prospect of nuclear war, the nuclear weapons issue often presented them with a vehicle to protest against British government policy more broadly.

From the mid 1970s, relations between the superpowers deteriorated, leading to the so-called Second Cold War and an intensification of fears of a nuclear conflict during the early 1980s. In the UK, these worries were exacerbated by new defence policies—most notably the 'Protect and Survive' civil defence programme and the purchase of the Trident nuclear missile system—and the closer relationship with the USA that Margaret Thatcher actively sought and which brought the deployment of American cruise missiles to Britain under the North Atlantic Treaty Organization's (NATO) 'double-track decision'. There was significant opposition to all these policies and a wave of sustained protests created some of the decade's enduring images.[1]

This was particularly clear in Wales. Local branches of the Campaign for Nuclear Disarmament (CND) staged protests at government bunkers, United States military installations and a Royal Ordnance Factory (ROF) in Llanishen (Cardiff), where components of the warheads for Trident missiles were manufactured. Local authorities established nuclear-free zones and published alternative information on the effects of nuclear war in protest at the line taken in the official civil defence campaign. A group of women organised a march from Cardiff to the base at Greenham Common where cruise missiles were to be stationed, thus laying the foundation for the women's peace camp outside that military installation. These protests drew together the Labour movement, Welsh nationalists, feminist groups, members of the peace movement and other radicals on the left.[2] Although this loose coalition helped give a sense of legitimacy to the anti-nuclear

---

This article has been republished with minor changes. These changes do not impact the academic content of the article.

lobby in Wales, it was also undermined by the broader political, linguistic and even ethnic tensions that defined parts of Welsh society.

This article explores the Welsh protests against British nuclear weapons policies. It seeks to promote a four-nations approach to the history of the British nuclear state in order to acknowledge the plurality of experience across the nations of the UK and illustrate the need for the nuclear threat to be understood as both a local and transnational issue.[3] The study builds on the work of scholars who have rooted their analyses of the Cold War within specific places or explored the spatial dimensions of anti-nuclear activism.[4] Such perspectives have helped establish that anti-nuclear protests were entwined with wider political and moral concerns and even individual circumstances.[5] In both Wales and the rest of the UK, while local authorities, individuals and extra-parliamentary groups certainly dreaded the prospect of nuclear war, the nuclear weapons issue often presented them with a vehicle to protest against government policy more broadly. Indeed, there were times when nuclear weapons were seen as manifestations of wider political problems rather than a self-contained issue in themself. The historiographical appreciation of the multi-causal nature of nuclear protest has also seen the emergence of work that ties nuclear questions to issues of Scottish and Welsh identities, politics and economics, thus demonstrating the plural character of protests across and within the British nations.[6]

However, as with so much of British history, Wales has been underrepresented in scholarship on Cold War and nuclear history.[7] This is despite the sometimes unique nature of the nuclear question in Wales, where it intersected with fears around the endangered cultural, political and economic status of the nation within the UK. Modern Welsh nationhood was built on the twin traditions and cultures of industry and the Welsh language but in the 1980s both were in decline. To the despair of nationalists, in a 1979 referendum, the Welsh electorate had rejected an opportunity to establish an Assembly that would have given the nation its first ever degree of democratic self-governance. The long-term decline in the numbers of Welsh speakers was continuing, especially in its rural heartlands which were simultaneously experiencing the out-migration of young Welsh speakers and the in-migration of older English monoglots. In industrial areas, manufacturing and the steel and coal industries were in retreat, leading to talk of the death of communities and a way of life. Much of this was blamed on Margaret Thatcher's Conservative administration but that government also received the support of almost a third of the Welsh electorate in 1979 and 1983, undermining another conception of Wales as a socialist nation.[8] In this context, nuclear weapons were one more destructive threat to a nation already concerned about its demise. Furthermore, they were another sign that the roots of Wales' fragility lay in governance by a British state run by a Conservative Party with values and a powerbase that lay beyond the Welsh border.

The importance of a Welsh study of nuclear protest goes beyond acknowledging the value of a four-nation approach to British history. Even within Wales, there were different and varying reactions determined by local conditions such as the importance of defence in a county's economy or the makeup of its local politics. Nuclear power might transcend borders but it was exercised and resisted at national, regional and local levels. The Cold War was, thus, an international conflict played out in a multiplicity of national and subnational levels and it has to be placed and understood within the contexts its participants lived in. It requires a polycentric narrative and Wales demonstrates how simultaneously unique and interconnected those different contexts and centres could be.[9]

Welsh protests against nuclear weapons

In 1980, the Home Office published *Protect and Survive*, an information pamphlet telling the public what to do in the event of a nuclear attack. It was first drawn up in 1976 but was then only available to local authorities and the emergency services and only intended to be made public if a war was likely. Its publication in 1980 followed public speculation about its content and whether it was secret.[10] When the government made it more widely available, it quickly became the subject of protest because it suggested that nuclear war could be survived and thus potentially minimised people's understanding of the scale of the threat. On behalf of CND, the historian and leading anti-nuclear-weapons campaigner E.P. Thompson penned a scathing and polemic response under the title *Protest and Survive*; it played an important role in mobilising anti-nuclear weapons protests and feeling across the UK.[11]

One such example was a 1981 booklet produced by Bridgend CND entitled *H-Bomb on Ogwr: A Study of a Nuclear Attack in Wales*. It examined the anticipated effects of two five-megaton hydrogen bombs on south Wales within a larger scenario involving nuclear attacks on 150 strategic and industrial targets across the UK. The sombre conclusion was that the existing civil defence measures advocated by the government would fail in the event of a nuclear attack on Wales, let alone Britain or Western Europe.[12] Its argument was more widely publicised in November 1981 when the radical Welsh magazine *Rebecca* dedicated a title story to local responses to *Protect and Survive*. It imagined thermonuclear attacks on the Royal Air Force (RAF) base at St Athan (South Glamorgan) and the steelworks at Port Talbot (West Glamorgan) in graphic detail, with 'craters 150 feet deep and a thousand yards wide swallow[ing] the radioactive remains of buildings, vehicles and people' and each bomb's flash 'melt[ing] people's eyeballs forty miles away' from ground zero. An accompanying map identified some 30 potential Welsh nuclear targets, thereby illustrating the anticipated vulnerability of Wales in a nuclear war. Besides military installations such as RAF Caerwent (Gwent), RAF St Athan and RAF Brawdy (Dyfed), the map featured urban-industrial centres like Cardiff, Newport and Swansea, and the nuclear power stations at Wylfa and Trawsfynydd (both located in Gwynedd).[13]

H-Bomb on Ogwr and the *Rebecca* article marked a specifically Welsh response to the defence policies of the British nuclear state. They illustrate that, while the nuclear threat may have been one faced by people across the globe, responses to it were very much localised. This was not only a rational way of understanding what otherwise was an abstract concept; it was also a way of mobilising opposition to the more general threat. Just as propaganda in the Second World War was at its most effective when it appealed to people's everyday lives rather than grandiose ideas of patriotism, anti-nuclear campaigning worked best when it pointed out the direct threat to people's own lives and homes.[14]

Given Wales' position on the political and geographical periphery of the UK, and the fact that Wales was long past its height as an industrial zone, it would have been easy for the Welsh population to imagine they were not on the nuclear frontline. Throughout the 1980s campaigners, thus, repeatedly stressed the likely targets in Wales. They also did so with good reason. In 1981, a study by three members of the School of Peace Studies at Bradford University identified Cardiff and Swansea, as well as the oil refinery in Milford Haven in west Wales as likely targets in a Soviet nuclear strike.[15] The government also envisioned Welsh targets. In 1982, it planned a home defence exercise entitled 'Hard Rock'. The details were meant to be secret but comprehensive information on the scenario imagined was published in the *New Statesman* and repeated in CND literature.[16] There were four targets in South Glamorgan (the ROF at Llanishen, Cardiff docks, the US Army transportation terminal at Barry docks and RAF St Athan) and another 12 across south Wales from the US munitions depot and ammunition maintenance facility at Caerwent in the east to the US submarine listening post at Brawdy in the west. CND thought that there might be more Welsh targets and it produced an alternative 'Burst List' that envisioned a total of 20 nuclear explosions in Wales.[17]

It was the presence of two American military installations that particularly convinced peace protesters that Wales was a likely target.[18] The American base at Brawdy, which John Cox, a Welsh chemical engineer, CND activist and author of the Pelican Books mass paperback *Overkill*, identified as 'probably the most important target in Britain', witnessed a major CND demonstration in 1981.[19] There were also fears that Wales was vulnerable to attack because of the possibility that the US military was storing nuclear weapons at its munitions depot at RAF Caerwent.[20] The secretive atmosphere around the military installations encouraged levels of speculation that reflected a wider distrust of government in Wales. A Plaid Cymru publication speculated that Caerwent's vulnerability to nuclear attack might have motivated plans by the Welsh Office to move a plastic surgery and burns unit from nearby Chepstow to a location west of Cardiff.[21] Concern about the site was exacerbated by revelations about nuclear contamination at a British Army base at Donnington near Telford (Shropshire), which, like Caerwent, was only supposed to be used for conventional arms.[22] In April 1982, members of CND set up a peace camp outside Caerwent; it lasted more than three months and drew threats of eviction from Monmouth District Council, and attacks by local residents.[23] This was an example of the plethora of small peace camps that existed across Britain and which have been marginalised in the historiography and popular memory by the much larger camp at Greenham Common. Yet, not only were they part of the same movement, they also featured many of the same people. Indeed, the origins of the Greenham Common camp was a group of Welsh women, calling themselves 'Women for Life on Earth: Women's Action for Disarmament', staging a march in 1981 from Cardiff to RAF Greenham Common (Berkshire), where American cruise missile were to be stationed. The women's camp there remained in place for almost two decades and continued to receive attention from and inspire anti-nuclear weapons activists in Wales.[24]

Both the Greenham march and peace camp have been retrospectively associated with feminist peace activism but the peace movement was also becoming a coalition of much wider political movements from the left and it cannot be separated out from the broader context of opposition to Thatcher's Conservative government and the alienation being generated by spending cuts and rising unemployment.[25] Thus, for example, when students marched through Swansea in a 1983 rally that formed part of CND Cymru's peace week the slogan chanted was 'jobs not bombs'.[26] CND Cymru also explicitly appealed to issues that might draw in those committed to other causes. Although the Ministry of Defence claimed 'that no "fissile" material' (the '"explosive" part of the bombs', as protesters put it) was handled at the ROF at Llanishen in Cardiff, CND still maintained that sub-critical uranium 238 and beryllium might be used there, endangering human health and the environment. Throughout the early and mid 1980s, it argued there was a danger of cancer from materials used in Llanishen and this helped draw in other groups such as the 'Friday Morning Women' to its protests at the site.[27] In late 1983, there was a two-day protest and blockade at Llanishen by CND, Christian groups, trade unions (the Transport and General Workers' Union and the Amalgamated Union of Engineering Workers), students and others, a clear example of the diversity of the peace movement.[28]

In 1985, CND Cymru wrote of how an unelected emergency committee would govern Wales in the event of a war, and pointed to the claims of a Plaid Cymru MP that this would be 'devolution without democracy'.[29] Welsh nationalists were an important part of the peace protests and in March 1984 Plaid Cymru held a major rally at the US installation at Caerwent.[30] The party, heavily influenced by Nonconformist ideals of peace, had always been sympathetic to CND and its leader Gwynfor Evans was prominent in the Welsh peace movement from its inception.[31] However, after the defeat of the 1979 devolution referendum, the party increasingly looked to issues that extended beyond its traditional concerns around Wales' political and cultural position and its three MPs were prominent in anti-nuclear campaigns in this era. This was partly about diversifying the party's political base but some activists did see direct connections between their political and cultural nationalism and the peace movement. One campaigner, for example, argued that nuclear weapons and attempts to destroy a language were both forms of oppression that must be fought to halt the 'destruction of what is dear to us'.[32] Nationalists also objected to nuclear weapons because they believed them to be about upholding British prestige and the veneer of being a world power rather than defence. Gwynfor Evans, thus, denounced Trident as an 'evil weapon which is a badge of British nationalism rather than a weapon of military defence'.[33]

CND itself also saw its campaign as part of a wider need for social and political justice. Most notably, Welsh members were active in raising money and food to support the miners in their 1984–1985 strike. This was partly because of how overtly anti-government that strike was but it was also rooted in an understanding that a strong coal industry undermined the need for nuclear power.[34] The Labour MP Hywel Francis argued that the 1984–1985 strike created a coalition of progressive forces and a stronger sense of national identity. One outcome of this was renewed support for Welsh devolution.[35] The peace movement deserves acknowledgement for its role in forging this coalition, too. Indeed, as Christopher Hill has shown, its contribution to bringing nationalists and the Labour movement together actually stretches back into the 1950s and 1960s, when CND in Wales and Scotland was entwined with emerging nationalist concerns and contributed to progressive left of centre visions for those nations.[36]

The interweaving of wider political issues with the anti-nuclear question did not always help the peace movement, leaving it vulnerable to accusations of being a 'lefty' cause. As a Cardiff student put it in 1980: 'I think this frightens a lot of people away'.[37] Similarly, the Greenham marchers worried that they were alienating those who might associate them with an anti-male feminism.[38] A majority of CND activists seemed to have been middle class and that may also not have helped it attract active participation from working-class sympathisers.[39] In rural areas CND was often associated with English in-migrants and especially what locals referred to as 'hippies'. In 1981, a magazine article by Ann Pettitt, one of the driving forces behind the establishment of the Greeham camp, conceded that most of the people in Carmarthen CND were English incomers. She pointed out that this was not surprising because it was the DIY movement and a desire to live a peaceful, self-sufficient lifestyle that had brought them to Wales in the first place.[40] Most English incomers into rural Wales were more conventional than that but, at a time when there was considerable concern about the cultural impact of in-migration into Welsh-speaking communities, the association of CND with English 'hippies' did not help its cause. In west Wales, such people were, in Pettitt's own words, 'outsiders'.[41] Even when campaigners tried to address such concerns through symbolic bilingualism, they could find themselves attacked. For example, a 1981 letter to a magazine complained about poor pronunciation by the compère at a CND protest at RAF Brawdy: 'I find the continual massacre of Yr Hen Iaith [the old language] by self-righteous well meaning outsiders extremely offensive', it declared.[42] Such tensions seem to have contributed to the formation of a CND group in Cardiff specifically to operate through the Welsh language. A report of its formation stated, in Welsh, that 'Welsh speakers of Cardiff no longer have an excuse, there is a Welsh group for them'.[43]

In the middle of the decade, anti-nuclear weapon campaigning in Wales lost some of its energy and focus. Amongst nationalists and trade unionists, the 1984–1985 miners' strike perhaps drew some attention and energy away from the peace movement. At the same time, superpower tensions eased in the mid 1980s, making the outbreak of nuclear war appear less likely.[44] In addition, the reactor accident at Chernobyl in the Soviet Union in April 1986 raised questions over the safety of the nuclear power stations at Wylfa and Trawsfynydd, and criticism grew over plans for a new reactor at the Hinkley Point nuclear plant opposite Cardiff across the Severn Estuary. The result was some shift in the attention of grassroots campaigners from the threat of war to the safety of nuclear plants and waste.[45]

In early July 1986, Newport CND and CND Cymru, thus, attempted to revive protests against the Caerwent base by organising two days of events there.[46] Protesters also renewed their campaign against the US Navy submarine tracking station at Brawdy in rural Dyfed, hoping to raise local opposition to the base. They focused on the fact that it formed such an important part of the USA's and NATO's capabilities to detect enemy submarines that it was highly likely to be a chief target in a nuclear war.[47] The Brawdy campaign also aimed to 'snowball' into a much broader platform of demands. Apart from calling on the Thatcher Government to vote for multi-lateral nuclear disarmament in the United Nations, it urged the British government to encourage the Reagan Administration to accept proposals to 'freeze' its existing nuclear stockpiles. Finally, this 'snowball' campaign demanded that Britain should take some steps towards unilateral nuclear disarmament, particularly cancelling the purchase of Trident nuclear missiles.[48]

The renewed protests against US military installations in Wales were again motivated by more than just concern at the nuclear threat. In the aftermath of Ronald Reagan's order to use British bases to bomb targets in Libya in retaliation for the Lockerbie bombing, British participation in the American Strategic Defense Initiative ('star wars') and proposals to store nerve gas at Caerwent, concern rose about Britain's general complicity in American military aggression. In 1986, protesters thus mounted a 'campaign to free Wales from US bases'. Cardiff CND's *Radio-Active Times* published a map, 'Wales under the Eagle—US Bases and Military Facilities'. Besides Caerwent, Brawdy and Barry, it also contained lesser known installations such as the Llanbedr missile range where US Air Force (USAF) F-111 nuclear bombers practised low-flying exercises, RAF St Athan and Cardiff Rhoose airport, both used as dispersal bases for the USAF and for flying in troops from the USA in the event of rising tensions with the Warsaw Pact. It also featured the nuclear power station at Wylfa on Anglesey, which allegedly bred plutonium for American nuclear weapons.[49]

Since the American bases were beyond the control of the British government and British law, they further raised questions of national sovereignty. In late 1986, it was thus reported that 17 Welsh Labour MPs, including the party leader, supported the 'unconditional' removal of US nuclear bases and a British veto over the use of the others.[50] Legal issues revolving around national security, secrecy and sovereignty also framed a significant part of protests at Barry dock. Central to these concerns was the 1983 US-UK Lines of Communications Agreement, which granted the US military a range of powers in case of war including the declaration of martial law on British soil. In light of Barry dock's role as a major communications and logistics link for American forces in the event of war on the European continent, CND, South Glamorgan County Council and other nuclear-free local authorities across Britain expressed serious concern over the infringement or even suspension of civil liberties of Barry's population to allow the US military to move troops and equipment quickly from Barry to airfields in Wales and England via the M4 motorway and the Severn bridge. The *New Statesman* thus suggested that 'Mrs Thatcher's government may have sold out British national interests'.[51] Under the title 'Our Future—A Secret!', local CND activist Carol Westall shared her personal experiences about replies to her letters regarding the position of local residents in Barry in the event of crisis and the arrival of large numbers of American troops. She had written to her MP, the Welsh Office, the armed forces, the Home Office and Ministry of Defence, Barry Dock, the US Army and Navy, the US embassy in London, local councillors, trade unions and the health authorities in Cardiff and Barry. None of this produced any answers since the role of Barry dock was classified and could not be made public.[52]

Welsh concerns about nuclear weapons were thus expressed within and about a localised context. This undoubtedly helped protesters connect with wider audiences but it also reflected how the fear of nuclear Armageddon was always imagined at a very personal level. People also connected their wider personal politics to the protests, infusing the peace movement with an association with the left in general, feminism, English in-migration and a distrust of the government's secrecy and motives. None of these issues was necessarily any more important than the others, and some certainly harmed the peace movement's popularity, but the nuclear question did bring together individuals and causes that might otherwise have remained disparate.

Local government and protests against nuclear weapons

'Though no nuclear weapons are stored there, the base at Brawdy is a certain target for attack and its presence destroys the credibility of Dyfed County Council's nuclear-free zone,' observed the *Radio-Active Times* in 1986.[53] Over the course of the decade, the nuclear question repeatedly added to criticisms of Welsh local government. The Conservative government elected in 1979 believed local authorities to be wasteful and overly left wing and, thus, cut both their powers and their funding.[54] In South Glamorgan County Council's annual report for 1981–1982, Rev. Bob Morgan, the authority leader, complained of a 'determined and concerted effort by the national government to denigrate and downgrade local government'.[55] Morgan had become leader of the council when Labour regained control of it in 1981. He was a vicar in a deprived part of Cardiff and had turned to local politics to improve his parishioners' lot in life and to serve them more effectively than just through being their parish priest. His faith shaped his political convictions and his opposition to nuclear weapons was part of that. The Labour group he led was young and inexperienced, with only seven members that had sat on the council before. Many were from middle-class professional backgrounds and ambitious. Like the party nationally, they were also to the left of where Labour had stood in the 1970s and part of a 'new urban left' movement. This emerged in the larger British cities in response to the central government attacks on local authorities and localised concerns at the stagnant and complacent way in which some Labour authorities were being run. It was characterised by the promotion of ideas of equality and inclusiveness and making a stance on international issues such as apartheid. Although some important local work on the promotion of gender and racial equality came out of the 'new urban left', it was often gesture politics against the UK's right-wing government by left wing authorities whose other responsibilities and limited resources prevented anything more substantial.[56]

The question of nuclear weapons was an obvious target for such local authorities who knew making a stance on the issue would annoy the same government that was curtailing their powers and resources. In November 1980, Manchester City Council's nuclear-free zone declaration received considerable public attention. This meant very little in reality but its symbolic appeal was significant to the 'new urban left' and other authorities followed. In October 1981, a meeting of nuclear-free councils from all over Britain took place, establishing a national steering committee to direct efforts.[57] In that same month, South Glamorgan County Council declared itself a nuclear-free zone and sought similar action from its twin cities in the Soviet Union and West Germany, Voroshilovgrad and Stuttgart respectively, as a 'sign of goodwill and peace'.[58]

In making its declaration the local authority said it would actively oppose the manufacture and siting of nuclear weapons within South Glamorgan and the transport of any material or components for nuclear weapons through the county. It also decided to publicise a synopsis of its '"War Plan" and any other relevant non-classified information', granted CND permission to mount exhibitions in its libraries and allowed the 'voluntary showing' of Peter Watkins' controversial documentary drama *The War Game* (1965) in the fifth and sixth forms of schools that requested it.[59] Such actions were intended to ensure that the nuclear-free declaration was more than just gesture politics. Most importantly, the council produced a pamphlet entitled *South Glamorgan and Nuclear Weapons*, which was distributed to 200,000 households and paid for from the county's government funding for civil defence and emergency planning operations, making it the first authority to use the money in such a way. The pamphlet was a direct response to the government's *Protect and Survive* literature and was intended to be based on research rather than rhetoric. The council had, thus, consulted expert organisations, including the Medical Campaign Against Nuclear Weapons and Scientists Against Nuclear Arms (SANA). The leaflet attracted considerable attention from within and outside South Glamorgan, especially from other local authorities.[60]

Based on the Home Office's 1980 Square Leg war game exercise, which designated Cardiff a prime target in a nuclear exchange with the Warsaw Pact, *South Glamorgan and Nuclear Weapons* envisaged a scenario where a one-megaton thermonuclear bomb exploded in an airburst above Cardiff City Hall with devastating consequences. 'Practically everyone within 2 miles of City Hall would be killed. Nothing would remain. The City Centre and buildings further away such as the Heath Hospital and Llandaff Cathedral would be levelled', the pamphlet claimed. Even in the Cardiff suburbs some 3.25 miles away from ground zero, five out of ten people would die and four of the remaining five would suffer injuries, with many survivors later dying from their injuries or from radiation. And in towns like Newport and Pontypridd, some 10 miles or so away from the explosion's epicentre, buildings would be damaged, and '[a]nyone looking in the direction of Cardiff at the moment of the explosion would be temporarily, or possibly permanently, blinded'.[61]

Yet, the leaflet was more than just information about the effects of a nuclear war and it tried to encourage popular activism against nuclear weapons, urging readers to take part in demonstrations, marches and conferences, and to sign petitions. The booklet declared: 'STAND UP AND BE COUNTED. THE ARMS RACE MUST BE REVERSED. NUCLEAR WEAPONS MUST BE DISMANTLED! SUPPORT NUCLEAR FREE ZONES'. Despite this rhetoric, it concluded: 'You may or may not agree with the County Council, but try to reach your own conclusion. Do not assume that someone else always knows better than you about things like this. The future is in all our hands.'[62] Ultimately, the object of the leaflet was to inform people that there was no defence against a nuclear attack.[63] Bob Morgan told a CND newsletter that 'This is part of our campaign to tell the people the truth. The debate is a public one—we are all in it together. It is our lives and the lives of our children—and the yet unborn—that national politicians are gambling with'.[64] The government itself, however, saw things rather differently. After the council wrote to the Home Secretary about its nuclear-free declaration, it received a curt reply stating the 'government is aware of the full horrors of war' but that the 'the aim of civil defence planning is to ensure the future of the millions that will survive'.[65]

South Glamorgan was the second Welsh county council to declare itself a nuclear-free zone. West Glamorgan had done so as early as July 1981 and Mid Glamorgan and Gwent followed suit in November 1981.[66] These three counties had large Labour majorities but all the other Welsh counties were independent or in the case of Clwyd no party had a majority. Yet, they, too, all declared themselves nuclear-free zones, a testament to the nuclear threat but also the resentment in local authorities over how they were being treated by central government, even if the Powys declaration was passed by just a single vote.[67] When Clwyd became the last Welsh county to declare itself a nuclear-free zone on 23 February 1982, it was claimed that Wales was Europe's first nuclear-free nation.[68] Clwyd's declaration was inscribed on vellum intended to resemble a mediaeval legal document and celebrated by a press reception that brought together figures from Labour, Plaid Cymru and the peace movement. The Chief Bard of Gorsedd y Beirdd, a Welsh-language cultural body, read a declaration of Wales as a nuclear-free nation 'to

Europe and the rest of the world'. A CND symbol was set ablaze at the highest point in each county and there were plans for signs reading 'YOU ARE NOW ENTERING A NUCLEAR FREE COUNTRY' to be put up at the border with England. This was all followed by a team of athletes taking a peace torch and the declaration to the President of European Parliament in Strasbourg.[69]

Nuclear-free Wales was not only home to two nuclear power stations in its north-west but its capital city was the site of an ordinance factory that made the casing for nuclear warheads. While South Glamorgan County Council investigated incidents at the ROF Llanishen to assess their potential impacts on the environment and human health and objected, in principle, to the manufacture of nuclear weapons components within its boundaries, it was not directly involved in protests by activist groups at that installation of the British nuclear state.[70] To have been so would have put the authority in the awkward position of undermining an important source of local employment, particularly at a time when it was seeking to boost its declining industrial and manufacturing sector. Other local authorities faced similar dilemmas. In the 1970s, Dyfed County Council had allowed the US naval installation at Brawdy, despite it encroaching onto the Pembrokeshire National Park. It welcomed the economic contribution made by the US and nearby RAF bases and the local press was also hostile to the peace protests targeted at the American facility, claiming they were unrepresentative of local feelings.[71] When the US munitions facility at Caerwent was first being planned in the late 1960s, there had been local concerns about the possibility of nuclear weapons being stored there but the local Labour MP had been won over to the cause by assurances that this would not be the case and a promise to discuss handing the land back if it was needed for industrial development.[72] The support of the Labour-controlled local authority was also won by promises of 800 civilian jobs at the site. Although only 150 ever materialised, the council's Labour group was so committed to the project that it expelled a councillor who spoke out against it.[73]

By the early 1980s, the political climate and the pressure that could be exerted on councillors made local authorities less favourable to these bases but local economic conditions had deteriorated in both rural and urban Wales. In particular coal mining and the steel industry suffered under government economic policies described by *Rebecca* as 'the most vicious attack on Welsh living standards since the Thirties'.[74] The actual economic contribution of the nuclear and defence industries may not have always matched the initial promises but anything that risked unemployment rising even further was not going to be popular and thus local authorities did nothing about any contradiction between their status as nuclear-free zones and the existence of American bases, nuclear power stations or even a manufacturer of nuclear weapon components in their counties. It was the symbolism of the zone that mattered.

The position of local authorities was also complicated by their legal responsibilities for emergency planning, which included the occurrence of a war. In the event of a nuclear attack, defence plans anticipated the UK being governed by a series of regional administrations of which Wales would be one. The Welsh regional government headquarters would be based at Brackla Hill near Bridgend but each county was also expected to function from its own nuclear bunker.[75] The early 1980s, thus, saw renewed government instructions on what local authorities should do and financial aid to achieve that. However, in the new era of nuclear-free zones, not all were willing to comply and

South Glamorgan County Council, for example, refused to upgrade its war room.[76] By summer 1982, a refusal by South, Mid and West Glamorgan, Gwent and Gwynedd, along with 15 local authorities in England, to participate in the 'Hard Rock' home defence exercise even forced central government to postpone it indefinitely. The Home Office worried in particular that the exercise was playing into the hands of CND and Labour councils by giving them an opportunity to oppose government policies on nuclear deterrence and civil defence. The fact that the three remaining Welsh county councils demonstrated only 'limited participation' in the war game exercise suggested that the Home Office's fears were right.[77]

In 1984, the year after the Home Office had issued another set of civil defence regulations to local authorities, South Glamorgan, in cooperation with CND Cymru and Cardiff CND, hosted a conference for local Welsh authorities on the new directives in an attempt to formulate a unified and coherent opposition.[78] The conference included a talk on nuclear winter by Michael Pentz of SANA and was preceded by a council-run 'Peace Week'.[79] By 1986, tensions between central and local governments in Gwynedd and Gwent escalated further when the Home Office threatened to withhold civil defence funding and to appoint commissioners for these two councils should they fail to abide by the regulations on civil defence planning.[80]

Not all local authorities were so reticent, however, and Dyfed and Mid Glamorgan both planned to upgrade or build new bunkers. The Labour Party had a large majority on the latter and its decision, taken at the exact same time as its nuclear-free declaration, was further evidence of how such a status was often intended as a symbolic gesture rather than an actual refusal to embrace every aspect of the nuclear state. It was also a reminder of how the 'new urban left' was concentrated in the cities rather than in traditional industrial communities such as Mid Glamorgan. However, not every councillor was in favour of the move and senior officials placed pressure on elected representatives to support the bunker, even arguing that not supporting the authority's civil defence responsibilities could be 'wilful misconduct' and that councillors might be disqualified and fined.[81]

Civil defence, with its ideological underpinnings and physical network of bunkers, formed an integral part of the infrastructure of the British nuclear state at the national, regional and local levels. It also undermined the coherence of the peace movement by bringing nuclear-free local authorities into conflict with grassroots protesters. Many anti-nuclear weapons activists viewed civil defence with great scepticism, criticising both its effectiveness against nuclear attack and its exclusivity in only granting selected senior officials access to bunkers. Moreover, they often warned against the imposition of anti-democratic martial law in the event of nuclear war.[82]

Local authority nuclear bunkers became focal points of protest, with CND Cymru arguing that they were 'all part of Thatcher's war plans'.[83] It was the bunkers in Dyfed and Mid Glamorgan that attracted the most significant protests. The work to upgrade Mid Glamorgan's existing war room at Warton led to a picket line at the entrance to the site and non-violent disruption of the construction work. This was led by the local CND but received support from Labour and trade union activists, the loose network of grassroots groups that called itself the Welsh Anti Nuclear Alliance, as well as religious groups, including the United Reformed Church, Welsh Congregationalists and Quakers. Such was the level of controversy caused that the council in the end abandoned its plans.[84] There was similar disruption and protests at Carmarthen in Dyfed where the county council was building a new bunker, with financial aid from central government. Protesters had the support of the town's former Plaid Cymru MP and its current Labour MP. The local authority, however, went as far as taking out a High Court injunction against 17 protesters to prevent them from accessing or blockading the construction site or inciting others to do so. It also claimed £250,000 in damages from them for conspiracy to trespass. This won the protesters much sympathy, and Dyfed County Council eventually dropped its case.[85] Again, the bunker was entangled with broader political concerns that drew support beyond the conventional peace movement. Dyfed County Council's actions seemed inflated and aggressive and its and Mid Glamorgan's intransigence over the bunker question gave the impression of authorities that were profligate and out of touch with their constituents, particularly in a wider climate of local authority service cuts. Local government was never a particularly popular or appreciated institution, and a banner at the Warton protest that read 'No Bunkers for Bureaucrats' was an emotive symbol of that.[86]

Conclusion

The protests that took place at military and nuclear installations across Wales are powerful illustrations of how active popular opposition to British, US and NATO nuclear policies during the 1980s was. They stood alongside a campaign of anti-nuclear propaganda whose arguments were conveyed through homemade banners, photocopied leaflets, the pages of the alternative press and slick mass-distributed council leaflets. Together this formed a vibrant protest culture that attempted to draw in wider support by entangling the nuclear threat with general concerns around both government policy and Welsh identity. This was not simply political pragmatism but rather a genuine outcome of how contemporaries made connections between the nuclear threat and the wider state of Welsh, British and global society. For campaigners, trade unionists, councillors, nationalists and concerned citizens, both feeling and articulating an opposition to nuclear war was all part of symbolically and practically opposing the cultural and political direction Thatcher was taking Wales and the wider UK, even if they did not necessarily agree on the precise nature of the problems or solutions. As such, the Welsh anti-nuclear movement demonstrates how the historiography of both the British nuclear state and the Cold War benefits from a polycentric approach to anti-nuclear weapons protests that places opposition to the nuclear threat within wider economies of political and socioeconomic concerns.

Hill has argued that the peace movement in the 1950s and 1960s contributed to the 'making of national identity' in Wales and Scotland by encouraging visions of those nations that were different to the dominant idea of post-imperial, nuclear-power Britain.[87] By the 1980s, the sense of Welsh nationhood that had intensified since the Second World War was under threat from deindustrialisation and linguistic decline. Nuclear weapons were not just another threat to the Welsh nation but one that was being imposed by the same external political forces deemed to be undermining the Welsh economy and culture. Thus, the commitments of many nationalists to a nuclear-free Wales intensified because it was a symbol of how Welsh nationalism could protect and create a better Welsh nation. The Labour Party was also increasingly sensitive to the political possibilities of Welsh nationhood and its increasing sense of Welsh identity and difference was visible in its anti-nuclear actions in local government.[88] However, whichever party was in charge, local authority anti-nuclear campaigns were also intended as deliberate gestures of resistance to a central government that was actively curtailing the powers and status of local government. Thus, by 1985, an estimated 173 British local authorities had declared themselves nuclear-free zones. This raised questions not only about whether such actions were sensible at a time of financial constriction for local councils but also about whether they made local government vulnerable to further attacks from a central government determined to reign in municipal profligacy and politicking.[89] Such actions were also perhaps not entirely popular. Although the general fear of nuclear war was real, it was only on occasions at the forefront of most people's minds and support for unilateral disarmament was never widespread.[90] Local government's expensive anti-nuclear campaigning may thus have even contributed to its vulnerability to central government cuts and curtailments.

As US-Soviet relations improved in the second half of the 1980s, some of the energy was lost from the Welsh anti-nuclear weapons protests. The Labour movement, in particular, became more focussed on supporting the 1984–1985 miners' strike. Local government, too, moved away from gesture politics to concentrating on protecting its service delivery and working on supporting economic development, something which required close co-operation with the Welsh Office. Yet, this does not diminish the significance of what happened in the early and mid-1980s. It remains an important example of how the anti-nuclear weapons movement should be put in a wider context that acknowledges the role of other causes in both contributing to and distracting from its vibrancy. One of those contexts is the multinational nature of the UK. There was no uniform understanding of or response to the nuclear weapons question within the UK. Indeed, the question was itself actually part of the long-term process where a multiplicity of issues were interpreted and responded to within a Welsh context, a process that ultimately led to Welsh devolution in 1997. Welsh protests against nuclear weapons in the 1980s not only signified an attempt to ensure the physical survival of the Welsh nation, but they also addressed a set of broader issues such as the preservation of Welsh identity, culture and language, as well as a struggle for survival between local authorities and central government over financial and governance issues. In this sense, resist and survive was not just about the hypothetical threat of future nuclear war.

Notes

1. Halliday, *The Making of the Second Cold War*, 203–64; and Heuser and Stoddart, "Großbritannien zwischen Doppelbeschluss und Anti-Kernwaffen-Protestbewegungen," 305–24.
2. On Welsh anti-militarism and pacifism in general, see Ellis, "A Pacific People—a Martial Race," 15–37; and Morgan, "Peace Movements in Wales," 398–430.
3. For a recent appraisal of four-nation approaches see Lloyd-Jones and Scull, "A New Plea for an Old Subject," 3–32.
4. On places see Hevly and Findlay, eds, *The Atomic West*; Hunner, *J. Robert Oppenheimer*; and Farish and Monteyne, eds, *Cold War Cities*. On the spatial dimensions of anti-nuclear

activism see Miller, *Geography and Social Movements*: Schregel, *Der Atomkrieg vor der Wohnungstür*; Schregel, "The Spaces and Places of the Peace Movement," 173–88.
5. On links between CND and morality see Burkett, "Re-defining morality." On individuals see Hughes, *Young Lives on the Left*.
6. Notably see Hill, "Nations of Peace," For other work on Scotland see Eschle, "'Bairns Not Bombs'," 139–51; Jamieson, "Britain's National Deterrent," 449–69; and Mort, *Building the Trident Network*.
7. For an introduction see Johnes, "Wales and the Cold War," 5–15. Also see Hill, "Nations of Peace," 26–50; Jones, "A Comparative Study of Local Authority Preparations for Nuclear War in North-Eastern Wales," 89–115; LaPorte, Reid, and Williams, Eds *Cold War Wales*; Olsson-Rost, "The Cold War Home Front, An Age of Anxiety?" 42–57; Pincombe, "'The Cold Brain of the Machine'," 62–83; and Whitham, "Sheep, Subs and Showcases," 168–86.
8. Johnes, *Wales since 1939*, 245–341.
9. For a comprehensive historiographical problematization of the concept of the "Cold War" see Nehring, "What Was the Cold War," 920–47.
10. Central Office of Information, *Protect and Survive*; HC Deb 20 February 1980 vol 979 cc625-30; Stafford, "'Stay at Home," 383–407. The booklet formed part of a wider civil defence programme that also included television infomercials to be broadcast if nuclear war appeared likely.
11. Thompson, *Protest and Survive*.
12. Simpson and Llewellyn, *H-Bomb on Ogwr*, 10.
13. "A Table for You: When the bomb drops the government says you should shelter from the blast, heat and radiation—under the kitchen table...," *Rebecca* (November 1981), 16–18.
14. Baxendale, "You and I—all of us ordinary people," 295–322.
15. Rogers, Dando, and van den Dungen, *As Lambs to the Slaughter*, 120–22. Magnus Clarke drew similar conclusions in *The Nuclear Destruction of Britain*, 106, 198, 273.
16. Duncan Campbell, "Bad Day at Hard Rock," *New Statesman*, 17 September 1982, 6, 8–9; "Hard Luck," *Radioactive-Times* (November-December 1982), 3. Note that the *Radio-Active Times* operated under different sub-titles over the years (*The Newspaper of Cardiff CND, CND's Paper for South Wales* and *CND's Paper for South Glamorgan*).
17. "Hard Luck Scenario. Burst List, Wales," n.d., London School of Economics Archives, London, United Kingdom, CND Papers, CND/2008/8/4/27.
18. Duncan Campbell, "Armies of the Night," *Radical Wales* 3 (Summer 1984), 14–15 (p. 14). Also see Campbell, *The Unsinkable Aircraft Carrier*.
19. John Cox, "Target Wales," *Arcade* 10 (20 March 1981), 13; Cox, *Overkill*; and Nigel Jenkins and Martin W. Roberts, "Will World War Three Start Here?" *Arcade* 16 (12 June 1981), 6–7.
20. "Mystery of U.S. Base," *Rebecca*, 10 (June 1982), 12–13.
21. "Burns Unit and the Bomb," *Welsh Nation*, 56, no. 3 (1984), 1.
22. Tony Simpson, "U.S. Base Threatens S. Wales," *Radioactive-Times* (March-April 1984), 1.
23. "N.A.T.O. Arms Dump," *Campaign Wales: CND Cymru's Paper for Groups* 26 (June 1986), unpaginated.
24. "News Extra," *Rebecca* 2 (October 1981), 14; "The Road to Peace," *Rebecca* 11 (July 1982), 16–18; Clare Hudson, "Greenham Women Sit Tight," *Radio-Active Times* (November-December 1982), 2; Sally Albrow, "Solidarity with Greenham Women," *Radio-Active Times* (January-February 1983), 6–7; Carol Westall, "All I Did Was Catch a Bus!," *Radio-Active Times* (April-May 1985), 3; Clare Hudson, "Jailed for Peace," *Radio-Active Times* (June-July 1985), 1, 12; and Rolph, "Greenham and Its Legacy," 97–122.
25. For a feminist reading of these protests see Liddington, *The Road to Greenham Common*. For challenges to such feminist interpretations see Pettitt, *Walking to Greenham*; Titcombe, "Women Activists," 310–29.
26. W.W., "Swansea CND," *Double Take*, 15 March 1983, 4.
27. "The Cancer in Cardiff," *Radio-Active Times* (November-December 1982), 1; "Ministry Lies about Bomb Factory Leak," *Radio-Active Times* (April-May 1985), 1.; Alex Farrow, "ROF Cardiff—Leukaemia Risk?', *Radio-Active Times* (March-April 1986), 3; "Plans for Action," *Radio-Active*

Times (March-April 1986), 3; The Friday Morning Women to ROF workers, 12 April 1983; The Friday Morning Women to ROF workers, September 1983, all in, Glamorgan Archives, Cardiff, Wales, United Kingdom, DD/AW/10; Tim Jones, "Candidate Rejects Left-Wing Charge," *The Times*, 4 April 1983, 2.

28. "Trident Made in Cardiff," *Radio-Active Times* (November-December 1983), 1; "ROF Cardiff—the Welsh Bomb Factory: Blockade & Demonstration, Dec. 2 & 3," *Radio-Active Times* (November-December 1983), 6–7; "R.O.F. Llanishen Cardiff: Wales' Bomb Factory. Blockade and Demonstration, 2nd/3 December 1983," *Radical Wales* 1 (Winter 1983), unpaginated back cover; "Three Minutes to Midnight," *Radio-Active Times* (January-February 1984), 1; Work for Life Group, "ROF Cardiff—the Welsh Bomb Factory: Blockade & Demonstration, Dec 2&3," *Radio-Active Times* (January-February 1984), 6–7; "C.N.D. Demo," *Double Take*, 7 December 1983, 2.
29. "Devolution without Democracy," *Radio-Active Times* (Febraury-March 1985), 6.
30. "Caerwent—The Sleeping Monster," *Welsh Nation*, 56, no. 2 (1984), 1; "Make Wales Nuclear-Free," *Welsh Nation*, 56, no. 4 (1984), 2.
31. See Evans, *Gwynfor*, 183, 436, 445.
32. Menna Elfyn, "The Link between the Welsh Language Society and the Peace Movement," *Campaign Wales* 4 (July-August 1987), unpaginated.
33. Evans, *The Fight for Welsh Freedom*, 160. On this aspect, see also Gwynfor Evans, "Welsh Nationalists Reject Bomb," *Sanity* 6 (December 1977-January 1978), 4.
34. "CND and the Coal Strike," *Radio-Active Times* (February-March 1985), 3.
35. Francis, *History on our Side*, 68–71.
36. Hill, "Nations of Peace," 26–50.
37. *South Wales Echo*, 1 November 1980. There were even allegations of the peace movement being pro Soviet; Nehring and Ziemann, "Do all Paths Lead to Moscow?" 1–24.
38. Pettitt, *Walking to Greenham*, 40.
39. Mattausch, *A Commitment to Campaign*, 148, 157.
40. Ann Pettitt, "Fighting the Nuclear Menace," *Arcade* 20 (7 August 1981), 12–13.
41. Pettitt, *Walking to Greenham*, 38. On opposition to English in-migration, see Cloke, Goodwin and Milbourne, *Rural Wales*; and Johnes, *Wales since 1939*, 385–411.
42. "Welsh Tokenism," *Arcade* 21 (4 September 1981), 10.
43. Translated from "Grŵp CND Cymraeg Caerdydd," *Radio-Active Times* (July-August 1983), 2.
44. Heuser and Stoddart, "Großbritannien zwischen Doppelbeschluss und Anti-Kernwaffen-Protestbewegungen," 324.
45. Greg Hill, "The Anti-Nuclear Family," *Arcade* 10 (20 March 1981), 14–15; Hugh Richards, "Chernobyl Thoughts from WANA: The Muddling Through Approach Must Stop," *Campaign Wales* 26 (June 1986), unpaginated; Janet Davies, "Nailing the Nuclear Lie," *Radical Wales* 14 (Spring 1987), 18–19; "Hinkley Points A PWR at Wales," *Campaign Wales* 5 (September-October 1987), unpaginated.
46. Carol Handcock, "What's at Caerwent?" *Radio-Active Times* (May-June 1986), 8.
47. "Welsh Base's Nuclear Role," *Radio-Active Times* (May-June 1986), 6–7.
48. Cynthia Morris, "Snowball of Protest," *Radio-Active Times* (May-June 1986), 7. See also Nigel Jenkins, "A Snowball's Chance in Hell," *Radical Wales* 17 (Spring 1988), 4–5.
49. "Campaign Grows against US Bases," *Radio-Active Times* (Summer 1986), 1; "N.A.T.O. Arms Dump," *Campaign Wales* 26 (June 1986), unpaginated.
50. "Growing concern about US bases in Wales," *Campaign Wales* 29 (October 1986), unpaginated. Also see Tony Simpson, "Fortress Wales: The Road from Penyberth," *Radical Wales* 12 (Autumn 1986), 4–6. On Cardiff Airport, see also "Welsh Airport's Secret War Plans," *Radio-Active Times* (December 1986-January 1987), 1.
51. Duncan Campbell and Patrick Forbes, "If War Came Close We Would Have New Masters," *New Statesman* (13 September 1985), 10–12; "War Base Barry?" *Radio-Active Times* (March-April 1986), 4–5; R.M.W. Taylor to Nuclear Free Zone County Councils, 22 November 1985, attached: "War Plans: County Chiefs Kept in Ignorance," n.d., Manchester City Council, Local Studies and Archives, Central Library, Manchester, United Kingdom (hereafter MCC), GMC/2

Box 45, PR11.3; M.D. Boyce to R.M.W. Taylor, 9 December 1985; G.A. Smith to M.D. Boyce, 7 February 1986, MCC, M711/3/9.
52. Carol Westall, "Our Future—A Secret!" *Radical Wales* 11 (Summer 1986), 14–15.
53. See above 47.7.
54. On the struggle between central and local government, see Butcher et al., *Local Government and Thatcherism*.
55. Council of South Glamorgan, *Annual Report and Accounts, 1981–82* (Cardiff: County of South Glamorgan, 1982), unpaginated.
56. See Gyford, *The Politics of Local Socialism*; and Lansley, Goss and Wolmar, *Councils in Conflict*; Payling, "City Limits," 256–73; Payling, "'Socialist Republic of South Yorkshire," 602–27.
57. Schregel, "Nuclear War and the City," 568–69.
58. County of South Glamorgan, Policy Committee, Industrial Development Sub-Committee, minutes, 17 November 1981, 456 (minute 1045), Glamorgan Archives, SC/C/1/9; Manfred Rommel to W.P. Davey, 18 February 1982, Glamorgan Archives, SC/PO/36.
59. "Minute 746. South Glamorgan County Council Meeting, 22 October 1981," attached to note, John Southern, Cardiff CND, n.d., CND Papers, CND/2008/18/11.
60. Council of South Glamorgan County, *South Glamorgan and Nuclear Weapons* (Cardiff: County of South Glamorgan County, [1983]), unpaginated, Glamorgan Archives, D/DCGC114/39; County of South Glamorgan, Policy Committee, minutes, 11 February 1983, 860 (minute 1957), Glamorgan Archives, SC/C/1/10; County of South Glamorgan, Public Protection Committee, minutes, 20 May 1983, 59 (minute 153), Glamorgan Archives, SC/C/1/11; "Council Tells the Truth about War," *Radio-Active Times*, (January-February 1983), 1.
61. Council of South Glamorgan County, *South Glamorgan and Nuclear Weapons*, unpaginated; "Ex. Square Leg—Phase III—Post Strike Section—Scenario and Time Scale," n.d., attached to P.F. Russell to United Kingdom Commanders-in-Chief Committees, 18 December 1980, the National Archives, Kew, Richmond, United Kingdom (hereafter TNA), HO322/950; P.F.J. Griffiths, "RSA Participation in "Square Leg': Region 8," 14 October 1980, TNA, HO322/951.
62. Council of South Glamorgan County, *South Glamorgan and Nuclear Weapons*, unpaginated.
63. Council of South Glamorgan County, *Annual Report and Accounts 1983–4* (Cardiff: Council of South Glamorgan County, 1984), 19.
64. "Council Tells the Truth about War," 1.
65. County of South Glamorgan, Policy Committee, minutes, 11 February 1983, 860 (minute 1955), Glamorgan Archives, SC/C/1/10.
66. Swansea CND, *Nuclear-Free West Glamorgan* (Swansea: Swansea CND, n.d.), CND Papers, CND/2008/18/11; "Mid Glamorgan County Council. Public Protection Committee. No. 9A, 10 November 1981;" "Mid Glamorgan County Council. Special Meeting of the Public Protection Committee, 10 November 1981: Report of the County Clerk and Co-Ordinator," all in CND Papers, CND/2008/18/11.
67. "Extract from Unconfirmed Minutes of Last Meeting of Powys County Council held on 26th November, 1981," attached to note, T.F.G. Young to P.M. Jeffries, 28 January 1982, all in CND Papers, CND/2008/18/11.
68. "The Clwyd Declaration," 23 February 1982, CND Papers, CND/2008/18/11; "The Red Dragon Leads the Way," *Rebecca* 7 (March 1982), 6–7 (p. 6).
69. "Press Information. CND: First Principality Declares Itself a Nuclear Free Zone, 23 February 1982," CND Papers, CND/2008/18/11.
70. County of South Glamorgan, Policy Committee, Industrial Development Sub-Committee, minutes, 17 November 1981, 457 (minute 1046), Glamorgan Archives, SC/C/1/9; County of South Glamorgan, General Purposes Committee and Council Summons, minutes, 27 January 1982, 935 (minute 2512), Glamorgan Archives, DCC/C/1/9.
71. Whitham, "Sheep, Subs and Showcases," 168–86.
72. Hudson, "Caerwent," 9. On the background of anti-nuclear weapons and peace activism at the Caerwent site from 1967, see Tony Simpson, "Caerwent Archive," *Radio-Active Times* (March-April 1984), 5.
73. Hudson, "Caerwent," 9.

74. Geraldine Hackett, "The Day Wales Stopped," *Labour Weekly*, 1 February 1980, 7; Chris McLaughlin, "Vale of Despair," *Labour Weekly*, 14 March 1980, 1; "The Iron Maiden's Steel Blitzkreig [sic]," *Rebecca* 11 (Spring 1980), 11; Mike Sullivan and John Osmond, "Sir Keith—Man or Maniac?" *Arcade* 2 (14 November 1980), 15–16.
75. Cocroft and Thomas, *Cold War*, 197–235; McCamley, *Cold War Secret Nuclear Bunkers*, 207–15; Simpson and Llewellyn, *H-Bomb on Ogwr*, 29.
76. W.P. Davey, "County of South Glamorgan Council, Public Protection Committee: 1st July, 1983. Report of the Chief Executive, County Wartime Headquarters," 20 June 1983, Glamorgan Archives, SC/PU/38; Althea Osmond, "Inside the Warbunker," *Radio-Active Times* (November-December 1982), 3.
77. County of South Glamorgan, Council Summons, 25 November 1981, 696 (minute 1844), Glamorgan Archives, DCC/C/1/9; David Heaton, "Defence and Overseas Policy Committee—Meeting on 13 July: Civil Defence Policy—OD(82)57. Brief for Home Secretary," 9 July 1982; "Exercise 'Hard Rock'—Local Authority Participation," n.d., 2, all in TNA, HO322/1000.
78. County of South Glamorgan, Public Protection Committee, minutes, 18 May 1984, 94 (minute 201), Glamorgan Archives, SC/C1/12; "CND Cymru. Working Group on Civil Defence, 27.3.84," CND Papers, CND/2008/18/11; "Civil Defence Summit," *Radio-Active Times* (August-September 1984), 1.
79. "S. Glam Pushes for Peace," *Radio-Active Times* (August-September 1984), 1; Julie Nedin and Alison Jackson, "Peace Week and Beyond," *Radio-Active Times* (August-September 1984), 3.
80. "Home Office Ultimatum to Councils," *Radio-Active Times* (May-June 1986), 8.
81. Simpson, *No Bunker Here*, 27.
82. See, for example, James Stewart, "War Plan U.K.," *Radio-Active Times* (January-February 1983), 8.
83. "More War Games by the R.O.C," *Campaign Wales* 29 (October 1986), unpaginated.
84. Simpson, *No Bunkers Here*, 15, 19.
85. Michael Reed, "The Carmarthen Nuclear Bunker," 7 June 1986, available at: http://www.mjreedsolicitors.co.uk/uncategorized/the-bunker-case/ [accessed 21 February 2018]; "No Bunkers in Wales," *Radio-Active Times* (October-November 1985), 1; "What Is CND Cymru?" *CND Cymru Individual Member's Newsletter* (August 1986), unpaginated; Hilary Blunden, "Bunker Politics: Civil Defence in Wales," *Radical Wales* 12 (Autumn 1986), 8–9; "The Bunker Campaign Continues," *Radio-Active Times* (December 1985-January 1986), 1.
86. Simpson, *No Bunkers Here*, 23–2.
87. Hill, "Nations of Peace," 26–50. Similarly, Berger and LaPorte have also demonstrated Welsh dimensions to the left's responses to the Cold War in "The Labour Party in Wales and the Cold War," 58–76.
88. For the growing sense of Welsh identity across postwar Welsh society, see Martin Johnes, *Wales since 1939*.
89. David Regan, "Nuclear Free—at a Price," *The Times*, 5 August 1985, 12.
90. See Sabin, *The Third World War Scare in Britain*.

Disclosure statement

No potential conflict of interest was reported by the authors.

Funding

This work was in part supported by the British Academy/Leverhulme Trust under Grant SG151932.

Bibliography

Baxendale, J. "'You and I – All of Us Ordinary People': Renegotiating 'Britishness' in Wartime." In *British Culture in the Second World War*, edited by N. Hayes and J. Hill, 295–322. Liverpool: Liverpool University Press, 1999.
Berger, S., and L. Norman. "The Labour Party in Wales and the Cold War." *Llafur* 10, no. 4 (2011): 58–76.
Burkett, J. "Re-Defining British Morality: 'Britishness' and the Campaign for Nuclear Disarmament 1958–68." *Twentieth Century British History* 21, no. 2 (2010): 184–205. doi:10.1093/tcbh/hwp057.
Butcher, H., I.G. Law, R. Leach, and R. Mullard. *Local Government and Thatcherism*. London: Routledge, 1990.
Campbell, D. *The Unsinkable Aircraft Carrier: American Military Power in Britain*. London: Michael Joseph, 1984.
Central Office of Information. *Protect and Survive.1976*. London: HMSO, 1980.
Clarke, M. *The Nuclear Destruction of Britain*. London: Croom Helm, 1982.
Cloke, P., M. Goodwin, and P. Milbourne. *Rural Wales: Community and Marginalization*. Cardiff: University of Wales Press, 1997.
Cocroft, W. D., and R. J. C. Thomas. *Cold War: Building for Nuclear Confrontation, 1946–1989*. Swindon: English Heritage, 2004.
Cox, J., 1977; revised, expanded and updated ed. *Overkill: The Story of Modern Weapons*. Harmondsworth: Penguin, 1981.
Ellis, J. S. "A Pacific People – A Martial Race: Pacifism, Militarism and Welsh National Identity." In *Wales and War: Society, Politics and Religion in the Nineteenth and Twentieth Centuries*, edited by M. Cragoe and C. Williams, 15–37. Cardiff: University of Wales Press, 2007.
Eschle, C. "'Bairns Not Bombs': The Scottish Peace Movement and the UK Nuclear State." In *The United Kingdom and the Future of Nuclear Weapons*, edited by A. Futter, 139–151. Lanham: Rowan & Littlefield, 2016.
Evans, G. *The Fight for Welsh Freedom*. Talybont: Y Lolfa, 2000.
Evans, R. *Gwynfor: Portrait of a Patriot*. Talybont: Y Lolfa, 2008.
Farish, M., and D. Monteyne, eds. "Cold War Cities." *Urban History* 42, no. 4 (2015): 543–685. doi:10.1017/S0963926815000607
Francis, H. *History on Our Side: Wales and the 1984–85 Miners' Strike*. Iconau: Ferryside, 2009.
Gyford, J. *The Politics of Local Socialism*. London: Allen and Unwin, 1985.
Halliday, F. *The Making of the Second Cold War*. 2nd ed. London: Verso, 1986.
Heuser, B., and K. Stoddart. "Großbritannien zwischen Doppelbeschluss und Anti-Kernwaffen-Protestbewegungen." In *Zweiter Kalter Krieg und Friedensbewegung: Der NATO-Doppelbeschluss in deutsch-deutscher und internationaler Perspektive*, edited by P. Gassert, T. Geiger, and H. Wentker, 305–324. Munich: Oldenbourg, 2011.

Hevly, B., and J. M. Findlay, eds. *The Atomic West*. Seattle, WA: Center for the Study of the Pacific Northwest; University of Washington Press, 1998.

Hill, C. R. "Nations of Peace: Nuclear Disarmament and the Making of National Identity in Scotland and Wales." *Twentieth Century British History* 27, no. 1 (2016): 26–50. doi:10.1093/tcbh/hwv033.

Hughes, C. *Young Lives on the Left: Sixties Activism and the Liberation of the Self*. Manchester: Manchester University Press, 2015.

Hunner, J. *J. Robert Oppenheimer, the Cold War, and the Atomic West*. Norman, OK: University of Oklahoma Press, 2009.

Jamieson, B. P. "Britain's National Deterrent: Scotland's Answer to the Cycle of Unemployment?" *Contemporary British History* 21, no. 4 (2007): 449–469. doi:10.1080/13619460601060454.

Johnes, M. "Wales and the Cold War." *Llafur* 10, no. 4 (2011): 5–15.

Johnes, M. *Wales since 1939*. Manchester: Manchester University Press, 2012.

Jones, T. L. "A Comparative Study of Local Authority Preparations for Nuclear War in North-Eastern Wales, 1948–1968." *Welsh History Review* 20, no. 1 (2000): 89–115.

Lansley, S., S. Goss, and C. Wolmar. *Councils in Conflict: The Rise and Fall of the Municipal Left*. London: Macmillan, 1989.

LaPorte, N., F. Reid, and G. Williams, eds. "Cold War Wales." *Llafur* 10, no. 4 (2011): 2–103.

Liddington, J., repr. Syracuse, NY: Syracuse University Press, 1991. *The Road to Greenham Common: Feminism and Anti-Militarism in Britain since 1820*. London: Virago, 1989.

Lloyd-Jones, N., and M. M. Scull. "A New Plea for an Old Subject? Four Nations History for the Modern Period." In *Four Nations Approaches to Modern 'British' History: A (Dis)United Kingdom*, edited by N. Lloyd-Jones and M. M. Scull, 3–32. London: Palgrave Macmillan, 2018.

Mattausch, J. *A Commitment to Campaign: A Sociological Study of CND*. Manchester: Manchester University Press, 1989.

McCamley, N. *Cold War Secret Nuclear Bunkers: The Passive Defence of the Western World during the Cold War*. Barnsley: Pen and Sword, 2007.

Miller, B. A. *Geography and Social Movements: Comparing Antinuclear Activism in the Boston Area*. Minneapolis: University of Minnesota Press, 2000.

Morgan, K. O. "Peace Movements in Wales, 1899–1945." *Welsh History Review* 10, no. 3 (1981): 398–430.

Mort, M. *Building the Trident Network: A Study of the Enrollment of People, Knowledge, and Machines*. Cambridge, MA: MIT Press, 2002.

Nehring, H. "What Was the Cold War?" *English Historical Review* CXXVII, no. 527 (2012): 920–947. doi:10.1093/ehr/ces176.

Nehring, H., and B. Ziemann. "Do All Paths Lead to Moscow? the NATO Dual-Track Decision and the Peace Movement – A Critique." *Cold War History* 12, no. 1 (2012): 1–24. doi:10.1080/14682745.2011.625160.

Olsson-Rost, A. "The Cold War Home Front, an Age of Anxiety? the Cold War Narrative in School Magazines from Holyhead Comprehensive School during the 1950s and 1960s." *Llafur* 11, no. 4 (2015): 42–57.

Payling, D. "City Limits: Sexual Politics and the New Urban Left in 1980s Sheffield." *Contemporary British History* 31, no. 2 (2017): 256–273. doi:10.1080/13619462.2017.1306194.

Payling, D. "Socialist Republic of South Yorkshire': Grassroots Activism and Left-Wing Solidarity in 1980s Sheffield." *Twentieth Century British History* 25, no. 4 (2014): 602–627. doi:10.1093/tcbh/hwu001.

Pettitt, A. *Walking to Greenham: How the Peace Camp Began and the Cold War Ended*. Dinas Powys: Honno, 2006.

Pincombe, I. "The Cold Brain of the Machine': North Wales and the British Warfare State." *Llafur* 12, no. 1 (2016): 62–83.

Rogers, P., M. Dando, and V. D. D. Peter. *As Lambs to the Slaughter: The Facts about Nuclear War*. London: Arrow Books, 1981.

Rolph, A. "Greenham and Its Legacy: The Women's Peace Movement in Wales in the 1980s." In *The Idiom of Dissent: Protest and Propaganda in Wales*, edited by T. Robin Chapman, 97–122. Llandysul: Gomer Press, 2006.

Sabin, P. G. A. *The Third World War Scare in Britain: A Critical Analysis*. Basingstoke: Macmillan, 1986.

Schregel, S. *Der Atomkrieg vor der Wohnungstür: Eine Politikgeschichte der neuen Friedensbewegung in der Bundesrepublik 1970–1985*. Frankfurt/Main: Campus, 2010.

Schregel, S. "Nuclear War and the City: Perspectives on Municipal Interventions in Defence (Great Britain, New Zealand, West Germany, USA, 1980–1985)." *Urban History* 42, no. 4 (2015): 564–583. doi:10.1017/S0963926815000565.

Schregel, S. "The Nuclear Crisis: The Arms Race, Cold War Anxiety, and the German Peace Movement of the 1980s." In *The Spaces and Places of the Peace Movement*, edited by C. Becker-Schaum, P. Gassert, M. Klimke, W. Mausbach, and M. Zepp, 173–188. New York: Berghahn, 2016.

Simpson, T. *No Bunker Here: A Successful Non-Violent Direct Action in A Welsh Community*. Merthyr Tydfil: Mid Glamorgan CND, 1982.

Simpson, T., and P. Llewellyn. *H-Bomb on Ogwr: A Study of A Nuclear Attack in Wales*. 2nd. 1981, Bridgend: Bridgend CND, n.d.

Stafford, J. "'Stay at Home': The Politics of Nuclear Civil Defence, 1968–83." *Twentieth Century British History* 23, no. 3 (2012): 383–407. doi:10.1093/tcbh/hwr034.

Thompson, E. P. *Protest and Survive*. London: CND. Nottingham: Bertrand Russell Peace Foundation, 1980.

Titcombe, E. "Women Activists: Rewriting Greenham's History." *Women's History Review* 22, no. 2 (2013): 310–329. doi:10.1080/09612025.2012.726118.

Whitham, C. "Sheep, Subs and Showcases: The American Military in Brawdy, 1974–1995." *Welsh History Review* 24, no. 4 (2009): 168–186.

'Nuclear prospects': the siting and construction of Sizewell A power station 1957–1966

Christine Wall

ABSTRACT
This paper examines the siting and construction of a Magnox nuclear power station on the Suffolk coast. The station was initially welcomed by local politicians as a solution to unemployment but was criticised by an organised group of local Communist activists who predicted how the restriction zone would restrict future development. Oral history interviews provide insights into conditions on the construction site and the social effects on the nearby town. Archive material reveals the spatial and development restrictions imposed with the building of the power station, which remains on the shoreline as a monument to the 'atomic age'. This material is contextualised in the longer economic and social history of a town that moved from the shadow of nineteenth century paternalistic industry into the glare of the nuclear construction programme and became an early example of the eclipsing of local democracy by the centralised nuclear state.

Introduction

In 1951, the Glasgow *Exhibition of Industrial Power* designed by Basil Spence as part of the Festival of Britain featured a 'spectacular presentation of the new power source—nuclear energy'.[1] The exhibition aimed to inform the visiting public of the history and theory of power generation, including water and coal, and culminated in the *Hall of the Future*, which explained the production of nuclear power as an upbeat 'national story' of scientific and technical progress harnessed for social betterment.[2] This popular narrative of nuclear energy harnessed for the benefit of humanity began immediately after the end of the Second World War. Christoph Laucht has described how prior to the Festival, in 1947, the Science Museum together with the Atomic Scientist's Association (ASA) had organised the highly successful Atomic Train: a travelling exhibition which 'educated Britons primarily about atomic energy'.[3] Throughout the 1950s the promotion of nuclear power as the clean, safe, energy of the future continued via touring exhibitions organised by the U.S. Atoms for Peace programme, as well as being regularly featured in articles in the mass circulation magazine *Picture Post*.[4] Even the accidental leak of radioactivity at one of the Windscale piles, which was given widespread media coverage, has been interpreted by Jonathan Hogg as increasing public anxiety, rather than resistance, towards the role of

---

This article has been republished with minor changes. These changes do not impact the academic content of the article.

nuclear energy.[5] In Hogg's estimation the initial secrecy and subsequent political cover-up of the event resulted in a growing awareness that individuals and local communities were powerless and had little democratic voice in the face of state-controlled production of nuclear energy.[6]

It is against this background that this article focuses on the decision, in 1957, to site a Magnox nuclear power station in a typically remote rural location, on the Suffolk coast. Archive documents together with previously recorded oral histories have been used extensively to research the factors leading up to, as well as local responses to, the siting decision, while newly recorded oral histories with former building workers are used here as the basis for descriptions of the physical reality of building and working on the nuclear power station.

The use of oral history testimony, contextualised with documentary evidence, provides a more nuanced account of the 'national story' of nuclear power generation. Personal memories can enhance, and also subvert, the official histories deposited in national archives and oral histories are distinctive, according to Paul Thompson in that they, 'to a much greater extent than most sources, allow[s] the original multiplicity of standpoints to be recreated'.[7] They can of course, never reproduce the entirety of the complex and contingent responses by people to the imposition of rapid and permanent change to their living and working environment exemplified by the arrival of a nuclear power station. They do however provide insights into a range of reactions, from acceptance to resistance. In particular, the experience of constructing the power station, related in the personal testimony of the men who built it, gives immediacy, and fleshes out the distant, bureaucratic, mechanism of the nuclear state. The harsh, primitive, unsafe working conditions experienced by the construction workers were an unknown and hidden aspect of the 'national story' of nuclear energy. These oral histories were recorded as part of a Leverhulme Trust funded project, led by the author, aiming to document the role of building workers in post-war reconstruction. Sizewell A was chosen as a case study, which exemplified nationalised industry in the Central Electricity Generating Board, and the very large infrastructure projects of the 1960s.[8] The project case studies were all chosen to explore different aspects of the built environment produced during the era of the post-war welfare state, a period which also coincided with the Cold War and the emergence of the nuclear state. Workers, in their oral histories, recollected how conditions on building sites were often at odds with the wider social betterment aims of the welfare state and nuclear construction sites exemplified this dramatically. Despite the rhetoric of modernity associated with nuclear energy as the clean, efficient energy of the future, working conditions for those who built the power stations were primitive and dangerous. The interviews recorded with former workers still resident on the Suffolk coast reveal their experiences of work on the site, and also document how the social fabric of a small town was first disrupted by, and subsequently adjusted to, the arrival of nuclear infrastructure.

The Sizewell decision: site selection in East Anglia

Rural East Anglia was, and still is, dominated by large arable farms owned by a small number of families, which in the post-war period witnessed increased mechanisation and a rapid shift from traditional to business methods for agricultural production.

Agricultural labourers in the region earned wages between 10% and 12% lower than equivalent labour in the rest of England and Wales, attributed by Howard Newby to local labour markets controlled by paternalistic farmers with tied cottages as part of the employment contract, thus restricting labour mobility and increasing dependency.[9] This contributed to a clearly defined class structure of landowning farmers and hired farm workers with conservative farmers and landowners dominating in local and regional politics, as magistrates and in other civic institutions.

This pattern, while true for most of the surrounding agricultural area, does not, however, describe the small, industrial town of Leiston, nor the fishing village of Sizewell: the two communities directly affected by the construction of Sizewell A. Leiston was distinctive in accommodating an existing group of Communists and a wider network of left-wing activists in the town who were at first, cautiously critical of the siting of the power station and later actively resistant to the further development of the site. By contrast Sizewell was [see Figures 1, 2 and 3] a small fishing village consisting of a short terrace of houses, a few Coastguard cottages and a pub, The Vulcan Arms. Ipswich lies 20 miles inland to the south and Lowestoft to the north with the popular seaside towns of Southwold and Aldeburgh on the nearby coast. Together Leiston and Sizewell, consisting of c.4,000 inhabitants in the 1950s, were administered by the Urban District Council of Leiston until local government re-organisation in 1974.

There were many objections to the early Magnox power stations, and Ian Welsh reveals that opposition to nuclear power appeared well before, and distinct from, the

Figure 1. Aerial photograph of site published in Electrical Times 2nd October 1959, used with permission of the *Electrical Times*.

Figure 2. View of site from Sizewell hamlet, c.1940s. Reproduced with permission Leiston Long Shop Museum.

Figure 3. View of site from Sizewell hamlet, 2017. Author''s photograph.

emergence of an organised anti-nuclear weapons movement in the early 1960s.[10] His analysis of the 1956 inquiry into the siting of the Magnox station at Bradwell on the Essex coast highlighted the contradiction inherent in reassurance by the authorities that nuclear power stations were perfectly safe and the policy of siting them in remote areas of low population density.[11] The Bradwell Inquiry lasted five days with impassioned speeches from well organised objectors including representatives of the local oyster industry, backed up by marine biologists, and focussed on potential danger to the local population, environmental concerns and the lack of information given to the public. The Inquiry ruled against the objectors and in Welsh's words; 'the unassailable position of the nuclear enterprise remained inviolate'.[12] This may have contributed to the lack of opposition to Sizewell A, and the widespread sense of hopelessness described by Hogg, but there were also, from the outset, a local group of outspoken voices critical of the centralised nuclear state.

Even before the arrival of Magnox the nuclear state had been in evidence on the Suffolk coast for some time. At the end of the Second World War most of the military defence installations along the coastline had been rapidly dismantled but with onset of the Cold War a significant number were put back into use. By the mid-1950s the airfields at Bentwaters and Woodbridge had been extended to make them suitable for the use of the U.S. Air Force and eight former Royal Observer Corps visual observation posts dotted along the coastline were converted, by the construction of new underground bunkers, to monitor fallout in case of nuclear war.[13] While most of Cold War sites were concerned with early warning and monitoring against a Soviet attack the former Ministry of Defence radar development site at Orford Ness, an offshore shingle spit only accessible by boat at the mouth of the River Ore, became a research and development centre for Britain's own nuclear arsenal. Orford was chosen because of its remoteness from major centres of population, the same criteria used in the siting of nuclear power stations. From 1953 until 1971 the Atomic Weapons Research Establishment (AWRE) ran a ballistics test site on the Ness although the public have always been assured that no actual atomic material was ever used there.[14] The site was always surrounded in secrecy, including in the late 1960s when it was used as site for Cobra Mist, a U.S. and British collaborative project on radar early detection.

Against this background of existing Cold War concealment the site for Sizewell A was chosen, ostensibly, on the grounds of its suitable fit from an engineering perspective. The factors in its favour were, according to Michael Gammon, the senior engineer at the CEGB responsible for finding sites in East Anglia, its geological formation able to take the weight of the station (c.65,000 tons), proximity to sea as a source for cooling water for the turbines, relatively close to the source of high demand for electricity (the South East), and a ready supply of potable water both for the boilers and use of station staff.[15] However, Gammon when interviewed as an elderly man for the British Library's Oral History of the Electricity Supply in the UK gave more background to the process. He stated that the selection of any nuclear power station in the 1950s started with one key restriction, a consideration of the density of the local population in the immediate area and recounted that there were at the time, strict but crude rules about how many people could be living within certain miles—sensible because if necessary, if all else failed, you had to be able to evacuate people or at least control their movements. As engineers we thought it would never fail but ... [16]

Gammon does not finish the sentence and the ensuing short silence indicates a moment of discomposure in his erstwhile fluent narrative. The unfailing belief by engineers in the total safety of the power stations underpinned much of the technical and engineering decision-making on siting. As Brian Wynne has noted this was part of often, flawed decision-making, but made without any deliberate malice as the engineers and scientists involved were part of a social-intellectual community with a shared beliefs and value system operating in a 'pervading atmosphere of scientific self-confidence'.[17] The infallibility of nuclear science and its practitioners was given public authority by assertions from politicians. For example, Nigel Birch, Minister of Works, stated in 1955:

I am advised that there is no danger at all associated with radioactivity from the use of atomic power for civil purposes. Such radioactive materials as are emitted are very weak and their effect is not cumulative. Their radioactivity ceases almost at once. I want to dispose of any suggestion that the use of atomic energy for civil purposes raises any danger.[18]

Nevertheless, at the same time, work by T. M. Fry at the Atomic Research Centre at Harwell had determined that as few people as possible should be exposed to any potential risk. This was envisaged so that for any 10 degree sector around the plant the population would have to be less than 500 within 1.5 miles, less than 10,000 within 5 miles and less than 100,000 within 10 miles.[19] These criteria were not however in the public domain, and as Openshaw has demonstrated, the initial guidelines and their subsequent revisions in 1959 and 1963 were anyway, completely disregarded by the CEGB in relation to Sizewell A.[20] Michael Gammon admits later in his interview that they were 'doing things rushed' in the 1950s, cutting corners and 'doing things' he would never allow junior engineers to do today, an approach also admitted by Sir Christopher Hinton and evident in the Windscale fire of 1957.[21]

Site investigations in Suffolk began early in 1957 with geological surveys to ascertain foundation conditions. Seven possible sites were identified on the coast including Dunwich and Orford. Dunwich was abandoned because of the difficulty of digging down a cliff and Orford was considered problematic because of the shifting shingle ridge in the River Ore preventing its use as a source of cooling water, although it would be interesting to know whether the presence of the AWRE also affected the decision. Gammon considered that Sizewell fulfiled the technical criteria and in 1958 proceeded to write the report proposing it as the best option. He remembered Christopher Hinton's sarcastic response to the news, when he made a biblical reference to the wisdom of building a power station on sand.[22] There was minimal environmental investigation at Sizewell and the East Suffolk Council, with the authority to call for an enquiry remained silent. Openshaw suggests that a deal might have been made between the Council and the CEGB to agree on Sizewell as the site that would have the least detrimental effect on the environmentally sensitive Suffolk coastline and also on the visual amenity of the nearby tourist centres of Aldeburgh and Southwold.[23]

An oral history recorded by two local historians reveals that the Town Clerk of Leiston also had a hand in the CEGB decision.

> I well remember the chappy from the CEGB... He popped in here one day and declared himself to be looking for sites for nuclear power stations on the east coast. He thought the best place would be off Orford Ness, because it was remote and it wouldn't be too difficult to put power lines across the river at that point. But we were so desirous of increasing opportunities for local employment that the Clerk of the Council, Mr. Bonham, persuaded him to take a visit down to Sizewell where there was ample foreshore, ample hinterland and unspoilt coastland, but nevertheless available. [24]

This account is backed up by a letter from Mr. Bonham written to the Ministry of Power, and dated 7 March 1957, which does not offer unqualified support but asks for more information.

> My council are interested in introducing new industry into the district and they may favour the establishment of an atomic power station, but it may be that our district has not some of the requisites necessary for such an establishment. On the other hand, when the requirements of such a station are made known it may appear that this district is eminently suitable as there is a wide expanse of sub-standard agricultural land and easy access to the sea.[25]

By early 1958, it is likely there were rumours circulating locally, indicating that Sizewell was under consideration, to the extent that one Leiston resident wrote in January, in a personal capacity, to Lord Mills, Minister of Power, making a plea for the station to be sited at Sizewell. The letter, typed on headed notepaper, describes how lay-offs at the local engineering works, the threat of a four day week and the recent closure of a small factory which had employed 200 people, have caused 'a sense of foreboding' to overshadow the town. After indicating that it is generally understood that Sizewell is under consideration as the site for the new power station the writer concludes,

> ... I want to tell you personally, as a private person, how desperately our people are hoping that this project may be realised. If, as we hope and pray, it could come about, a heavy cloud will be lifted, and our morale will soar. If, on the other hand, the decision should go against us, I hesitate to think of the effect on our little community, for then, indeed, it would be hard to see anything to which we could fasten our hopes of an improvement.[26]

Inhabitants of the fishing village of Sizewell itself were less desirous of the power station. In her memoir Boni Sones, who grew up in the village, remembers helping her mother gather 70 signatures from every Sizewell resident who all objected to the coming of the power station.[27] There is no record of the petition from the Sizewell villagers in the National Archives file on Sizewell A and it is not mentioned in the meeting, held at the Ministry of Power in September 1958, to finalise the selection of Sizewell.[28] At this meeting only four of the six objections that had been lodged were deemed worth discussion and as they were easily resolved the meeting agreed on the site without the necessity of a public enquiry.[29] The site therefore was typical of the later Magnox stations in not having an enquiry and in being cautiously welcomed at local level.[30] Instead a half-day exhibition of plans for the new power station was held in Leiston with CEGB staff on hand to answer any questions. It appears that tenders for the construction were sent out even before planning permission was granted.[31] The building of Sizewell A was forgone conclusion by the time East Suffolk County Council announced the decision early in 1959. This was reported in the local Eastern Daily Press with the Chair of the Planning Committee commenting that he recommended the site, 'with great regret and as the least of all the evils'.[32]

The Leiston left

Up until the mid-twentieth century Leiston was a one-company town, the main employer being Garrett's Engineering Works, which had an international reputation for producing steam traction engines, as well as a local reputation for not allowing trade union membership among its employees.[33] By the 1920s, demand for steam engines had declined, the firm's attempts to diversify failed and it was forced to rationalise its assets.[34] In the process one of the Garrett family houses in Leiston together with its surrounding gardens and fields, was put on the market. It was bought by A.S. Neill, renamed Summerhill, and became the famous progressive school. The arrival of A.S. Neill attracted a number of left-wing radicals and Communist Party members to the town who taught at the school including Paxton Chadwick who joined the school as art teacher in 1933, together with the historian A.L. Morton.[35]

Local Communist Party members produced a newssheet called the *Leiston Leader*, published monthly and which began in 1934 and continued until 1999, containing articles on both national and local issues.[36] Its peak circulation was probably in the late 1930s when 1,200 copies were distributed and it was the only Communist produced publication throughout the Second World War, including the years the *Daily Worker* was banned.[37] During the war, while their husbands were in the forces, Lee Chadwick and Vivien Morton joined other women munitions workers at Garretts where they played prominent roles in the Transport and General Worker's Union and by the end of the war the Leiston branch of the Communist Party (CP) had 40 members.[38]

From the 1930s onwards, Leiston developed a longstanding co-operation between Labour and Communist Party activists resulting in a local council without the Conservative majority typical of rural Suffolk.[39] The first success of this collaboration was when Paxton Chadwick, locally known as 'Chad', became the first Communist councillor in Suffolk when he was elected in 1938. The combined forces of Communist and Labour party members successfully fielded Socialist candidates to every local election and in 1946 wider success was achieved when Lee Chadwick became the first Communist elected to East Suffolk County Council. Later, in 1956, she became secretary of the East Anglian Federation of Women for Peace in response to the siting of U.S. Air Force nuclear bombers at Lakenheath.[40] By the late 1950s, when the CEGB began investigating Sizewell as a possible site for a Magnox nuclear power station, there was an extant and organised nucleus of politically informed and active residents just over a mile down the road from the coast. Paxton's position as a popular local councillor enabled him to respond formally to anxiety among the local population concerning radioactive leaks and contamination. These were expressed in a letter written by Chadwick in his capacity as Secretary of the Leiston branch of the Communist Party, to E.J. Turner, Secretary, CEGB, in which he stated that,

> ...while we do not oppose, and never have opposed, in any way the building of a Nuclear Power Station at Sizewell, we do not think that the general assurances so far published by the Central Electricity Generating Board are sufficient.[41]

Chadwick's letter on the subject of the siting of the new nuclear power station stayed within the guidelines of Communist Party's manifesto *The British Road to Socialism* which supported the peaceful use of atomic energy with its potential for 'bringing into being immense new productive forces, making substantial economies in labour and transport, and paving the way for abundance and more leisure for the people'.[42] However, the letter also clearly reflected the concerns of local people and the questions asked were well informed. Queries were raised over the safeguarding of public drinking water supply, the build-up of radioactivity in the sea, and, given the life of the station was presumed to be only for 20 years, whether plans were in place to restore the countryside when it ceased production. The final paragraph was a plea for less secrecy from both the Ministry of Power and the CEGB:

> We urge the Board to take the public into its confidence and give details of measures to be taken to prevent any possible biological effect on the population. For example, we would like to know what degree of safety, in terms of röntgen units, is the Board working when it says the wastes will contain no harmful degree of radiation? [43]

At the time the nuclear power industry did not have any information on 'degrees of safety' of exposure to radiation and it was a scientifically contested field.[44] The letter reflects increased public awareness of the risks attached to nuclear power generation after the Windscale accident in 1957, which released air-borne radioactive material. The extent of the release and the subsequent destruction of milk from local dairy herds had received significant media coverage including the fact that the CEGB had delayed informing the public of the accident.[45] Chadwick's letter, copied to the Minister of Power, urged the Board to 'take the public into its confidence and give details of measures to be taken to prevent any possible biological effect on the population'.

While there is no record of a response from the Ministry the CEGB replied promptly and politely.

> Thank you for your letter of the 18th March from which it is noted that the Leiston Branch of the Communist Party are not opposed to the building of a nuclear power station at Sizewell.[46]

The CEGB's reply addressed the concerns raised at length, with general reassurances on both drinking and seawater quality, and stating that there would be no significant rise in sea-water temperature. There were also reassurances that any harmful radioactive discharge would not result in a 'harmful build-up of radioactivity' but there were no technical details forthcoming.

> It is regretted that, at this stage, no actual levels of radioactivity can be stated but these will, in any case, be matters which will be dealt with by the Ministry of Power under the Nuclear Installations (Licensing and Insurance) Bill in the course of the licensing procedure when this becomes law.[47]

Perhaps the most important revelation for the local community in the CEGB's reply was information on the future of the Sizewell site. The letter specified that when Sizewell A ceased production it was going to be replaced by a new power station and that, 'the Sizewell site will continue to be used indefinitely for power generation'.[48] This statement predicted the inevitable arrival of Sizewell B in the 1980s.[49]

This remarkable exchange of letters, in 1959, despite Cold War anxieties about the Soviet nuclear threat, reveals how Communist Party members were working openly at a local level to challenge state decisions. Christopher Andrew's authorised history of MI5 states that by the early 1950s the Secret Service had almost fully penetrated the Communist Party. Using informers and other sources they had compiled a list of 90% of members throughout the country and were well aware of Communist involvement in trade unions.[50] Paxton Chadwick was, by the late 1950s, well-known nationally as the illustrator of an acclaimed series of Puffin natural history books for children and the Leiston Communists, openly elected councillors and local activists, were likely of minor security significance. Peter Hennessey's history of Cold War Britain suggests that at this time the real threat to national security was perceived to be from a small number of senior men, with no obvious links to the CP, in influential positions within the civil service, and thus able to pass intelligence to the Soviet military.[51]

Notwithstanding its highly politicised group of activists, by the end of the 1950s, Leiston had moved from the mantle of local, paternalistic nineteenth century industrialism into the remote, and even more disenfranchising and secretive, realm of the twentieth century nuclear state.

Short-term gain: long-term stagnation

For some the arrival of the power station was seen as a business opportunity. The new landlords of the White Horse Hotel moved to Leiston in 1959 precisely because of its 'nuclear prospects', making a gamble that came off as trade increased greatly after the decision was ratified by the Ministry of Power early in 1960.[52] Relatively high unemployment in Leiston and the surrounding countryside was cited widely, in the press, by the Ministry of Power, and by the Leiston U.D.C as a compelling reason why the power station should be welcomed. It remained for the local Communists to sound a note of warning:

> The new power station will bring trade to the shops but with a few exceptions the jobs will be temporary. Don't be misled into thinking the power station is the answer to Leiston's problems. ... Leiston is likely to become a town of aging people instead of a balanced community. New Industries are vital![53]

At the opposite end of the political spectrum local farmers and landowners became worried at the prospect of men leaving the land for the higher wages of the construction industry. This was epitomised in an angry letter sent to local M.P. Col. Harwood Harrison from a local farmer asking that no agricultural workers be employed on the site as 'they seem to think they will all have jobs offered them, and they will be roping in big money (which we can ill afford) at the government's expense'.[54] The *Leiston Leader* meanwhile continued to point out that the government was deliberately siting nuclear power stations away from highly populated urban areas and this might result in future difficulties for Leiston developing in other directions.[55]

Both Leiston UDC and East Suffolk County Council seem to have been blinkered, or perhaps misled, as to the long-term effects of the siting of a nuclear power station within a mile and half of the town. Conflict between local government procedures and policy decisions emanating from a nationalised industry and central government became evident when plans for the expansion of the town were released.

The town's population had declined from 4,611 in 1921 to 4,056 in 1951 and the Leiston and District Plan, published in October 1961 (see Figures 4 and 5), intended to address inherent social and economic problems by attracting new industry and building new housing.[56] It considered that the effect of building of a nuclear power station nearby would be 'felt mainly in the short term' and was 'bound to have a livening effect on trade in Leiston', and to not have a lasting effect on land use apart from the station itself and the new housing planned for CEGB staff.[57]

Planning permission was already in place to build 350 new houses, and the CEGB had asked that at least 200 of these be allocated to manual staff required for the station maintenance. Interestingly, in the light of Leiston's many well-built Victorian villas, it was assumed that professional and salaried staff would not live in Leiston, but further out in the surrounding countryside and only manual staff working shifts, would need to live close to the station.[58]

However, the development plan was halted when, early in 1962 the Ministry of Housing and Local Government (MHLG) issued a circular to planning authorities stating that all applications for new development near a nuclear power station had to be referred directly to the Minister. After extensive negotiations among the County Planning Officer, Leiston UDC, the CEGB and Ministries of Power and MHLG, a revised and much reduced plan was re-calculated using Ministry of Power safety criteria and the CEGB also reduced their demand for 200 houses to 100.[59] As these new criteria resulted in the revocation of planning consent for residential and industrial development of 45 acres the CEGB agreed to reimburse the County Council by payment of compensation.[60] Meanwhile, the Minister of Power wrote in January of 1962 warning the County Planning Officer that 'generally, the increase in the population of Leiston should be kept to a very modest level'.[61] Although the original County Plan hoped to increase and diversify industry in Leiston a revised plan

Figure 4. Leiston, Post Office Square, c1950s. Reproduced with permission Leiston Long Shop Museum.

Figure 5. Leiston and District Plan, 1961. Reproduced with permission Leiston Long Shop Museum.

published in 1962 stated unequivocally that the government's policy of siting nuclear power stations away from large centres of population had to be followed.

This factor would now appear to require emphasis to the extent that future development in Leiston itself must be strictly limited. This is in order that the Ministry of Power safety criteria regarding the size of population in the vicinity of the power station are not infringed. The object of these criteria is to ensure that any people living in the vicinity can be safely evacuated should an accident occur at the nuclear power station.[62]

The spectacle of the construction site: 5,000 men over five years

Sizewell A was one of the 12 nuclear power stations outlined in the 1955 White paper 'A Programme of Nuclear Power' (Cmd.9389). The Magnox programme, its technical problems, inefficiency and problems of communication among the designers, the Atomic Energy Authority and the newly constituted body with the responsibility for their running and maintenance, the Central Electricity Generating Board, have been described and analysed in depth elsewhere.[63]

The design and construction of the plants was carried out by consortia consisting of several private firms and on completion the stations were handed over to the Central Electricity Generating Board who then became responsible for running and maintenance. Five industrial consortia were established to compete for the reactor orders, although the domestic market was not large enough to sustain all five, and Sizewell A was built by Nuclear Design and Construction (NDC), comprising English Electric, Babcock and Wilcox and Taylor Woodrow Construction.[64]

There are very few sources for examining the building process from the perspective of the workers themselves, and while there exist some sympathetic accounts of the lives of Irish building workers in post-war Britain, generally, the workers who brought the major infrastructure projects of the 1960s to completion are invisible.[65] The accounts here provide insights into the social world of constructing a nuclear power station, where industrial relations, working conditions, friendships and hardships are recalled by the men who built Sizewell A. They also provide a range of voices in relation to the nuclear power station, those who abhorred what it represented, those who willingly worked for short-term high wages, those who used it as an entry to a career in the construction industry, and those who benefitted from its arrival as a new source of steady employment. The recordings of their working lives were detailed and animated and full of anecdotes, for most of these men work on the power station construction site had been only a short stage in their working lives, but all of them still lived in the town of Leiston or nearby. Their accounts, including personal photographs of the construction site, were published at the end of the project in a small booklet intended as a keepsake for all the participants.[66]

The first stage of construction was the building of the concrete foundation, a reinforced concrete raft 8 feet thick, surrounded by the 'biological shields' to prevent radiation escaping from the reactor which were 100 feet high and 10–14 feet thick. One of the young Irishmen who arrived to work on the site was Patrick O'Kane, who had sailed to England, as thousands of his countrymen did, to look for work in the 1960s.[67] He arrived at Sizewell in the early stages of construction and lived in the site accommodation, which he remembered as very cramped. There were four in a room with two beds to a cubicle separated by a hatch so that 'you could speak to one another... like some animals could look over in a shed where they were living there, you know'.[68] Pat worked on the concrete gangs and earned about £20 a week, as he put it 'You had to work long hours to try and get a week's wages'. Conditions were harsh especially in the winter when the temperature dropped below that required for concrete to set:

> The working day was long. It was very, very long. And I think the coldest experience that I ever witnessed was at Sizewell Power station in 1963 when it used to thaw in the morning and freeze at night and we used to make fires to keep the concrete warm, to keep the heat in the concrete.[69]

Pat was then moved to tunnelling work: constructing the cooling water tunnels for the inflow and outflow of seawater, running from the pump house on the main site under the sea to two offshore rigs. Here he contracted an injury to his hand which landed him hospital where he met a local nurse he later married. The minor injury probably saved his life as it said locally that within 10 years nearly all the tunnelers were dead from complications arising from decompression sickness.[70] As a young Irishman Pat was part of a strong network of Catholic Irish building workers where the 'elders' helped the younger men along in getting work and building careers in construction. The site camp had a resident Catholic priest and mass was said every day, but Leiston was without a RC church. Pat and a number of other Irish workers volunteered their labour in building a new church for the town, partly paid for by Taylor Woodrow the civil engineering contractor, and which still stands as a permanent reminder of the Irish men who worked on the first nuclear construction site.

[Figure 6 and 7]

Taylor Woodrow also built the off shore rigs positioned over the inflow and outflow seawater tunnels. A small gang of local men worked on this section of the works, based

Figure 6. Patrick O'Kane, third from right, and friends on site of Catholic Church. Photograph reproduced with permission Patrick O'Kane.

Figure 7. Leiston RC Church, 2017. Author's photograph.

on the beach and employed because of their experience as boatmen they ended up doing a very wide range of jobs. Pat Cable, a former merchant seaman from Aldeburgh two miles down the coast, became ganger to these local men all of whom he knew personally.[71] After a slipway had been built and the rigs assembled and towed out to sea Pat became a diver and spent many hours underwater bolting together the off shore platforms. He was not trained for this job and had never done any diving before, and his account is typical of the gung-ho approach in the construction industry of the mid-1960s before improved Health and Safety legislation came into force.

> No, I never had any training for it... My general foreman was a Dutchman who was a naval wartime salvage diver, and he just said to me one day, 'Have you done any diving?' So I said 'No.' He said, 'Do you want to have a go?' So [laughing], I said, well, try anything...so he said, 'Well, put the suit on and go down and see what you think of it.' So I did...[72]

Pat was clear that the incentive was a very good wage: for the two years he spent diving he earned £60 a week, money that went towards buying a house for his young family. When the offshore work was completed he worked as a labourer for English Electric on the next phase of construction, fitting graphite blocks into the reactor core, a completely new type of work and again without any formal training. Pat recalled, 'It was all clean conditions, where you changed all your clothing—underwear, overalls, you wore hats and silk gloves and everything, to work inside the reactor'.[73] He remembered this process,

> In each reactor, there's 11 layers of graphite blocks, and the blocks are about three foot tall, about a foot diameter, and there's 11 layers of them in each reactor, and there was 3,000-some-odd blocks in a layer and we used to have to lay all these blocks in a certain sequence, because there was a chart that you had to lay them to, to make up a certain pattern, because they're all machined, these blocks, to make up a certain pattern. Once you'd done the whole layer, which you used to do in about two 12-hour shifts, one shift would lay

about half of them, and the other shift would lay about the other half, and they were all in...one [layered partition], and then there was integral steelwork that went all the way round the outside to keep them all clamped together, and then you went and done your next layer, and so it went on till you got to the top.

When the reactor began generating he became one of the few local men who ended up with 'a job for life' with the CEGB, working on Sizewell A as a rigger with the maintenance team. He took early retirement on a good pension at the age of 54 and was very positive about how much the CEGB and Sizewell had contributed to the town: a social centre, swimming pool and sports centre, and also to his own working life, including regular health-checks from CEGB doctors.

The construction process was an enormous undertaking and was widely publicised in the national, local and technical presses. Photographs of the site including shots of the cranes, night-working in the snow and lifting of the pile cap into place, represented the site as a spectacle of technological progress and featured regularly in the local press.[74] This sense of the site as a spectacle was encouraged when the construction consortium erected a 40 feet high observation platform just inside the site boundary in the summer of 1961 so that visitors could look out over the works towards the sea. This attracted over 3,000 visitors over the August Bank holiday with many brought to the coast by the Eastern Counties Omnibus Company who were running tours from 44 places in East Anglia to view the construction works.[75] The Town Council had recently bought the foreshore of Sizewell beach, as part of the negotiations for the power station site, to ensure that the beach remained open to the public during construction for the use of holidaymakers and fishermen.[76] A small car park, public conveniences and a tea shack were installed, while the local pub, the Vulcan Arms, was accommodating both visitors and construction workers in an extension erected in the garden to cater for the increased numbers of drinkers.

The extraordinary scale of the reactor and its components was recognised in a series of photographs taken by a welder, Charlie Dennis, his photographs conveying the construction site from the perspective of one of the workers (see Figure 8 and 9).

When the concrete superstructure was completed a very different workforce began to arrive. These were the highly paid and highly skilled welders needed to assemble the boilers manufactured by Babcock and Wilcox, a separate British subsidiary of the U.S. firm founded in 1891, at their Renfrew works. Made of 2.25 inch thick steel they were shipped in sections to Lowestoft from where they were then hauled by road to Sizewell. This work attracted highly skilled welders from further afield, although there were also local men and those who abandoned the Garrett's Works in favour of the construction site.

Ian Roberts and John Mittel were both local men who sought out the higher wages available at Sizewell, but while wages were high, working conditions were hellish. Up to 20 welders at a time worked inside a boiler, where, with no individual air filtration masks and just one main extractor, it was hot, dusty and very noisy. The welders were given salt tablets and only allowed to work for up to two hours at a time without a break. John Mittel recalled that the plates were, 'pre-heated up to about 200, 250 degrees centigrade, before welding could commence, and it was hot, very hot'.[77] Ian Roberts

Figure 8. Crane towering over site huts. Photograph copyright Charlie Dennis and reproduced with permission.

Figure 9. Workers on site. Photograph copyright Charlie Dennis and reproduced with permission.

remembered the heat of the plates that were being welded was so high that the welders were supplied with asbestos mats:

> the mats were about…eight inches deep, sprung mattress, all covered in blue asbestos, so that you didn't have to lay on the heated plates, you know, and that was a bit uncomfortable, the sweat and that, you know.[78]

The responses of former workers who were exposed to asbestos varied. While John did not comment on the presence of asbestos Ian knew of two men who had died of asbestos related disease and said he 'often wondered if that's going to be my lot'. John and Ian also worked on preparing the reactor by machining the openings for the reactor tubes, which pierced the reactor dome. This was very precise work to dimensions of within three-thousandths of an inch. John tried to describe the conditions in the dome:

> There would be 20 welders, about 20 machinists, and don't forget, with double-shifting there would be about 40, and then you've got other ancillary trades, … So, there would be about 10 or 12 scaffolders, who were constantly moving boards and equipment,. …just imagine a great big dome of steel 90 feet across, and there's all this scaffolding, and then there's the welders and a mass of electrical equipment—all the welding equipment, the wires, etc. …terrific voltages in there, and then there's us fitters, with the machines, and we're all connected up to electricity, …
>
> And then the other thing was … I mean, we were cutting metal. So…all 20 of the machines, blasting away! So, you've got horrendous noise!… [79]

Welders were members of the Boilermakers Union and renowned for determinedly arguing their wage rates at the outset of any project. Ian Roberts had been working as a welder in the Ipswich engineering works of Ransomes and Rapier for around £18 but at Sizewell he immediately earned £60–70 a week.[80] John Mittel considered that 'the welders, the boilermakers, were the kingpins, they held the key to the salaries…'[81] In terms of wages Sizewell A was typical of large civil engineering sites in the 1960s, prior to a unifying industrial agreement, with a large number of different unions on site and wide disparities in wages between occupations. The site saw a number of strikes and disputes but these were all resolved through a very efficient site committee so there were no overruns, and Sizewell opened on time. Jim Ward, a labourer and union convener who travelled in every day from Lowestoft, summed up the industrial organisation of Sizewell as a balance between local men desperate for high wages over a short period of time and the 'travelling men' used to fighting hard to maintain their pay and conditions from site to site.[82] He reflected that

> Generally speaking, the East Anglian workforce were more, if you like, gentle—that's the wrong word… peaceful, peaceable, than the travelling men, who were used to the hard, rough way of working and getting what they wanted, and I think the two things helped each other. There was the reticence of the local, earning good money, and there was the hardness, if you like, of the travelling men, and the two went together very well, I thought.[83]

Apart from mechanised lifting and other plant, much of the physical process of nuclear construction, including the 'clean conditions' required for assembling the reactor core, was undertaken by manual workers and on reflection, many years later, they still took pride in their work. As Jim Ward reflected, 'Sizewell was a good job and it was well done, and I've got no qualms about it. I did a small part of it, a very small part'.

Working on the Sizewell A site provided a window on a world very different from the rigidly controlled, low paid employment in local engineering works and the even lower pay of agricultural work. For some local men it was not just an introduction to the harsh life of the construction industry but, through working alongside incoming workers, the wider world beyond rural Suffolk, which arrived as a consequence of nuclear power. Dick Nettlingham, who had left his job at Garrett's, had joined the local 'boys' on the off-shore rigs and remembered it as an intense time:

> well, it was an eye-opener and an experience, hell of an experience, because I hadn't worked with those sort of men and that before, you know, and I suppose it…sort of broadened your outlook a bit but I still think the job…on the offshore was the best lot of boys I worked with.[84]

In 1966, when the station began operating Bill Howard moved to Leiston to take up a job as a fitter after working at a coal-fired power station near Liverpool.[85] He found the working conditions at Sizewell 'a dream' in comparison and was well aware of how nuclear power had been pushed in the media as the clean, safe, energy of the future. Bill had decided on the move partly because Leiston had an active branch of the Communist Party, which he joined as soon as he started work at Sizewell. One of his first political campaigns in Leiston was to lead a successful rent strike against the CEGB with the discovery that manual workers living in council houses were paying far higher rents to the CEGB than their neighbours were to Leiston UDC.

Later disputes with CEGB over wages involved mass meetings on Sizewell beach, but Bill left the CEGB after six years, finding the link between power generation and nuclear weapon production increasingly difficult to reconcile with his politics and his conscience. He became involved with local politics, and one of the last editors of the *Leiston Leader*, and was elected to the UDC for many consecutive years, first as a Communist candidate and later as an Independent councillor. Bill's experiences, as an elected local councillor and as an objector in the enquiry for Sizewell B, had made him very aware of the role of the state in promoting nuclear power. His personal experience of political campaigning for his local community has brought him into close contact with the nexus of state secrecy, which surrounds the production of nuclear power. He gave evidence at the Sizewell B enquiry and recounted how his post was regularly opened before he gave evidence to support Dr. Alice Stewart and her research findings on the clusters of leukaemia deaths found in former nuclear power workers.[86] More recently he has publically criticised the role of the armed civil nuclear constabulary, a force he considered were outside local democratic control. With a remit to protect the station from terrorist attacks they patrol the dunes on Sizewell beach but also have jurisdiction within five kilometres of the power station, which includes the town.[87] He remains actively opposed to further development of nuclear and power and is part of the local campaign group organising against the building of Sizewell C.[88]

Nuclear construction: acceptance, anxiety and resistance

When the photographer, Libby Hall, moved to Leiston in 1962 to work as a housemistress at Summerhill School, she noted some resentment among the local male workforce towards the incomer workers at the power station.[89] Throughout the 1960s she, and other Summerhill staff members, drank at the Engineers Arms, a pub opposite the gates of the Garretts Works and frequented by the Garrett's workers, agricultural workers and a few American Air Force servicemen stationed at nearby U.S. airfields.[90] The Sizewell construction workers drank elsewhere, and a number of interviewees recounted that many of the 'hard, travelling men' drank excessively and recalled Saturday night brawls on the Leiston streets between American servicemen and Irish construction workers.

Throughout the period she lived in the town Libby did not remember much concern expressed about the safety of the station, but that people were more interested in the wonderful new technology of nuclear power. After Sizewell became fully operational in 1966, she and other Summerhill staff would regularly swim in the sea at Sizewell because the water was 'almost tropical', the sea warmed by the outflow from the power station. Local people were not enthusiastic about swimming there because, as Libby recalled, they believed the seawater was warmed from radioactivity leaking from the power station.[91] This was a belief held for many years and Sizewell beach, as late as 1988, was described in the *Companion Guide to East Anglia* as having seawater temperature raised by 10 degrees by the 'monstrous' nuclear power station.[92]

The stories of Boni Stones who grew up in Sizewell, including her childhood memories of practising emergency evacuation procedures, recount the cynical acceptance of the villagers to the industrialisation on their doorstep and new anxieties about nuclear accidents. The uneven pace of nuclear modernity is perfectly expressed in Figure 10. It was some time

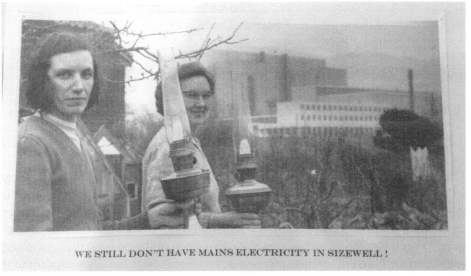

Figure 10. Newspaper cutting in album compiled to accompany exhibition of photographs, *Leiston 1966*, by Libby Hall, 27th August – 11th September 2016. Photographer unknown. Reproduced with permission Leiston Long Shop Museum.

after Sizewell A began operating and exporting power to London and the Southeast that electricity was installed for the villagers living in the shadow of the nuclear power station.

By the mid 1960s, most of the construction workforce had moved on, many following the work to the next Magnox power station in North Wales at Wylfa. Leiston adjusted to a decrease in population but suffered a further setback to its future prospects when the railway station was closed as part of Beeching's rationalisation. The East Suffolk line that looped between Leiston and Aldeburgh was closed in 1966 and all the tracks lifted apart from a five and half mile length stretching from the main Ipswich to Lowestoft line which ran through the southeast corner of Leiston directly to Sizewell A. This was retained as the route for spent nuclear fuel rods to be transported to Sellafield and remains intact and in use today.

Paxton Chadwick's early plea for increased communication was realised in the setting up of a liaison committee between CEGB staff at the power station and local community representatives, which met for many years. It was only in 1986 that community members of the committee discovered that the CEGB had failed to mention that radioactive waste was being stored at Sizewell, and had been from the very first year that Sizewell A began operating.[93] After Paxton's death in 1961 Lee Chadwick remained living on the heathland just over a mile behind the nuclear power station where she wrote *In Search of Heathland*, a meticulous study of a rapidly vanishing habitat, published in 1982.[94] A few years later she gave evidence at the Sizewell B enquiry against the siting of another power station on environmental grounds pointing out the irony of the recent designation of the area as heritage coast because of its outstanding natural beauty and the immediate plan to turn it into 'a nuclear park'.[95] She had anticipated the enquiry would be 'the focus for yet another form of popular struggle concerning the use of one-time open land'.[96] This land, deemed in the 1950s of poor agricultural value by both the CEGB and the then Town Clerk, was for Lee Chadwick and many others, environmentally rich and a precious remnant of open 'commens': unenclosed land which remained free for the use of local people. Viewed from the beach and surrounding heathland the group of buildings, which make up the station are unashamedly monstrous in scale. Sizewell A, now decommissioned and no longer producing electricity will stay in place until it is safe to be dismantled, now estimated to be in 2110.[97]

Conclusion: when 'a new world' came to Leiston

> It was a new world when Sizewell A started... It was a new world for the people here. It was a new world at the end of the day.
>
> Patrick O'Kane, building worker.

The construction of the first wave of nuclear power stations, the Magnox reactors, brought the 'atomic age' abruptly into the lives of rural communities. While the decision on siting the power station at Sizewell was not contested at the level of county politics, resistance and criticism were expressed locally through the pages of the Communist broadsheet, *The Leiston Leader*.[98] Meanwhile, the organisation of the construction of the power station, supposedly representing the fusion of scientific progress and modernity, was broadly equivalent to the way in which the canals and railways of the eighteenth and nineteenth centuries were built. Thousands of workers were bussed in or accommodated on site where long hours of hard physical labour in harsh conditions were the norm, and the strange new world of the atomic age materialized through the traditional, physical processes of production: pouring concrete, welding metal, drilling holes, and putting up scaffolding. The widespread media coverage of construction, and the employment of local men at Sizewell A, is likely to have contributed to a sense of 'ordinariness' in relation to the power station building site: a factor that enabled the local community to carry on their lives with the attendant risks of nuclear power.[99] Centralised decision-making, and Welsh's notion of the 'nuclear juggernaut', ensured that nuclear power generation, its waste and contamination, would affect generations of people living within the ambit of Sizewell. At a local level, the use of oral histories has enabled a range of voices to comment on the arrival of nuclear power. For some it gave a 'job for life', for others a temporary period of relative affluence, but the majority were left to live their lives in a town frozen by restrictions placed on its development, and exposed to the secrecy and surveillance surrounding the station.

Leiston, at the time of writing and unusually compared to other similarly sized towns close to the heritage coast of Suffolk, remains without an influx of second homeowners. It could be argued that the presence of the power station has saved it from the fate of gentrification, and in many ways it is a thriving community with library, schools, local shops and a small industrial estate of local businesses. Leiston's historical legacy of socialist activism survives and it is still a locus of resistance to the nuclear state. Power generation, including a new off-shore wind-farm, continues to provide local employment, while Sizewell A (see Figure 11) sits on the shoreline, adjacent to the huge dome of Sizewell B, as a monument to the labour of thousands of men and, for generations to come, a reminder of the nuclear state.

Figure 11. Sizewell A, March 2017. Author's photograph.

Notes

1. Conekin, Mort, and Waters, eds., *Moments of modernity*, 242.
2. Jolivette, "Representations of Atomic Power", 121.
3. Laucht, "Atoms for the people", 591–608.
4. See, Krige, *Atoms for Peace, Scientific Internationalism, and Scientific Intelligence*, 161–181; Alario and Freudenburg, "Atoms for Peace, Atoms for War", 219–240; and Laucht, "'Dawn— Or Dusk?' Britain's Picture Post Confronts Nuclear Energy," 117–148.
5. Hogg, *British nuclear culture*, 92.
6. Ibid.
7. Thompson, *The Voice of the Past*, 101.
8. The Leverhulme Trust funded project *Constructing Post-War Britain: building workers' stories 1950–70* was led by the author who was Principle Investigator together with Co-Applicant Linda Clarke, at the University of Westminster. The project archive can be viewed at http//: www.westminster.ac.uk/probe/projects/constructing-post-war-britain
9. East Anglia Economic planning Council, *East Anglia: A Study*, HMSO, 1968, 4; and Howard Newby's classic text, *The Deferential Worker*, 1977, London, Allen Lane, 186.
10. See chapter 3, Resisting the Juggernaut: opposition in the 1950s, in Welsh, *Mobilising Modernity*.
11. Ibid., 73–82.
12. Ibid., 81.
13. *Suffolk's Defended Shore, Coastal Fortifications from the Air*, Cain Hegarty and Sarah Newsome, 2007, English Heritage, 77.
14. Ibid. p 86.
15. Gammon and Pedgrift, "The selection and investigation," 130–160.
16. Gammon, Mike (3 of 9). An Oral History of the Electricity Supply in the UK. Accessed March 9, 2017 http://sounds.bl.uk/Oral-history/Industry-water-steel-and-energy/021M-C1495X0025XX-0003V0.
17. Wynne, in *Rationality and Ritual. The Windscale Enquiry and Nuclear Decisions in Britain*, 1982, uses the term 'cosmologies' to describe a system of thought rooted social practice and belief and with intellectual frameworks which must be articulated without contradiction or doubt, pp. 12–13 and p. 19.
18. http://hansard.millbanksystems.com/commons/1955/mar/22/nuclear-explosions-genetic-effects, *Hansard* (1955), 'Nuclear explosions (genetic effects)', HMSO.
19. Marley and Fry, "Radiological hazards from an escape of fission products,".
20. Openshaw, "Nuclear power," 99–109.
21. Wynne, *Rationality and Ritual*, 20–21.
22. Gammon, Mike (3 of 9). An Oral History of the Electricity Supply in the UK.
23. Openshaw, "Nuclear power,"167.
24. David Gooderham interviewed by Daphne Yasodhara in, May and May, *From Flint Knappers to Atom Splitters*, 237. Openshaw reveals that the CEGB many years later expressed an interest in Orford Ness but that any application was embargoed until the Sizewell site was fully developed.
25. NA/*AB*/16/3825 Folder: CEGB Power Station, Sizewell.
26. Ibid.
27. Sones, *"The Mermaid's Tale"*, 28.
28. NA POWE 14/1406 min of a meeting held at the Ministry of Power, September 18th, 1958. Headquarters Committee on the Siting of Power Stations. Sizewell Nuclear Power Station. This was declassified in 1988, three years after the end of the Sizewell B Enquiry.
29. NA/*AB*/16/3825 min of a meeting held at Ministry of Power, 19 September 1958.
30. Welsh, *Mobilising Modernity*, 90.
31. See note 20 above.
32. Eastern Daily Press, February, 1959.

33. Set up by Richard Garrett (the great grandfather of Elizabeth Garrett Anderson) in 1778, in what was then a small agricultural village, the Garrett's works expanded over the nineteenth century as their steam-driven threshing machines were exported throughout Europe. R. A. Whitehead, 1964, *Garretts of Leiston*, London: Percival Marshall and Co. Ltd., 193 and see also Richard Webster, n.d., *Leiston: the sickle, the hammer and the progressive school*, www.suffolkcottage.net/**leiston**_garretts_summerhill.pdf downloaded April 2010.
34. A major setback to the financial viability of the firm occurred in 1918 when the contemporary equivalent of tens of millions of pounds invested in Russian Imperial bonds, which, after the Russian Revolution, were cancelled by the Central Committee of the Communist party.
35. These included Vivien Jackson (daughter of T. A. Jackson), A. L. Morton (author of *A People's History of England*), Richard Goodman, Cyril Eyre and Lee Bosence who later married Paxton Chadwick. See Saville's biography, *Paxton Chadwick. Artist and Communist 1903–1961*.
36. Suffolk Archives hold some copies of the *Leiston Leader*, at Ipswich Records Office, HD2272/309/162.
37. Chadwick, "Leiston Communists and the 1939 War", 14–21.
38. Ibid., 16.
39. Little, "Report back—Early Socialism in East Anglia".
40. Dictionary of Labour Biography, v9 p37.
41. NA/*AB*/16/3825 Folder: CEGB Power Station, Sizewell. Letter from Paxton Chadwick, Secretary of the Leiston branch of the Communist Party, to E.J. Turner, Secretary, CEGB and copy to Lord Mills, Minister of Power, 18 March 1959.
42. *The British Road to Socialism*, 1958, Communist Party of Great Britain, accessed from Marxist Internet Archive, March 08 2017, www.marxists.org/history/international/comintern/sections/britain/brs/1958/58.htm.
43. See note 41 above.
44. In 1958 *New Scientist* published an article stating that given the long-term effects of radiation, 'it is impossible to be sure of safety levels at this stage'. Quoted in Wynne, 1982, 23.
45. See Taylor, *The Fall and Rise of Nuclear Power in Britain*, 12.
46. NA/*AB*/16/3825 Folder: CEGB Power Station, Sizewell. Letter dated 27 April 1959 from H.V. Barnett, CEGB to the Secretary of the Leiston Branch of the Communist Party, copy to Leiston U.D.C.
47. NA/*AB*/16/3825 Folder: CEGB Power Station, Sizewell. Letter from CEGB, Winsley St. London W.1. to the Secretary of the Leiston branch of the Communist Party, 27 April 1959, signed H. V. Bartlett.
48. NA/*AB*/16/3825 Folder: CEGB Power Station, Sizewell. Letter from CEGB.
49. Friends of the Earth refused to take part seeing the building of Sizewell B, Britain's first PWR station, as a foregone conclusion. See.
50. See Section D, Chapter Five, The Communist Party of Great Britain, the Trade Unions and the Labour Party, in *The Defence of the Realm. The Authorized History of MI5*, 2009, London: Allen Lane, 400–419. Hennessey, *The Secret State*, 105, points out that Soviet intelligence also knew that King Street was bugged via Anthony Blunt's presence in MI5.
51. Hennessey, *The Secret State*, 100.
52. *The Times*, April 5th, 6.
53. Ipswich Public Records Office, HD 2272/161/113 Communist Party leaflet for local election, Lee Chadwick and Daphne Oliver, no date.
54. NA/*AB*/16/3825 Folder: CEGB Power Station, Sizewell, letter dated March 6th, 1959, from A. Cooper, Manor Farm, Framlingham.
55. *Leiston Leader*, (September/October 1960), Ipswich Public Records Office, HD 2272/161/ 113.
56. *Leiston and District Plan, Factual Survey and Outline Plan*, 1961, T.B. Oxenbury, County Planning Officer, County Hall, Ipswich. Copy held at Leiston Long Shop Museum.
57. Ibid. para 36 The nuclear power station.
58. See note 29 above.

59. These deliberations involving meetings, letters, visits from representatives of the Ministry of Power to Leiston and threatened delegations from Leiston UDC to the MHLG in order to speed up the decision process, are recorded in the minutes of Leiston UDC and held in the Town Clerk's office in Leiston.
60. The Leiston/Aldeburgh Development Plan. Amendment Report. T. B. Oxenbury County Planning Officer, June 1962, East Suffolk County Council.
61. Leiston UDC, Minutes of the Meeting held on January13th, 1962.
62. The Leiston/Aldeburgh Development Plan. Amendment Report. T. B. Oxenbury County Planning Officer, June 1962, East Suffolk County Council. Pt. 4.
63. The Magnox program has been described and analysed by many commentators, the following titles cover policy, technical, economic and social aspects: Walker, "The Road to Sizewell," 44–50; Williams, *The Nuclear Power Decisions*; Steward and Wield, "Science Planning and the State"; Wearne and Bird, "UK Experience of Consortia Engineering for Nuclear Power Stations"; Hannah, *Engineers, Managers, and Politicians*; and Green, "The Cost of Nuclear Power," 513–524.
64. Cowley, *The Men Who Built Britain: A History of Irish Labour in British Construction*; and Sykes, "Navvies: Their Social Relations," 157–172.
65. See, Wall, "It was a new world: building Sizewell a nuclear power station,".
66. Author interview with Patrick O'Kane, Leiston, 3 March 2011.
67. Ibid.
68. Ibid.
69. Trevor Branton, in a talk to the East Anglian branch of the IEE in great Yarmouth on March 10 2011, recounted that local people told him that ten years after the tunnels were finished none of the men who worked on them were still alive due to them short-cutting the de-compression process.
70. Author interview with Pat Cable, Aldeburgh.
71. Ibid.
72. Ibid.
73. Ipswich Records Office, 1176/2/2/19/662, *The Lowestoft Journal*, 5 April 1961, through to views inside the finished reactor in 1967.
74. *The Times*, 21 September 1961, 20.
75. Leiston UDC, Minutes of the Meeting held on July 13th, 1961.
76. Author interview with John Mittel.
77. Ibid.
78. Ibid.
79. Author interview with Ian Roberts, Kesgrave, 15th September, Suffolk, 2011.
80. Author interview with John Mittel, October 12th, Kesgrave, Suffolk, 2011.
81. Author interview with Jim Ward, Lowestoft, 13th September, 2011.
82. Ibid.
83. Author interview with Dick Nettlingham, Leiston, May 2011.
84. Author interview with Bill Howard, Leiston, February, 2011.
85. See, Greene, *The Woman Who Knew Too Much*.
86. See *East Anglian Daily Times*; http://www.eadt.co.uk/news/leiston-concern-over-nuclear-police-responding-to-incidents-1-823471 first accessed 10 October 2016.
87. Together Against Sizewell C (TASC) campaign literature can be found on their website: http://tasizewellc.org.uk/.
88. Author interview with Libby Hall, Hackney, London, March 2017.
89. Libby Hall's photographs of Leiston and drinkers at the Engineers Arms were exhibited at PhotoEast Festival and later in Leiston at the Long Shop Museum, in August 2016.
90. See note 89 above.
91. *The Companion Guide to East Anglia*, 1988, John Seymour, Collins, 37.
92. Ipswich Records Office, Newspaper Cuttings on Sizewell A. *Ipswich Star* 26th March, 1986. It was understood that spent fuel rods were being transported to Sellafield for re-processing, but Sizewell staff were stripping the fins from the rods in order to fit more in to the

transporting canisters. The radioactive fins and other low-level waste was stored on site in water-filled vessels enclosed in thick concrete.
93. Chadwick, *In Search of Heathland*.
94. She argued passionately against further destruction of the unique habitat formed by the windswept, grass duneland above the shoreline. See *The Guardian*, 13th January, 1983.
95. Ibid., 66.
96. https://magnoxsites.com/wp-content/uploads/2014/03/Sizewell-A-Lifetime-Plan.pdf Accessed 11 August 2017.
97. Jonathan Hogg identified these characteristics of nuclear culture in the 1950s 'defined by the limits of democracy'. See Hogg, 2016, 82.
98. East Anglian Daily Times, "*Never talk to a Mermaid*", Saturday, 19 July 2010.
99. Parkhill, Pidgeon, Henwood, Simmons, and Venables, "From the familiar to the extraordinary," 39–58.

Acknowledgements

I am very grateful to all those who talked at length of their experiences of Leiston and Sizewell in the 1960s and allowed their testimony to be reproduced here. Thanks also to Paul Chandler and the staff and volunteers of the Leiston Long Shop Museum, to Boni Sones for her help with the photograph, to Bill Howard, the staff at Ipswich Records Office and the Town Clerk and Secretary of Leiston Town Council as well as to Charlie McGuire, Research Fellow on the Leverhulme funded project. This paper could not have been written without your help.

Disclosure statement

No potential conflict of interest was reported by the author.

Bibliography

Alario, M. V., and W. R. Freudenburg. "Atoms for Peace, Atoms for War: Probing the Paradoxes of Modernity." *Sociological Inquiry* 77 (2007): 219–240. doi:10.1111/soin.2007.77.issue-2.
Burn, D. *Nuclear Power and the Energy Crisis*. London: Macmillan, 1978.
Chadwick, Lee. "Leiston Communists and the 1939 War: A Grassroots View." *Socialist History Journal* no. 19, (May 1992): 14–21.
Chadwick, Lee, *In Search of Heathland*. Durham: Dobson Books Ltd, 1982.
Conekin, B., Mort, F., and Waters, C., eds. *Moments of Modernity: Reconstructing Britain 1945–1964*. London: Rivers Oram, 1999, 242
Cowley, U. *The Men Who Built Britain: A History of Irish Labour in British Construction*, Dublin: Wolfhound Press, 1998.

Edgerton, D. "The 'White Heat' Revisited: The British Government and Technology in the 1960s." *Twentieth Century British History* 7, no. 1 (1996): 53–82. doi:10.1093/tcbh/7.1.53.
Edgerton, D. *Warfare State: Britain, 1920–1970*. Cambridge: Cambridge University Press, 2006.
Foley, G. *The Energy Question*. Harmondsworth: Penguin Books, 1982.
Gammon, K. M., and G. F. Pedgrift. The Selection and Investigation of Potential Nuclear Power Station Sites in Suffolk, *Proceedings of the Institute of Civil Engineers*, 21, Session 1961–2, Jan. 130–160, 1961.
Glasson, J. "Better Monitoring for Better Impact Management: The Local Socio-Economic Impacts of Constructing Sizewell B Nuclear Power Station." *Impact Assessment and Project Appraisal* 23, no. 3 (2005): 215–226. doi:10.3152/147154605781765535.
Glasson, J., and A. Chadwick. "Auditing the Socio-Economic Impacts of a Major Construction Project: The Case of Sizewell B Nuclear Power Station." *Journal of Environmental Planning and Management* 42, no. 6 (1999): 811–836. doi:10.1080/09640569910849.
Gowing, M. *Independence and Deterrence. Britain and Atomic Energy, 1945–52*. Volume 1: Policy Making (assisted by Lorna Arnold). London: Macmillan, 1974.
Green, R. "The Cost of Nuclear Power Compared with Alternatives to the Magnox Programme." *Oxford Economic Papers, New Series* 47, no. 30 (1995): 513–524. doi:10.1093/oxfordjournals.oep.a042185.
Greene, Gayle. *The Woman Who Knew Too Much*, Revised Ed.: Alice Stewart and the Secrets of Radiation. University of Michigan Press, Ann Arbor: University of Michigan Press, 2017.
Hecht, G. *The Radiance of France: Nuclear Power and National Identity after World War II*. Cambridge Mass: MIT Press, 1998.
Hogg, J. *British Nuclear Culture: Official and Unofficial Narratives in the Long 20th Century*. London: Bloomsbury Publishing, 2016.
Hogg, Jonathan. *British Nuclear Culture: Official and Unofficial Narratives in the Long 20th Century*. Bloomsbury Publishing, 2016, 92
Hannah, L. *Engineers, Managers, and Politicians: The First Fifteen Years of Nationalised Electricity Supply*, London: Macmillan, 1982
Hennessey, Peter. *The Secret State. Preparing for the Worst 1945–2010*. London: Penguin, 2010, 105.
Jolivette, Catherine. "Representations of Atomic Power at the Festival of Britain." In *British Art in the Nuclear Age*, edited by C. Jolivette, 121. Routledge, 2017.
Krige, J. *Atoms for Peace, Scientific Internationalism, and Scientific IntelligenceAuthor(s): Osiris*. 2nd Series, 21, 161–181. Global Power Knowledge: Science and Technology in International Affairs, Chicago: University of Chicago Press, 2006.
Laucht, C. "Atoms for the People: The Atomic Scientists' Association, the British state and Nuclear Education in the Atom Train exhibition, 1947–1948." *The British Journal for the History of Science* 45, no. 4 (2012): 591–608.
Laucht, Christoph. "'Dawn—Or Dusk?' Britain's Picture Post Confronts Nuclear Energy." In van Lente, Dick, (Ed.) *The Nuclear Age in Popular Media*, 117–148. New York: Palgrave Macmillan, 2012.
Leader, L. "Suffolk's Little Moscow," 1981. downloaded March 2011, http://country-standard.blogspot.com/search/label/leiston
Little, Bob. "Report back - Early Socialism in East Anglia," *History Workshop Journal*, 1982. hwj.oxfordjournals.org/content/13/1/180.full.pdf
May, D. Y., and K. May. *From Flint Knappers to Atom Splitters; A History of Leiston-cum-Sizewell*. Leiston: Quickthorn Books, 2001.
Marley, W. G., and T. M. Fry. "Radiological Hazards from an Escape of Fission Products and the Implications in Power Reactor Location," *Proceedings of the International Conference on the Peaceful Uses of Atomic Energy*, Geneva, United Nations, 1955.
Ministry of Fuel and Power A Programme of Nuclear Power, Cmd 9389, HMSO. Great Britain. Privy Council. ; Great Britain. Ministry of Fuel and Power. London : H.M.S.O., 1955.
Nehring, H., and C. War. "Apocalypse and Peaceful Atoms, Interpretations of Nuclear Energy in the British and West German Anti-Nuclear Weapons Movements, 1955–1964." *Historical Social Research* 29, no. 3 (2004): 150–170.

Parkhill, K. A., N. F. Pidgeon, K. L. Henwood, P. Simmons, and D. Venables. From the Familiar to the Extraordinary: Local Residents' Perceptions of Risk When Living with Nuclear Power in the UK. *Transactions of the Institute of British Geographers* 35, no. 1, 2010, 39–58.

Saville, J. *Paxton Chadwick. Artist and Communist 1903–1961*. Leiston: Leiston Leader, 1993.

Sones, B. *The Mermaid's Tale. A Portrait of Suffolk*, 2009 http//:www.pradio.co.uk.

Steward, F., and D. Wield. "Science Planning and the State." In *State and Society in Contemporary Britain*, edited by G. McLennon, D. Held, and S. Hall. Cambridge: Polity Press, 1984.

Sykes, A. J. M. "Navvies: Their Social Relations." *Sociology* 3, no. 2 (1969): 157–172.

Thompson, Paul. The Voice of the Past, 3rd edn, Oxford: OUP, 2000, 101.

Taylor, Simon. *The Fall and Rise of Nuclear Power in Britain*. Cambridge: UIT, 2016 12.

Walker, J. "The Road to Sizewell." *Contemporary British History* 1, no. 3 (1987): 44–50.

Wall, Christine, et. al. "*It was a new world: building Sizewell a nuclear power station*," University of Westminster. 2012. It can be downloaded here http//:www.westminster.ac.uk/probe/projects/constructing-post-war-britain/sizewell

Wearne, S. H., and R. H. Bird, *UK Experience of Consortia Engineering for Nuclear Power Stations*, School of Mechanical, Aerospace & Civil Engineering, University of Manchester, Dalton Nuclear Institute, 2009. downloaded April 2011. http://www.dalton.manchester.ac.uk/about-us/reports/consortia-engineering/

Webster, R. n.d. www.suffolkcottage.net/**leiston**_garretts_summerhill.pdf

Welsh, I. *Mobilising Modernity: The Nuclear Moment*. Routledge, 2003.

Williams, R. *The Nuclear Power Decisions. British Policies 1953–78*. London: Croom Helm, 1980.

Wynne, B. *Rationality and Ritual. Participation and Exclusion in Nuclear Decision-Making*. London: Earthscan, 2011.

Reports and Inquiries

Power stations. Report of the Committee of Inquiry into Delays in the Commissioning CEGB Power Stations. Cmnd.3960. 'The Wilson Report', London: HMSO1969.

Large Industrial Sites, Report, 1970, National Economic Development Office.

Britain, West Africa and 'The new nuclear imperialism': decolonisation and development during French tests

Christopher Robert Hill

ABSTRACT
This article explores how the Macmillan government managed opposition to French nuclear tests at the end of empire in West Africa and prior to its first application to join the European Economic Community in 1961. It focuses in particular on the use of scientific aid and development as a means by which West African states could be re-assured and won over to British diplomacy. This was calculated to appeal to ideas of modernity on the eve of Nigerian and Sierra Leonean independence, yet also reflected forms of imperial knowledge and power that can be traced back to the nineteenth century.

The dawn of independence for British colonies in West Africa coincided with what can be regarded as the dawn of the nuclear age on the African continent, signified by the detonation of 17 atomic devices by France in the Algerian Sahara between 1960 and 1966. These tests began in the midst of the Algerian War for Independence in February 1960 and extended 4 years beyond its conclusion, as permitted by a secret provision of the Évian Accords signed by France and the Provisional Government of the Algerian Republic in 1962. At the same time that Ghanaians, Nigerians and Sierra Leoneans established and imagined their futures as independent people, they also lived in fear of radioactive fallout from the tests and what Africans and international activists described as ' the new nuclear imperialism'—' an imperialism more menacing than anything you have ever known', as a propaganda leaflet circulated by the activists in four languages put it.[1] When Sierra Leone prepared for Independence Day celebrations in April 1961, for example, it was plagued by the prospect of a French test, so much so that Harold Macmillan felt it necessary to write a letter of warning to President Charles de Gaulle. 'A further nuclear test taking place during [the celebrations]', he claimed, 'might … precipitate some action hostile to both your country and mine'.[2]

The methods that the Macmillan government employed to overcome dissent against French nuclear tests in West African states are highly revealing for how the position of Britain in the world was being re-negotiated in the late 1950s and early 1960s. These methods and this re-negotiation were rooted in an imperialism not so far removed from that of the nineteenth century, yet were being used to further a diplomatic strategy that espoused a shift away from empire and towards membership of the European Economic

Community (EEC). The imperialism in question drew on scientific knowledge and technology as a form of cultural and political power, which in the context of decolonisation and independence was highly persuasive. Through introductions to nuclear sciences and technologies and the wielding of imperial expertise, it will be argued, the Macmillan government was able to subordinate Nigeria and Sierra Leone to its diplomatic agenda, while at the same time supporting the French right to test in the United Nations (UN) ahead of their first application to join the EEC. The exception to this argument is post-colonial Ghana, which refused to accept what its prime minister Kwame Nkrumah described as 'scientific sweeteners' and drew upon sources of anti-colonial expertise to repudiate the scientific and technological authority of the British.[3] These narratives of science and technology, entangled in Cold War and colonial politics, came to a head in a dispute over the radioactive fallout from the French tests and the turn of Ghana towards the Soviet Union as it carried out its own investigations into nuclear power.[4]

In this article, therefore, 'the new nuclear imperialism' is seen not so much as a propagandistic slogan as a compelling framework by which British and French power can be interpreted at the end of empire. An attempt will be made in the opening section to define this imperialism with more precision, distinguishing it from the techno-politics of nuclear powers without imperial histories and viewing it in relation to the imperial sciences of the nineteenth century.[5] Through these perspectives, 'the new nuclear imperialism' can be seen as a product of what environmental historians have called the 'political ecology' of late empire, whereby the natural assets of less powerful territories were exploited by foreign actors.[6] The characteristics and functions of nuclear imperialism will then be examined in the context of West Africa and Anglo-French relations, referring in particular to aid and development, information services and universities as channels through which West African concerns about radiation were counteracted and managed. The article concludes with an assessment of investigations into nuclear energy and the role of Ghana as an epicentre of anti-colonial networks of expertise. In this way, the article locates the nuclear age 'within the history and practice of science' of West Africa, to borrow from Timothy Mitchell, 'not outside it' as if that science had already been fully formed in the west and was merely transplanted.[7]

Nuclear imperialism

By exploring British and French nuclear energy and weapons programmes within the framework of imperialism, it is necessary from the outset to re-scale—to depart from histories concerned with the scientists and research centres of the metropole and to explore ones concerned with the environmental and human sacrifices of the periphery. In relation to Britain, this framework brings into view a range of under-researched subjects—from the illegal mining of uranium in Namibia to the suffering of aboriginals and islanders in Australian and Pacific tests—and each of these highlights the global entanglements of a project that was driven by ideas of British importance in the world.[8] As Gabrielle Hecht put it in her research on the global uranium trade, an approach that broadens the field of nuclear history blurs the very notion of what it means to 'be' nuclear. Gabon, Niger and Namibia may have recently supplied as much as one-fifth of enriched uranium to Europe, Japan and the US, for example, but nowhere did official reports designate them as having 'nuclear activities'.[9]

This ambiguity of 'being nuclear' can be applied to the effects as well as the production of nuclear technologies. The science of what constitutes radioactive contamination or exposure is actively contested in Anglo- and Francophone worlds to this day. Australian aboriginals or French Polynesians were not 'nuclear victims' according to British and French courts and governments, since they did not possess sufficient evidence to correlate their illnesses to fallout from the tests.[10] As Britain and France employed a range of strategies to avoid compensation for the damage caused by the tests, it has often fallen upon their former colonies and dominions to foot the bill. The British government, conscious of wider liability for tests in Australia and the Pacific, was in fact the last of the Commonwealth states to create a reparations scheme for ex-servicemen who took part in the tests, 2 months after Fiji in March 2015.[11] These disagreements over compensation stem from the same conflicts of expertise and power that surrounded testing in the first place: in particular over the link between radioactive fallout and the proliferation of cancers among indigenous peoples and veterans. In the same way as compensation claims for colonial crimes has been one legacy of imperialism, compensation claims for the effects of nuclear tests has been another. In this way, the nuclear age very much had its own 'reparatory history', as yet largely unwritten.

The designation of what is 'nuclear' or what or who has been 'irradiated' has therefore been based on a series of hierarchic values about environmental and human worth. These values were tied to ideas of progress and power relations that derive not only from imperialism, but also from what can be called the 'techno-political' state. After all, it was not only Britain and France who exploited far-away lands and people to further their nuclear ambitions. At the review conference of the Non-Proliferation Treaty in the UN in 2015, a representative from the Marshall Islands elaborated on the fate of these territories while under UN trusteeship. In a period spanning 12 years, the US carried out 67 tests in the Islands, with a combined explosive yield that equated to 1.6 Hiroshima bombs every day.[12] Following the first H-bomb test in 1954, the US returned the people of Rongelap to their atoll, heavily contaminated by unexpected levels of fallout. 'It would be very interesting to go back and get ... environmental data ... when people live in a contaminated environment', claimed one scientist. 'While it is true that these people do not live, I would say, the way Westerners do, civilised people, it is nevertheless also true that they are more like us than mice'.[13] Since the US Department of Energy began to declassify documents on human radiation experiments over 20 years ago, it has become clear that ethical abuses were endemic.[14] Bruno Barrillot, a French anti-nuclear campaigner, has claimed that these documents expose a picture of scientific transgression not dissimilar to that revealed by the Nuremberg Trials in Nazi Germany.[15]

If the designation of what was nuclear has been shaped by forms of power embedded in imperialism and the techno-political state, it was legitimised by pretences to scientific objectivity. It was only possible for Britain, France and the US to test their weapons overseas, in other words, by making claims about radiation and safety that were rooted in authority and expertise. The reliability of these claims was in practice incredibly suspect. As the US mistakenly anticipated that hydrogen and atomic bombs differ for the most part by heat and blast rather than by radiation, for example, their first

H-bomb test in 1954 ended up irradiating a Japanese fishing boat—the unfortunately named *Lucky Dragon*—beyond the exclusion zone.[16] For France, outside the agreements that facilitated information sharing between the US and the UK, additional risks also had to be taken. When the French embarked on underground testing in granite mountains in Algeria, they did not possess the engineering knowhow to render the site secure.[17] As a consequence, they blew off the top of a mountain, exposing dignitaries and soldiers to radioactive fallout in what became known as the Béryl incident.[18] In order to avoid a public controversy, the state broadcaster, *Radiodiffusion-Télévision Française*, simply recycled film footage taken from the first underground test, Agathe, in its news items.[19]

The scientific objectivity that seemed to legitimise testing overseas was shaken by the *Lucky Dragon* incident in particular. This event was highly influential in breaking a consensus within the scientific community and led to the formation of the Pugwash Conferences on Science and World Affairs as a rival forum of global expertise.[20] It exacerbated a dispute between scientists who believed in permissible thresholds of exposure and ones who believed that all increases in radiation have the potential to harm. While the majority of experts today endorse the latter position, the ambiguity created by this dispute has been exploited by what investigators and scholars of the Fukushima disaster have referred to as the 'nuclear village': a powerful coalition of scientists, investors, the media and politicians.[21] Ever since the Hiroshima and Nagasaki bombings, this coalition has in one form or another attempted to deny the harmful effects of nuclear power.[22] In the aftermath of the *Lucky Dragon* incident, for example, the Churchill government arranged for Joseph Rotblat, a physicist, to downplay fears about radiation from H-bombs on television. When he encountered evidence that H-bombs in fact emitted far more radiation than atomic ones, he was blacklisted by the government, excluded from the scientific establishment and denied a platform for his views.[23]

The scientific complexes and laboratories where ideas of progress were at their keenest and most motivated by power were also the places where conceptions of human worth could be at their most disparaging and racialised. In Britain and France, these ideas of progress—and the environmental and human costs they entailed—intersected with imperial experiences that distinguished them from one another and indeed the US.[24] For Britain, the role of nuclear power as a vanguard science and technology gave it a diplomatic utility that shared similarities with other discoveries and inventions in the imperial past. It could be used to further imperial and international agendas that were entrenched in traditional practices of colonial administration, especially as they pertained to political control and development.

The role of scientific knowledge as a form of power has been a recurring theme in the historiography of imperial Britain, from instrumentalists who have seen British modernisation as incompatible with colonial economies to post-colonial theorists who have seen British science as a hegemonic symbol for 'dominating, restructuring and having authority', to borrow Edward Said's well-known phrase.[25] Roy Macleod has argued that the New Imperialism of the late nineteenth century was fuelled and shaped by the natural sciences in particular, constituting a 'scientific imperialism' that emanated from institutions, networks and personnel in Cambridge, Edinburgh, London and Oxford.[26] The increasingly constructivist approaches that were being taken towards the governance of empire in the twentieth century also placed an emphasis on science, particularly in relation to welfare and development, leading in the late colonial period to a so-called 'technological turn' in colonial policy.[27] In the words of Michael Worboys, it was 'expected that science and scientists would be catalysts of development by discovering economic opportunities, making the tropical environment safe, solving technical problems in production, processing and distribution, directing and improving productivity and investment, and generally demystifying the tropics and their people'.[28]

It is in this context that the nuclear diplomacy of Britain in West Africa in the 1950s and 1960s can be meaningfully interpreted. The threat of French tests was negotiated by presenting knowledge of nuclear energy and weapons in terms linked to aid and development, a strategy that enabled Britain to retain control over decolonisation while at the same time furthering relations with France. As Jordanna Bailkin has demonstrated, the position of West Africa in colonial policies that were informed by science, technology and expertise was particularly prized. 'Independence in South Asia and federation in the West Indies cast their own shadows over life in Britain', Bailkin argued, 'but it was the fraught and urgent trajectory of African independence ... that drew most avid governmental attention. ... British investment in African development and Africa's perceived significance in the Cold War meant that their impact was disproportionate'.[29] Sir Hilton Poynton, Permanent Under-Secretary of State for the Colonies, underlined the importance of West Africa in correspondence about French tests with the Foreign and Commonwealth Office (FCO) in August 1959: relations between Britain and Nigeria had been 'one of the most encouraging features of our colonial policy', he claimed: 'a shining light in a naughty world of Mboyas, Bandas, *et hoc genus omne*'.[30]

Nuclear diplomacy and Britain in the world

The announcement in October 1958 that French tests were planned and likely to take place in the Algerian Sahara provoked a minor crisis for Britain, wedging it between the interests of Ghana, Nigeria and Sierra Leone on the one hand and France on the other.[31] This crisis continued to escalate until the late summer and autumn of 1959, in part due to the failure of the Macmillan government to commit to concerns on either side. When the foreign secretary, John Profumo, clarified in the House of Commons that he had merely 'passed on' Nigerian complaints about the tests to the French and had not supported them, the West African states were incensed.[32] Despite refusing to provide information about the precise location, timing and yield of the tests, the French were equally irritated by British fence-sitting, with French newspapers alleging that the Macmillan government was mounting opposition to the tests through the press. It is 'as if the British newspapers are playing to the beat of an invisible conductor', claimed *L'Information*. This aggravation was worsened by a lead article against the tests in *The Times*, described by the Gaullist *Combat* as 'virulent'. 'Here is *The Times* ... well-known to be of an official nature ... joining the pack', remarked *Le Figaro*.[33]

The response of the Macmillan government to this crisis provides an insight into how the role of Britain in the world was being re-negotiated at the time, seemingly offering a stark choice of whether to align with West African states and the Commonwealth or with France as a gatekeeper of the EEC. When Britain manoeuvred to support France against a resolution calling upon her to 'refrain' from the tests in the UN in November, it demonstrated that its strategic priorities were ultimately with the latter. In view of the importance that de Gaulle attached to nuclear weapons, their role in the process of European integration in the 1950s and 1960s has been somewhat neglected, as research by Gunnar Skogmar has highlighted.[34] Lord Gladwyn, a diplomat and Liberal peer, argued in a confidential essay drafted on the eve of Britain's first application to join the EEC that de Gaulle had a tendency 'to think in political terms and entirely disregard economics'. 'Should we be able to help him in the construction of his nuclear striking force', claimed Gladwyn, 'it is probable that a deal could be fixed up without further delay'.[35] The unwillingness of Britain to conceive of Europe as a nuclear-armed 'third force' between the US and Russia, however, may have been a factor in de Gaulle casting a veto over the British application, with France also withdrawing from the North Atlantic Treaty Organisation (NATO) in 1966.[36] 'NATO is preferably a word that should never be used in conversation with the General', remarked Gladwyn in his essay.[37]

Just as the French interpreted the British position on tests in the Sahara in relation to the EEC, the West African states did so in relation the Commonwealth and empire. In a debate on the tests in the Nigerian House of Representatives on 11 August, it was Jaja Wachuku, ambassador to the UN following Nigerian independence in October 1960, who stressed British responsibilities most forcibly. 'If no official support is given to … this country and to this motion [against French tests]', he claimed, 'then … the younger generation will reserve the right to opt away from the Commonwealth'. He was also cognisant of British interests in Europe, suggesting that a European bloc led by France and Britain would be disastrous. 'Are we going to allow France to destroy us?', he asked in response to shouts of 'no!'. The speech also linked British inaction over the tests to other colonial indiscretions, all of which seemed to expose the double-standards of a British justice system for which Wachuku had some admiration. He referred, for example, to the Devlin Commission, which despite finding that excessive force had been employed in colonial policing was largely rejected by the Macmillan government. 'If it were one British who had died', he proclaimed in relation to 11 deaths at the Hola Detention Camp in Kenya, 'the whole machinery of justice would have been adopted'.[38] By the end of summer in 1959, the position of Britain in West Africa was therefore highly unstable, with prospects for a Commonwealth undermined by French tests.

Nuclear science and technology in West Africa

The most effective means by which the Macmillan government could defuse tensions in West Africa was by demonstrating that their fears about radiation were misplaced and not grounded in scientific fact. Such a strategy built directly upon the imperialist function of Britain as an arbiter of knowledge and could be executed through channels of colonial administration, including aid and development, information services and West African universities. British interpretations of the dangers posed by radioactive fallout, however, were hindered by French secrecy and subverted by anti-colonial networks of expertise that revolved around the same infrastructures of knowledge that Britain had helped to develop. The official line—that French tests were taking further away from West African states than those of the Americans from Los Angeles or the British from Adelaide—was heavily contested by expatriate scientists based in the University of Ghana and University of Ibadan in Nigeria, both of which were established as colleges of the University of London in 1948.[39] If the tests were so safe, Ghanaians and Nigerians concluded, then France should conduct them on the outskirts of Paris.

In the period after the announcement of French tests, then, a rival set of claims about radiation were forming in Ghana and Nigeria, emerging out of the same centres of knowledge in which Britain had invested and linked to a worldwide shift in scientific opinion that had been stimulated by the *Lucky Dragon* incident. These rival claims were far more considerate of the interaction of radioactive fallout with environmental and meteorological conditions in the surrounding regions. In the view of scientists from Ibadan, for example, the dependence of Nigerians on cereal and vegetables rather than meat and dairy for their diet might make them more vulnerable to fallout from the tests.[40] In a similar manner, Professor Walker, Director of Meteorological Services in Ghana, drew attention to the potential for Saharan wind cycles to disperse the fallout over significant distances. The Harmattan, in particular, was described as a 'terrible wind', carrying 'Saharan dust a hundred miles to sea, not so much as a sandstorm, but as a mist or fog of dust as fine as flour filling the eyes, the lungs, the pores of the skin, the nose and throat'.[41] In a fact sheet designed to address African concerns, circulated before the UN debate in November, the French made a commitment to test 'in the period of no winds'. In private, however, British scientists acknowledged that the winds 'blow throughout the year', with Sir William Penney, chief adviser to the United Kingdom Atomic Energy Agency (UKAEA) claiming that the fact sheet did not offer much 'solid information'.[42]

Neither was the site of the first series of tests merely a barren desert, as the French and British maintained. On the contrary, the test site, not far away from Reggane in the Adrar province of south western Algeria, was home to a complex eco-system that depended on underground channels known as *foggaras*. In the words of Odette du Puigaudeau, a French ethnologist who had lived and researched in the Sahara, the test site was in fact a fertile valley irrigated by strings of oases and inhabited by 200,000 Arabs, Jews, Berbers and Africans. It was part of what was known as the 'date super-highway' because of the abundance of date trees that lined the thoroughfare between Reggane and Colomb Bechar. As Puigaudeau struggled to publish the article in France, she sent it to British pacifists in the Direct Action Committee against Nuclear War, a non-violent anti-nuclear group who were organising an international campaign against the tests. The article was used by *The Observer*'s foreign correspondent, William Millinship, and printed at length alongside a map in *Reynold's News*, a radical weekly with pacifist sympathies. *The Observer* news clipping was subsequently circulated and referred to in the Nigerian House of Representatives in August.[43]

Yet not all the concerns that West Africans had about radiation were rooted in scientific knowledge and research: these were articulated by only a small and influential minority. For the majority, radioactive fallout was an emotional subject that tended to succumb to hysteria and political manipulation. The debates in the Nigerian House of Representatives provide an exemplar of the sorts of sensationalism that the tests provoked, with one politician claiming that a French H-bomb test would 'almost wipe out the 32 million people of this country'.[44] Such fears derived in part from Communist propaganda from the late 1940s, disseminated through international networks by the World Peace Council.[45] It was due to the efficacy of this propaganda that police forces monitored West Africans who were 'known to receive regular supplies of Communist literature' so closely in the period prior to the first test.[46] The British Commonwealth Office was also increasingly perturbed at the tendency of West Africans to ascribe natural disasters to nuclear testing. A report described how in certain areas of Nigeria 'the 1918 influenza epidemic is attributed to the use of gas in the First World War and the more recent Asian flu to ... tests ... by Western powers'. 'There are signs', warned a separate report about social unrest in Northern Nigeria, 'that people may soon start to associate natural phenomena, especially those with adverse effects such as a long drought or excessive rain, with the test. The eclipse of the sun on 2 October ... total in North Eastern Bornu, may be associated with the test by those who seek an explanation for it'.[47]

In the context of these fears and scientific misinformation, the Macmillan government was able to advance its own position, utilising its superior expertise and resources to demonstrate how rival claims about radiation were erroneous. As concerns about radioactive fallout reached their height in the late summer of 1959, the FCO drew upon the British Broadcasting Corporation (BBC) and information services to confront the spread of moral panics and misguided science head on. In the same period, a French official described to the foreign office how he had been pleased to hear the BBC Arabic service putting across the French position 'perfectly'. 'The French would like to see more ... [of this] coming from the BBC and other British sources', remarked one FCO official.[48] The British propaganda was especially effective in territories under colonial rule, where the FCO continued to exercise a degree of control over the press and radio. Patrick Dean, the Permanent Representative of the United Kingdom (UK) to the UN, highlighted 'the striking influence of radio in areas where newspapers and books are in short supply and the illiteracy rate is high'.[49]

It was through radio that the Macmillan government were able to challenge ideas about scientific knowledge in relation to radioactive fallout. Colin Maclaren, a colonial administrator who was involved in the Nigerian Broadcasting Corporation, believed that a lot of the fear among Nigerians was 'attributable' to the statement made by the scientists from Ibadan.[50] In a broadcast on *Topic for Today*, a popular current affairs programme airing on 31 July, he argued that 'scientists, because they know a good deal about one particular thing, ... suppose that this gives them some sort of qualification to pronounce in other subjects, political subjects [such as radioactive fallout] for instance'. After referring to tests conducted by the US, Russia and Britain, he concluded that 'there are not many places in the world where conditions suitable for atomic testing exist. Presumably the Sahara desert ... is one of them'.[51]

This propaganda offensive was combined with an attempt to court and re-assure Nigerian ministers by inviting them to meet senior politicians and scientists in Britain in September; an expenses-paid trip that led to the donation of air sampling equipment and the establishment of monitoring stations across Nigeria, Sierra Leone and the Gambia. In a meeting on the 17 September, Macmillan made it clear that 'Her Majesty's Government were ready to do all they could to help Nigeria with technical information on the effects of nuclear explosions', which included a visit to the Atomic Energy Research Establishment (AERE) at Harwell, where the Nigerians directed questions to William Penney and his team. The following day it was agreed that a Joint UK–Nigerian Scientific Committee would be established to monitor fallout from the tests, modelled on a safety committee established between the UK and Australia during British tests.[52] By the end of the trip, the Nigerian prime minister, Abubakar Balewa, was 'convinced' alongside his fellow ministers 'that there would be no danger' from the tests.[53]

The role of Britain as scientific benefactor and patron might have eased concerns in Nigeria, Sierra Leone and the Gambia, all of which had sought representation against the French, but it failed to do the same in independent Ghana. For Nkrumah, the tests offered a prime opportunity by which Africa could be united, with Ghana in the vanguard of a Pan-African politics. He was passionate about nuclear disarmament, establishing the Ghana Council for Nuclear Disarmament towards the end of 1959, offering residence to international activists seeking to prevent the tests and hosting a Positive Action Conference on Peace and Security in April 1960 after the first test. On the back wall to the platform of this conference were the words 'no nuclear imperialism'. When Nkrumah learnt that the Nigerians had accepted air sampling equipment from the British, he was outraged. The *Ghana Times*, founded by Nkrumah upon Ghanaian independence, went so far as to accuse Balewa of succumbing to 'lollipops' under a heading that proclaimed 'A Betrayal of Africa'.[54]

At the same time that Nkrumah rallied against the nuclear imperialism of the British and French, he also pursued the Ghanaian interest in nuclear energy. This interest went back as far as September 1951, when the Ghanaians first approached the UKAEA about the possibility of being given an experimental reactor.[55] As the Ghanaians became disenchanted with British testing, however, they began to explore the possibility of technical assistance from Canada. In October 1959, a month after the meeting between the British and the Nigerians, the Ghanaian Permanent Secretary for the Ministry of Defence, Annan, and a British physicist from the University of Ghana, Professor Wright, visited Canada, where they also secured air sampling equipment and technical support.[56] Through the Canadians, Nkrumah was able to engage Ghana in cutting-edge research and science without having to collaborate with its former colonial master or one of the so-called 'bomb club'.

When relations between Canada and Ghana broke down a year later over the Canadian refusal to donate an experimental reactor, it was to the Soviet Union that Nkrumah turned. The move away from Canada—a power with which Britain corresponded regularly on matters of nuclear diplomacy—represented a significant setback for the British.[57] In an effort to prevent the Soviet Union from gaining a foothold in West Africa, the British Board of Trade and UKAEA even contemplated offering Ghana an experimental reactor of their own. In an inter-departmental meeting among British officials in late 1960, however, this transaction was deemed unwise. The British government would not be able to match the Russian terms of credit, did not want to stoke competition over nuclear-related aid and development and did not want to encourage similar requests from other West African countries. Despite this reluctance, British officials did ask representatives of Hawker Siddeley, a manufacturing company that had recently taken over British Nuclear Engineering, to explore the possibility of selling a reactor to the Ghanaians. The prospects of business between Hawker Siddeley and the Ghanaians were ruled out by negotiations between Ghana and the Soviet Union, who agreed to Cooperation in the Utilisation of Atomic Energy in February 1961.[58]

While the Hawker Siddeley initiative did not come to fruition, it begs wider questions about the relationship between the British state, expatriate scientists and private companies at the end of empire. In particular, it is tempting to wonder how far there was a privatisation of power, as well as how far the British state sought to create the conditions in which British companies could continue to wield economic and scientific influence. Robert L. Tignor, in his study into the influence of organised business over the end of empire in Kenya and Nigeria, has argued that 'European-based firms ... planted themselves firmly in the African economic landscape'. These firms 'were accustomed to being consulted on all matters, political as well as economic, and were determined to influence the outcome of decolonisation'.[59]

The first French test

In entering into a scientific partnership with the Nigerians and establishing monitoring stations across West Africa, the Macmillan government sought not only to entice or re-assure states on the brink of independence with high-profile knowledge or technology, it also sought to exercise control over how fallout from French tests was interpreted. To this end, it ensured that the Joint UK–Nigerian Scientific Committee was composed of scientists who 'had the confidence of [the AERE at] Harwell'.[60] In contrast, the credentials of British scientists in independent Ghana, now under the service of Nkrumah rather than Harwell, were subject to increasing criticism from the scientific establishment in Britain. Professor Walker, the meteorologist who had drawn attention to the dangers posed by Saharan winds, was the target of particular ridicule: 'I cannot estimate his standing as a meteorologist', claimed one FCO official in correspondence, 'but, applying the maxim that good wine needs no bush, it may be relevant to observe that he has a large handlebar moustache'.[61] To break away from the imperial line on radioactive fallout, it seemed, was also to risk personal and professional credibility.

In the event of 'Blue Jerboa', the first French test on 13 February 1960, these disagreements over radiation intensified, as fallout from the test was much higher than anticipated. A report published in April by the Joint UK–Nigerian Scientific Committee described how 'abnormal wind currents resulted in the deposition in Nigeria of measurable quantities of radioactive debris within two days of it being detonated'. As British scientists in this period tended to interpret radiation in terms of permissible thresholds, however, the report 'concluded that the amount of fallout in Nigeria was far below that likely to cause harm'. Another notable conclusion—that repeated tests by the French could have harmful effects—did not make it into the final report.[62] If the Joint Committee tended to understate the danger posed by the first test, then the British scientists in Ghana tended to overstate it—their findings forming the basis of scare stories about 'death dust' in the Nkrumah press.[63] J.A.T. Dawson, who led the Joint Committee and travelled to Ghana after the first test as part of a scientific delegation, believed that readings of these scientists, 'though not falsifying facts', would be presented in the form 'most likely to cause alarm'.[64] How fallout from the first test was interpreted was inextricably linked to the politics of decolonisation and development.

In maps of fallout from the first test, recently de-classified by the French Ministry of Defence, it seems that African concerns about radiation have been vindicated. A map de-classified in 2013, for example, demonstrated that abnormal levels of radiation could be detected in north-east Nigeria, over 2000 km away, a day after the test. The health risk posed by this radiation may have been negligible, but it had the potential to escalate through repeated incidents. Another map, de-classified in 2007 for the purposes of compensation, suggests that fallout closer to the test site was dangerous indeed. The map shows an increase in surface radiation levels of over 50 millisieverts, stretching 220 km south-east from the site of the test towards the border with Libya and Niger.[65] According to the World Nuclear Association, an organisation that serves to promote the interests of the nuclear industry, an increase of this proportion is sufficient to establish a causal link with cancer.[66] On the fiftieth anniversary of the first test in February 2010, it was alleged at an international conference in Algiers that widespread illnesses had been caused by the tests and had gone undocumented. The site near Reggane remains so contaminated, however, that a full investigation into the environmental and human impact of the tests has been unable to take place.[67]

Conclusion

The scientific aid and development that the Macmillan government offered to West African states during French tests was largely successful in stabilising the region, ensuring that systems of colonial patronage could survive the process of decolonisation. In the context of the tests, these systems of patronage served to perpetuate forms of knowledge that were largely conducive to the interests of Britain and inimical to those of West Africa. It is widely agreed today that a fundamental premise of this knowledge—that radiation is only harmful when it reaches a given threshold—was erroneous and misconceived. Ironically, on the verge of their independence, the Nigerians submitted to a partnership over nuclear energy and technology that was characteristic of scientific imperialism and largely one-sided in favour of the British. The lure of such a forward-facing field of science seemed to disguise the backward-facing diplomacy and politics on which is introduction depended. Only independent Ghana shunned British patronage and the scientific logic it engendered. The unwillingness of the British to oppose the French tests seemed to be a major reason behind Nkrumah's shift towards Russia. As a result of his agreement with the Soviet Union, the Ghanaian leader was able to inaugurate the Ghana Nuclear Reactor Project in November 1964, an initiative that was abandoned when he was ousted by a military coup less than 2 years later.[68]

Notes

1. Bennett, *Radical Pacifism*, 234; and See: Allman, "Nuclear Imperialism and the Pan-African Struggle for Peace and Freedom", 83–102.
2. PREM 11/4242, Harold Macmillan to Charles de Gaulle, no date.
3. CO 968/701, Ghana news agency transcript, no date.
4. On 'entangled' Cold War and imperial histories; and see: Hecht (ed.), *Entangled Geographies*.
5. Hodge, "Science and Empire", 3–29.
6. Ross, *Ecology and Power*, 2.
7. Mitchell, *Rule of Experts*, 7–8.
8. On Namibia, see: Hecht, *Being Nuclear*, 147–170; on aboriginals: Australia, *The Report of the Royal Commission into British Nuclear Tests in Australia*, Volume 1, 151–173; on pacific islanders see: Maclellan, "Grappling with the Bomb", 21-38.
9. Hecht, *Being Nuclear*, 3.

10. Ministry of Defence v *AB and others* [2012] UKSC 9; Barrillot, *Note Sur Les Documents Déclassifiés*, 1–10.
11. See: *Fiji Times*, 29 January 2015; *The Guardian*, 30 January 2015; *The Sunday Times*, 13 June 1999.
12. Debrum, 9th Review Conference of the States Parties to the Treaty on Non-Proliferation of Nuclear Weapons, General Debate, 27 April 2015.
13. Alvarez, "The Legacy of US Testing in the Marshall Islands", Hearing before the Subcommittee on Asia, the Pacific and the Global Environment.
14. US Department of Energy, *Human Radiation Experiments Associated with the Department of Energy and its Predecessors*.
15. Barrillot, *Note Sur Les Documents Déclassifiés*, 1–10.
16. Wittner, *Confronting the Bomb*, 52–81.
17. PREM 11/4242, J.H. Robertson to P.F de Zuleata, 15 November 1961.
18. See the documentary: Djamel Ouahed, *Gerboise Bleue* and the television drama: Jean-Pierre Sinapi, *Vive La Bombe!*.
19. See footage at the *Institut National* de *l'Audiovisuel*: www.ina.fr.
20. Brown, *Keeper of the Nuclear Conscience*, 135–148.
21. Samuels, *3.11: Disaster and Change in Japan*; The Fukushima Nuclear Accident Independent Investigation Commission, *The Official Report*.
22. Beyea, "The Scientific Jigsaw Puzzle", 13–28; and Charles Perrow, "Nuclear Denial", 56–67.
23. WAC, T32/1201/1, Leonard Miall to Michael Barsley, 22 July 1955.
24. On the relationship between science, politics and international relations see: Bell, "Beware of false prophets".
25. On instrumentalism, see: Headrick, *The Tentacles of Progress*; on postcolonialism, see: Said, *Orientalism*, 1–3; and Alvares, *Science, Development and Violence*.
26. Macleod, "On Visiting the Moving Metropolis", 220.
27. Clarke, "A Technocratic Imperial State?", 453–80; and Hodge, *Triumph of the Expert*.
28. Worboys, "British Colonial Science Policy", 108.
29. Bailkin, *The Afterlife of Empire*, 5.
30. CO 968/700, A.H. Poynton to F.H. Millar, 4 August 1959.
31. CO 968/700, Nigerian House of Representatives Debates, 24 February 1959.
32. CO 968/700, P. Dean to H.M. Gladwyn Jebb, 5 August 1959.
33. *The Observer*, 5 July 1959; le *Monde*, 12 August 1959; *The Times*, 21 August 1959.
34. Skogmar, *The United States and the Nuclear Dimension of European Integration*, 1–9.
35. PREM 11/3789, "The Giraffe and the Lion", 21 May 1962.
36. Kohl, *French Nuclear Diplomacy*, 251–258.
37. See note 35 above, 1962.
38. CO 968/700, Nigerian House of Representatives, 11 August, 1959.
39. On the official position, see: CO 968/700, G. Petty-Fitzmaurice to A.V Alexander, 29 July 1959; on the British empire and universities, see: Pietsch, *Empire of Scholars*.
40. CO 968/700, Reuters cables, 13 July 1959.
41. Cwl DAC 5/7/10, Notes on the Sirocco and the Harmattan, no date.
42. PREM 11/2694, M. Moch to H.C. Hainsworth, no date.
43. The only French newspaper to publish the article was *Tribune Des Nations*, a left-wing weekly with a small circulation; Cwl DAC 5/7/10, Charles Davy to April Carter, 18 July, 1959; Cwl DAC 5/7/1, April Carter to Odette du Puigaudeau, 24 September 1959; Cwl DAC /5/7/15, Michael Randle to Kingsley Martin, 28 February 1960.
44. See note 38 above, 1959.
45. J.D. Bernal Peace Library, *Des Hommes* de *Paix Du Monde Entier Arrivent Au Grand Rendez-Vous* de *Sheffield*, no date.
46. CO968/700, Report from the Office of the Inspector General, Nigerian Police, 11 August 1959.
47. On nuclear fear and cultural assimilation of nuclear testing, see: Harrison, "Popular Responses to the Atomic Bomb in China", 98–116.

48. CO 968/700, Record of Conversation on French Nuclear Tests between C. O'Neill and M. Tiné, 19 August 1959.
49. CO 968/701, P. Dean memo, no date.
50. CO 968/700, C. Maclaren to O. Morris, 8 August 1959.
51. CO968/700, Transcript of *Topic of the Week* with C. Maclaren, no date.
52. CO 968/701, Outward Telegram from the Secretary of State for the Colonies to the Federation of Nigeria, 18 September, 1959.
53. CO 968/701, Note of a Meeting in the Secretary of State's room at the Colonial Office at 5.30. pm on 18 September, 1959.
54. *Ghana Times*, 24 September 1959.
55. DO 195/45, T.W. Jones to J.O. Moreton, 23 February 1961.
56. Ibid.
57. On Canada, see: Regehr and Rosenblum (eds), *Canada and the Nuclear Arms Race*.
58. On Ghana's nuclear energy ambitions, see: Adeniji, *The Treaty of Pelindaba on the African Nuclear-Weapon-Free Zone*, 29–30.
59. Tignor, *Capitalism and Nationalism at the End of Empire*, 15; and Hilary, "Britain's Global Power Empire".
60. CO 968/701, R.J.Vile to J.A.T. Dawson, 23 September 1959.
61. DO 35/9341, from the Commonwealth Relations Office to the High Commission in Accra, no date.
62. DO 177/19, Report by the Joint United Kingdom-Nigerian Scientific Committee on the Monitoring of Radioactivity, April 1960.
63. DO 35/9341, Inward Telegram to Commonwealth Relations Office, 25 February 1960; *Evening News*, 26 February, 1960.
64. DO 35/9341, Inward Telegram to Commonwealth Relations Office, 24 February 1960.
65. Barrillot, *Note Sur Les Documents Déclassifiés*, 1–10.
66. See: http://www.world-nuclear.org/information-library/safety-and-security/radiation-and-health/radiation-and-life.aspx.
67. Reuters, 19 February 2007 and 23 February 2010, accessible via: www.itnsource.com.
68. Nyarko, Akaho and Ennison, 'Nuclear Power for Future Electricity Generation in Ghana'.

Disclosure statement

No potential conflict of interest was reported by the author.

Bibliography

Adeniji, O. *The Treaty of Pelindaba on the African Nuclear-Weapon-Free Zone*. Geneva: United Nations Publication, 2012.
Allman, J. "Nuclear Imperialism and the Pan-African Struggle for Peace and Freedom: Ghana, 1959-1962." *Souls* 10 (2008): 83–102. doi:10.1080/10999940802115419.
Alvares, C. *Science, Development and Violence*. Dehli: Oxford University Press, 1991.
Arnold, L., and M. Smith. *Britain, Australia and the Bomb: The Nuclear Tests and Their Aftermath*. Basingstoke: Palgrave Macmillan, 2006.
Auton, L. "Opaque Proliferation: The Historiography of Australia's Cold War Nuclear Weapons Option." *History Compass* 11, no. 8 (2013): 561–572. doi:10.1111/hic3.v11.8.
Bailkin, J. *The Afterlife of Empire*. Berkeley: University of California Press, 2012.

Barrillot, B. *Note Sur Les Documents Déclassifiés Le 21 Mars 2013*. Lyon: Observatoire des armements, 2014.
Bell, D. "Beware of False Prophets: Biology, Human Nature and the Future of International Relations Theory." *International Affairs* 82, no. 3 (2006): 493–510. doi:10.1111/j.1468-2346.2006.00547.x.
Bennett, B. M., and J. M. Hodge, eds. *Science and Empire: Knowledge and Networks of Science across the British Empire, 1800–1970*. Basingstoke: Palgrave Macmillan, 2011.
Bennett, S. H. *Radical Pacifism: The War Resisters League and Gandhian Nonviolence in America, 1915–1963*. New York: Syracuse University Press, 2003.
Beyea, J. "The Scientific Jigsaw Puzzle: Fitting the Pieces of the Low-Level Radiation Debate." *Bulletin of the Atomic Scientists* 68, no. 3 (2012): 13–28. doi:10.1177/0096340212445025.
Brown, A. *Keeper of the Nuclear Conscience: The Life and Work of Joseph Rotblat*. Oxford: Oxford University Press, 2012.
Clarke, S. "A Technocratic Imperial State? The Colonial Office and Scientific Research, 1940–1960." *Twentieth Century British History* 18 4 (2007): 453–480. doi:10.1093/tcbh/hwm017.
Cooper, F. *Colonialism in Question: Theory, Knowledge, History*. Berkeley: University of California Press, 2005.
Dubow, S. *A Commonwealth of Knowledge: Science, Sensibility and White South Africa, 1820–2000*. Oxford: Oxford University Press, 2006.
The Fukushima Nuclear Accident Independent Investigation Commission. *The Official Report*. Tokyo: The National Diet of Japan, 2012.
Gill, D. J. *Britain and the Bomb: Nuclear Diplomacy, 1964–1970*. Stanford: Stanford University Press, 2014.
Gowing, M. *Independence and Deterrence: Britain and Atomic Energy, 1941–52, Volume 1: Policy Making*. Basingstoke: Palgrave Macmillan, 1974.
Gowing, M. *Independence and Deterrence: Britain and Atomic Energy, 1941–52, Volume 2: Policy Execution*. Basingstoke: Palgrave Macmillan, 1974.
Grabosky, P. N. *Wayward Governance: Illegality and Its Control in the Public Sector*. Canberra: Australian Institute of Criminality, 1989.
Harrison, H. "Popular Responses to the Atomic Bomb in China, 1945–1955." *Past & Present* 218 (2013): 98–116. doi:10.1093/pastj/gts036.
Headrick, D. *The Tools of Empire: Technology and European Imperialism in the Nineteenth Century*. Oxford: Oxford University Press, 1981.
Headrick, D. *The Tentacles of Progress: Technology Transfer in the Age of Imperialism, 1850–1940*. Oxford: Oxford University Press, 1988.
Hecht, G., ed. *Entangled Geographies: Empire and Technopolitics in the Global Cold War*. Cambridge, MA: MIT, 2011.
Hecht, G. *Being Nuclear: Africans and the Global Uranium Trade*. Cambridge: The MIT Press, 2012.
Hilary, J. "Britain's Global Power Empire", *Red Pepper*, 1 November, 2006.
Hodge, J. M. *Triumph of the Expert: Agrarian Doctrines of Development and the Legacies of British Colonialism*. Athens, OH: Ohio University Press, 2007.
Hodge, J. M. "Science and Empire: An Overview of the Historical Scholarship." In *Science and Empire: Knowledge and Networks of Science across the British Empire, 1800–1970*, edited by B. M. Bennett and J. M. Hodge. Basingstoke: Palgrave Macmillan, 2011.
Hogg, J., and C. Laucht. "Introduction: British Nuclear Culture." *The British Journal for the History of Science* 45, no. 4, December (2012): 479–493. doi:10.1017/S0007087412001008.
The Independent Investigation Commission on the Fukushima Daiichi Nuclear Accident. *The Fukushima Daiichi Nuclear Power Station Disaster: Investigating the Myth and Reality*. Chicago: Routledge, 2014.
Kohl, W. L. *French Nuclear Diplomacy*. Princeton: Princeton University Press, 1971.
Maclellan, N. "Grappling with the Bomb: Opposition to Pacific Nuclear Testing in the 1950s" in P. Deery and J. Kimber (eds) *Proceedings of the 14th Biennial Labour History Conference*, Melbourne: Australian Society for the Study of Labour History, 2015, 21–38.

Macleod, R. M. "On Visiting the Moving Metropolis: Reflections on the Architecture of Imperial Science', in Michel, Dieter. 'Villains, Victims and Heroes: Contested Memory and the British Nuclear Tests in Australia." *Journal of Australian Studies* 27, no. 80 (2003): 221–228. doi:10.1080/14443050309387928.

Mitchell, T. *Rule of Experts: Egypt, Techno-Politics, Modernity*. Berkeley: University of California Press, 2002.

Nadesan, M. H. *Fukushima and the Privatisation of Risk*. Palgrave Macmillan: Basingstoke, 2013.

Nehring, H. *The Politics of Security. West European Protests against Nuclear Weapons and the Cold War*. Oxford: Oxford University Press, 2013.

Nyarko, B. J. B., E. H. K. Akaho, and I. Ennison. *Nuclear Power for Future Electricity Generation in Ghana: Issues and Challenges*. Vienna: International Atomic Energy Agency, 2009.

Perrow, C. "Nuclear Denial: From Hiroshima to Fukushima." *Bulletin of the Atomic Scientists* 69, no. 56 (2013): 56–67. doi:10.1177/0096340213501369.

Pietsch, T. *Empire of Scholars: Universities, Networks and the British Academic World, 1850–1939*. Manchester: Manchester University Press, 2013.

Regehr, E., and S. Rosenblum, eds. *Canada and the Nuclear Arms Race*. Toronto: James Lorimer & Co., 1983.

Reingold, N., and M. Rothenberg, eds. *Scientific Colonialism: A Cross-Cultural Comparison*, 220. Washington: Smithsonian Institution Press, 1987.

Ross, C. *Ecology and Power in the Age of Empire: Europe and the Transformation of the Tropical World*. Oxford: Oxford University Press, 2017.

Said, E. *Orientalism*. New York: Pantheon Books, 1978.

Samuels, R. *3.11: Disaster and Change in Japan*. Ithaca: Cornell University Press, 2013.

Schaffer, G. *Racial Science and British Society 1930–62*. Basingstoke: Palgrave Macmillan, 2008.

Scheinman, L. *Atomic Energy Policy in France under the Fourth Republic*. Princeton: Princeton University Press, 1965.

Shiva, V. *Staying Alive: Women, Ecology and Development*. London: Zed Books, 1989.

Skogmar, G. *The United States and the Nuclear Dimension of European Integration*. Basingstoke: Palgrave Macmillan, 2004.

Tignor, R. L. *Capitalism and Nationalism at the End of Empire: State and Business in Decolonizing Egypt, Nigeria, and Kenya, 1945–1963*. Princeton: Princeton University Press, 1998.

Tynan, E. R. "Maralinga and the Journalists: Covering the Bomb Tests over Generations." *LiNQ* 38 (2011): 131–145.

Wittner, L. S. *Confronting the Bomb: A Short History of the World Nuclear Disarmament Movement*. Stanford University Press, 2009.

Worboys, M. "British Colonial Science Policy (1918–1930)." In *Colonial Sciences: Researchers and Institutions*, edited by P. Petitjean. Paris: Orstom Editions, 1996.

Archival Sources

The British Broadcasting Corporation Written Archives Centre at Caversham
    T32/1201/1: Current Affairs and Nuclear Weapons.
The J.B. Priestley Library, University of Bradford
    Cwl DAC: The Archive of the Direct Action Committee against Nuclear War
The Marx Memorial Library, Clerkenwell, London
    The Papers of J.D. Bernal (uncatalogued)
The National Archives
    CO 968/700: Official Representations against French Nuclear Tests in the Sahara
    CO 968/701: Official Representations against French Nuclear Tests in the Sahara
    DO 35/9341: Ghana Protest at Proposed French Atomic Explosion in Sahara
    DO 177/19: Nigerian Reaction to French Nuclear Tests in the Sahara
    DO 195/45: Request for Nuclear Reactor
    PREM 11/2694: French Nuclear Tests in the Sahara: UN Debate; UK Position

PREM 11/3789: Attitude of President de Gaulle to UK membership of EEC: Paper by Lord Gladwyn

PREM 11/4242: French Nuclear Tests in the Sahara: Parts 2 and 3

Documentaries and Films

Djamel Ouahed, *Gerboise Bleue* (2009)

Jean-Pierre Sinapi, *Vive La Bombe!* (2006)

Newspapers

Fiji Times

Le Monde

The Guardian

The Observer

The Sunday Times

Official Publications and Reports

Alvarez, Robert. 'The Legacy of US Testing in the Marshall Islands', Hearing before the Subcommittee on Asia, the Pacific and the Global Environment, House of Representatives, 110th Congress, first session, 27 March, 2007.

Debrum, Tony. 9th Review Conference of the States Parties to the Treaty on Non-Proliferation of Nuclear Weapons, General Debate, 27 April 2015.

Délégation à l'Information et à la Communication de la Défense, *Dossier* de *Presentation* Des *Essais Nucléaires et Leur Suivi au Sahara*, 2007.

Ministry of Defence v *AB* and others [2012] UKSC 9.

The Report of the Royal Commission into British Nuclear Tests in Australia, Canberra: Australian Government Publication Services, 1985.

Websites

Independent Television News Source: www.itnsource.com

The *Institut National* de *l'Audiovisuel*: www.ina.fr.

The World Nuclear Association: www.world-nuclear.org

Index

Air Raid Precaution Act 28
anti-nuclear activism 6, 16, 67
atom bomb 4, 29, 31–32, 48–49, 52–56, 58–60, 116

'Babies Against the Bomb' (BAB) 15–17
Banks, Tony 14, 20
Brink, Joram Ten 16
Britain 5–6, 12, 28–30, 57, 59–60, 66, 68–69, 71–73, 86, 90, 114–124
Britain's Civil Defence Corps 27–39
Brooke, Stephen 20

Campbell, Duncan 11
CEGB 90–94, 96, 101, 104, 106
Chadwick, Lee 93, 106
Churchill, Winston 30
civil defence 5–6, 12, 18, 28–39, 49, 73, 76
Civil Defence Corps (CDC) 5, 27–30, 32–33, 35–39
Civil Defence plan 5, 11–13
civil defence rehearsals 34–37
civil defence training 28, 30–31, 37–38
Cold War 4–6, 28, 30, 39, 67, 87, 90, 94, 118
Commonwealth 118–119
Communist Party 93–95, 104
Cordle, Daniel 11–12
Cuban Missile Crisis 36
cultural circuit 36
cultural policy 10–12, 14–15

Davis, Tracy 28
Douthwaite, Jessica 4–5, 27

East Anglia 87, 90, 101, 105
emotional politics 48–60
emotional responses 4, 10, 52, 54, 58
emotions 4–5, 7, 16, 31, 35, 48–50, 52, 54, 56, 58–59
European Economic Community (EEC) 115, 118–119

feelings 4, 17, 28, 48–60, 68, 77
first French test 123
France 114, 116–120
French tests 114–115, 118–120, 123–124
Fry, T. M. 91

Gammon, Michael 90–91
Ghana 115, 118–120, 122–123
Glasgow 2, 31, 34
GLC Peace Year 10–13, 20
Greater London Council (GLC) 5–6, 10–12, 14–16, 18–21

H-Bomb 68, 117
heathland 106
Hill, Christopher 6
Hinton, Sir Christopher 91
Hogg, Jonathan 29, 49, 86, 90
Hughes, Jeff 3

imperialism 114–116
Imperial War Museum 18–19

Johnes, Martin 6

Kennard, Peter 12–13

Langhamer, Claire 4–5
Laucht, Christoph 6, 30
Leiston 5, 88, 91–93, 95–96, 98–99, 104–107
London 5, 10–15, 17–21, 52, 72, 106, 117, 120
London Wall 18–19
long-term stagnation 95

Maclaren, Colin 121
Macleod, Roy 117
Macmillan government 114–115, 118–119, 121, 123–124
Mass-Observation 4, 48–54, 58–60
Mittel, John 101, 103
Morton, Vivien 93
motherhood 15–17

new nuclear imperialism 114–115
Nigeria 118–123
Nkrumah, Kwame 115, 122–123
North Atlantic Treaty Organisation (NATO) 119
nuclear anxieties 10, 20, 49, 52, 60
nuclear attack 5–6, 11, 17, 20, 28–29, 31, 33–39, 68–69, 74–76
nuclear cultures 3–7, 49
nuclear danger 11, 30, 38
nuclear diplomacy 3, 118, 122
nuclear exceptionalism 3–4, 6
nuclear-free zones 11, 18, 66, 73–75, 78
nuclear imperialism 115, 122
nuclearisation 3–4, 6
nuclearity 30, 39, 48–49, 52, 60
nuclear juggernaut 107
nuclear narratives 12, 18, 20, 32
nuclear power 67, 70, 86, 88, 98, 104–105, 107, 115, 117
nuclear power stations 2, 68, 71–72, 75, 87, 90, 92–96, 98, 105–106
nuclear science 4, 30, 32, 91, 115, 119
nuclear war 2–3, 5, 11–12, 16, 18–19, 27–29, 31, 33, 36, 38, 66–68, 71, 74, 76–78
nuclear weapons 6, 16, 19–20, 28, 30–31, 33, 38–39, 67–70, 72–75, 77–78, 119

Openshaw 91
oral histories 4–5, 36, 39, 87, 91, 107

peace camp 2, 13, 69
peace movement 15, 66, 69–72, 74, 76–77
Peace Year 11–12, 14, 18, 20
Penney, Sir William 120
political climate 75
power 49, 56, 58, 72–73, 78, 95–96, 104, 116–117, 122–123
power station 2, 5, 86–88, 91–92, 95, 98, 104–107
protests 11, 59, 66–68, 70, 72, 75–77
public space 10, 18

radiation 11, 29, 31, 33, 35, 37, 74, 94, 115–117, 119–121, 123–124
Radio-Active Times 73
radioactivity 86, 91, 94
Rawlings, Jini 16
reparatory history 116
Roberts, Ian 101, 103
Rotblat, Joseph 117

scientific knowledge 3, 115, 117, 120–121
scientific sweeteners 115
Second World War 28–29, 32–36, 49, 68, 77, 86, 90, 93
Shapira, Michal 52
short-term gain 95
Sierra Leone 114–115, 118, 121–122
Sizewell A power station 86–107
sociality, of feeling 55–56
South Glamorgan 68–69, 73–74, 76
South Glamorgan County Council 72–73, 75–76
South London Press 19

techno-political state 116
Thompson, E. P. 11
Thompson, Paul 30, 87
Tomkins, Alan 12
training 5, 15, 27–28, 31–33, 36–39, 100

Wall, Christine 5, 86
Ward, Jim 103–104
The War Game (Watkins) 73
wartime feeling 52
wartime group control centres 12
Watkins: *The War Game* 73
Wellsian nightmare 55
Welsh 6, 67, 69, 71–73, 75, 77–78, 107
Welsh protests 66–68, 78
West Africa 6, 114–115, 118–119, 122–124
women's peace activism 18–19
Women's Peace Mural 19–21
workers 87, 98, 101, 106
working-class sympathisers 71